Scripture quotations are from the English Standard Version (ESV)
© Crossway Publishing, 2008.

ISBN 979-8-9917844-0-5

Library of Congress Catalog: TXU2467498

Find and Get
Your Ideal Ministry Job

By Dr. Joel D. Hathaway

www.joelhathaway.com

Dear Reader

I welcome the opportunity to interact with you. If you have questions as you engage the ministry search process or feedback on this book, please email me. I will attempt to reply to requests in a timely manner: joelhathaway@joelhathaway.com. And please remember to leave a review at Amazon.com or Goodreads.com.

Acknowledgements

Thank you to the Laine Schmidt Coaching team—Laine, John, Louanne, Sean, Hace and especially Gigi who first challenged me to prioritize this work. I'm deeply grateful to Kent Needler who regularly asked about my writing, and to Covenant Theological Seminary for the job which fueled this research. With appreciation for Shannon Hathaway (wife) and Alice Hathaway (mother), who edited versions of this work. And ultimate gratitude to the Lord Jesus who is working good in His Church and through His people (Eph. 4).

CONTENTS

INTRODUCTION

When a corporate firm seeks new financial advisers, the company publicly posts a clearly defined job description listing areas of responsibility, necessary skills and certifications, and a salary range. Applicants know what documents to give, where, and to whom. Human Resources confirms receipt of the application and schedules an interview. Within 48 hours of the first interview, the candidate knows whether he or she will be further interviewed or is no longer a candidate. Once hired, the new employee goes through a formal onboarding process. This process is quick, thorough, and efficient.

The ministry hiring process is rarely quick, thorough, or efficient. Simply finding available ministry jobs is difficult enough. Job postings are decentralized, scattered across dozens of electronic job boards. Many jobs never make it onto a board and are filled by people who were personally referred. Some churches hire exclusively from within, while others only consider candidates coming from the outside.

After the first interaction comes the application process and multiple rounds of interviews. Job descriptions don't follow standard formats. Organizations don't share information uniformly, making it difficult for candidates to get accurate information.

Ministry positions may be vacated at any time of the year, affecting how and when candidates give time and energy to the job search. Meanwhile, committees working to fill those positions conduct most candidate assessments and interviews between January and June. New ministry candidates may find their need for a job and the hiring timetable does not overlap.

Then there is the length of time a pastoral search process takes. Compared to the business world, candidates describe it as painstakingly slow. The discussion of compensation is usually held until the very end of the process, leaving candidates unsure whether a church will pay them enough to live "free from worldly cares" (Presbyterian Church in America, Book of Church Order, 20-6).

Interactions between candidates and a church spans months and sometimes more than a year. These interactions involve the exchange of documents—like a Ministry Data Form (MDF) or a Pastor Information Form (PIF), a resume, and a Church Profile—as well as phone interviews, site visits, and public speaking or preaching. The flow, pace, and nature of these interactions vary between churches of different sizes, in different regions, and of different denominations. Some conduct almost exclusively digital and data-oriented approaches, while others adopt a more personal-relational approach. And besides all this, there are personality, preference, and theology issues—yours and those of the church you are considering.

Reading this can leave you feeling critical of the inefficiency of ministry search processes and the people who run them. In all fairness, few search committee members are adequately trained for their role. They are volunteers who give their time and energy out of love for their community. And they aren't hiring someone simply for technical skills. Character, emotional intelligence, managerial competence, leadership, and relational capacity are essential for success in vocational ministry.

Considering these facts, many candidates despair. You don't have to. This book provides practical steps toward developing a differentiated approach to finding your desired ministry position. In 20 years of candidate consulting, I have seen that few candidates intuitively develop an effective process when seeking ministry positions. Most assume a scatter-shot approach: apply everywhere using the same resume packet. Or wait for churches to pursue them. Or resign themselves to an unpleasant situation.

You need a better system, and I offer you one on the following pages. There are other possible methods, and you may decide only to incorporate some of the recommended steps. But I believe the process described below—what I call *Intentional Networking*—is unique in its integration of reinforcing efforts. *Intentional Networking* saves you time, allows you to focus your energy on positions you want, and provides clarity as you navigate the unique landscape of finding a ministry position. As a result, you stand out from other candidates, and you can make more informed decisions throughout the vocational ministry job search.

Book Structure
This is a "How To" book. It's designed to be a resource you consult when you need specific information or guidance. Some readers don't need to read it from beginning to end, though others of you might. Give yourself the freedom to skip around to the section that addresses where you are in the search process. The goal is to know where to find the information you need when you need it.

This book has four main sections.
- Chapters 1-3 focus on the aspects of the job search: where to find open ministry positions, *Intentional Networking*, and when to search for a new ministry position.
- Chapters 4 and 5 focus on understanding yourself and creating a resume packet that captures your uniqueness, differentiating you from other similarly qualified candidates.
- Chapters 6 and 7 provide insight into the committees and people with whom you will interact, with emphasis on how to evaluate and assess the churches to which you apply.
- Chapters 8 and 9 focus on preparing you for job interviews and site visits.

Over the past 20 years, I've talked with over 1,000 pastors and consulted over 100 churches. I have used those rich experiences to create fictional people, situations, and stories to illustrate challenges common in the job search process—art imitating life. To that extent, nobody can say, "He's writing about me," while dozens of readers should be able to say, "I've had an experience similar to that one." The stories about myself are historical, with key details changed to protect individuals involved.

More of the stories focus on the challenges of navigating the ministry job search rather than the joys. When things go well, we celebrate. But we don't learn about navigating challenges from success. Golfer Bobby

Jones is quoted as saying, "I never learned anything from a match I won." I hope your job search will be easy; don't expect it to be. Put a sinful ministry candidate together with a broken organizational system, and you have the recipe for difficulty and heartache. To that end, my examples are intended to encourage you through the resistance you face so that you never lose heart in your desire to serve God and His people.

Conclusion
No job search is free of frustration but have hope. The process outlined in the following text will provide you with the support necessary to map the confusing landscape and keep you oriented toward your ultimate goal: to find and get your ideal ministry job.

1

HOW TO USE AND NOT USE JOB BOARDS

Chapter Summary
Ministry candidates find jobs in one of two places: either from electronic job boards or from other people's referrals to a relational network. Candidates who focus on job boards experience more disappointment. These candidates don't have access to many of the best ministry positions because most are never posted on a public job board. Job boards also do not expose candidates to the highest quality jobs. But job boards should not be neglected entirely since they provide ministry candidates with essential information necessary to navigate the non-profit job search effectively. Understanding what job boards can and cannot do for you in the ministry search will reduce frustration and alleviate wasted effort. Instead, you can focus on the steps for the best positions.

Starting the Search
Ministry candidates find jobs either through electronic job boards (e.g., Indeed, LinkedIn, denominational or seminary websites) or through a relational network. Candidates who focus primarily on positions listed on a job board encounter three limitations.

1. These candidates cannot access the largest number of ministry positions because most are never posted on a public job board. By some measures, as few as 30% of ministry jobs are posted on a job board.
2. Job boards do not expose candidates to the highest quality jobs. Larger churches have the resources to develop more thorough and professional candidate evaluation processes used more regularly. As a result, these churches rarely post their jobs

5

publicly. Larger churches employ relational networks for finding candidates without doing a public search.

3. Job boards do not expose candidates to the best positions. Organizations aware of the impersonal nature of job boards tend to avoid them, opting instead for a networked approach to candidate identification. When a church posts a job publicly, it expects that only qualified candidates self-select into the application process. Smaller churches often do not have the necessary relational network or financial capital to conduct relational networked searches. By default, they post their positions on public job boards.

But job boards should not be neglected completely. They provide ministry candidates with information essential for navigating the ministry job search.

1. Job boards confirm that you are looking for a ministry position. A survey of job descriptions posted publicly provides candidates with a realistic perspective on the types of work typical in the non-profit sector.
2. Inexperience can limit candidates' ability to consider the full scope of ministry positions. Job boards broaden candidates' awareness of the types of ministry positions available.
3. Job boards enable candidates to develop an Ideal Job Description.
4. Job boards build familiarity with how most churches manage the hiring process.

Understanding what job boards can and cannot do for you in the ministry job search reduces frustration and alleviates wasted effort. Instead, you can focus on the steps for the best positions.

I grew up in the Pine Belt region of Southern Mississippi near what I considered to be my own 100 Acre Wood. As far as any of us knew, they had never been explored. A boy could set off after breakfast and, with some luck, get lost until almost supper time. There were no maps, no guideposts. But the wood had four distinct boundaries. A cattle field stretched along the east side, the road along the south, the mill pond along the west, and The Unnamed Creek to the north. Strike upon one of these, and we knew at once where we were.

Spoiler alert! In the following pages, I'll make a case that most ministry jobs—both quantitatively and qualitatively—are not found on job boards. Instead, these jobs are found, assessed, and gained through relational interactions I call *Intentional Networking*.

Intentional Networking is a complex system. There is no map, and every path is a new adventure. In this system, job boards serve something of a boundary marker to set limits on the perimeter of this endeavor.

What Job Boards Can't Do

Much of the frustration you will experience when applying to jobs found on boards is the result of unrealistic expectations. We expect more from non-personal, electronic job boards than they can give. We need to clarify what job boards can't do for us during the job search.

It may seem odd to start with what job boards cannot do, but by dispelling unrealistic expectations, we minimize frustration. The ministry job search is already fraught with enough disappointment— waiting for committees to respond and dealing with rejection. Adjusting your approach allows you to gain the benefits of job boards without the burden of unrealistic expectations.

Job boards cannot provide you with a job search process consistent with the nature of ministry.

Job boards are impersonal by design. They exist "out there"—on websites and in databases. They collect and present information, primarily technical information. Job boards cannot evaluate the highly relational, soft skills necessary for the ministry. Because job board listings are available to everyone, the nature of the interaction between a candidate and a committee is also impersonal and transactional. Relationship is mediated through process: an organization asks for specific documents, and an applicant provides them; the organization evaluates the documents and decides which calls for further evaluation. Some candidates are asked to continue in the process, while others never hear anything. Job boards define the terms of interaction between organizations and candidates.

Many churches recognize their relational hiring outcomes are at odds with the impersonal dynamics of job boards. Still, job boards often remain the best avenue for candidate identification for Under-Resourced Churches. Churches that post jobs publicly cannot be expected to practice the same level of personalized engagement as those conducting a networked approach because of the high response rate. Based on my 20 years of experience, public job listings can receive up to 70 applications. The greater the number of potential candidates, the more likely the application and communication processes feel mechanical and impersonal.

On the other hand, the ministry is relational. Ministry leaders may be employees, but they are never just employees. Every industry has baseline requirements for character, skill, and competency, but this is especially true for ministry. An electrician without character may be an exceptional electrician. A minister without character and skills cannot be an exceptional minister.

A pastor looking to hire an assistant would never put his cell number in a public job description but gladly shares his cell number with a select group of friends from whom he asked for references. And there lies the tension. How does an organization use an impersonal job board— transactional more than relational—to evaluate the subjective aspects of a candidate?

Churches typically use a public job board in two situations. Either the church is not connected well enough to rely on relationships for recommendations, or the church has run out of candidates gathered through referral. As such, these churches usually assume a job board exists to feed them candidate names. The process becomes personal, but it does not begin that way. I call these churches "under-resourced."

Under-Resourced Churches
What are the traits of an Under-Resourced Church? Under-Resourced Churches tend to be small in terms of both size and budget. They have a small staff, often with only one ordained person. They expect their pastors to be generalists who do everything. Under-Resourced Churches are in a hurry to find their next pastor, so they cannot afford to be overly selective. The urgency of their search requires them to look as broadly as possible from the beginning. Under-researched churches tend to post their ministry jobs on public boards from the get-go.

In my experience, candidates expect different things from job boards than most churches do. Candidates assume job boards are intended to connect them to organizations willing to treat them with a degree of relational consistency. This is not the case, nor is it possible for the above reasons. On the other hand, Under-Resourced Churches assume job boards will connect them to numerous candidates quickly. When you keep this distinction in mind, you are likely to avoid frustration with the impersonal nature of the job board and the potential discouragement arising when organizations do not respond to inquiries or applications.

Job boards cannot grant you access to the most jobs.

The second thing job boards cannot do is provide candidates with access to most available ministry positions (quantity). In an ongoing longitudinal study, I noted listings on ministry job boards declined 82.7% from 2001 to 2011. During the same period, actual placement rates across theological schools remained high. How do we account for this apparent discrepancy? I believe that candidates looking for ministry positions during this decade were heavily dependent upon networking, not on job boards.

When interpreting this data, we must consider cultural trends. In 2001, very few industries had figured out how to use the Internet for hiring. Most companies and organizations still relied heavily on publicly accessible job boards in physical places: on university campuses or in binders on the desks of headhunters. Organizations could post their job, but they were at the mercy of applicants to inquire or apply.

The next decade would see incredible growth in the scope and capacity of the Internet. Most industries embraced the idea that networking produced better hiring results than the job-board approach. Medical practices, legal firms, and non-profits moved jobs away from public boards. They shifted their focus to referrals from friends, alumni, and trusted leaders, accounting for the radical decline in publicly posted job descriptions. Notably, this visible decline in public job listings did not reflect a real decline in available ministry positions or candidates securing ministry positions. There remained an abundance of ministry positions. Candidates just couldn't apply for them unless they knew someone who knew someone involved in the hiring process.

Then the Great Recession hit, and the quantity of ministry positions *actually* declined. Practically, many churches did not begin hiring or rehiring until 2011. When they did, they moved to a hybrid hiring approach: a prolonged networking period for candidates at the beginning of the search, followed by a shorter, public job-board phase near the end. This data explains the visible increase in ministry jobs as reflected in job board numbers after 2011.

In 2019, job boards reflected around 60% of available jobs compared to 2001. Practically, candidates who depended on job boards were still not privy to 40% of open ministry positions. Of course, these numbers vary greatly based on whether a church is denominationally affiliated, how that denomination conducts hiring (i.e., sent or selected, placed or called), and the size and location of the congregation in question.

> *Job boards cannot grant you access*
> *to the highest quality jobs.*

Most churches know that picking one candidate out of a stack of paper applications is not the best way to find a qualified candidate. However, some churches still believe this gets the best results. In 2010, I found the following announcement posted online. Notice the description of the process the church followed in identifying and calling its next pastor:

> [We] published the search in a variety of venues and received over 100 inquiries. Of these, 70 individuals completed the application process. From the 70 applicants, the committee selected 10 candidates with whom it conducted 45-minute phone interviews. From those interviewed, it selected 5 "semi-finalists" with whom the committee conducted more extensive interviews (by phone and in person), checked references, and received additional written input. From the semi-finalists, we made our final selection.

This newly Senior Pastor left the congregation nine months after his installation. There are many reasons a pastor leaves a ministry position, so I don't want to draw too many conclusions. What we can be sure of is that nobody considers this a ministry *success*. Certainly, not the committee working for more than a year on this process, nor the candidate who disrupted his life and uprooted his family to move to a new place. As Arthur W. Jones put it, "All organizations are perfectly designed to get the results they get."[1]

Job boards cannot provide candidates with access to the best ministry positions (quality). I don't mean the *quality* of the work, the *health* of the ministry, or the *caliber* of people at the church. By "best," I mean positions crafted with an understanding of the work, clarity in articulating the job description, alignment with organizational values, and a thorough process for evaluation. Churches with the corporate knowledge necessary to craft such positions are more resourced. Money and people give these churches an advantage when preparing a job description and running a professional process. These churches rarely post their position on a job board and often elect to hire from the pool of candidates gathered through referral.

Resourced Churches
Resourced Churches are larger in terms of congregational size, staff size, and budget. More extensive staff means a more precise division of duties and responsibilities, leading to specialization. A Solo Pastor is expected to do everything, while a Senior Pastor over a large staff has a narrower and more defined role. And when you have a large staff, there are more people to shoulder the responsibilities of a vacant position during a transition period. Larger budgets mean churches can afford to be more thorough and selective in their process, whether by taking a more protracted hiring approach or hiring a search firm. These churches tend to be in major cities or suburbs which positions them to be more networked within their geographic area or denomination.

These assets mean a Resourced Church tends to deliberate more thoroughly about the people it hires. They know that selecting from a pool of candidates who asked to be considered (open application process) is less effective than inviting qualified people to apply. Resourced Churches rarely post their jobs publicly, at least at the beginning. Remember that the average public job posting receives more than 30 applications. Within this group, many who apply know they are not qualified. Some are just desperate for employment or a new job. Others assume their education can compensate for their lack of experience. Sometimes they are in denial about the demands of a position and their lack of preparation to meet those demands.

11

Resourced Churches are conscious of these facts and so only pursue qualified candidates. They do not need to trust a candidate to have high self-awareness, honest self-assessment, and proper self-disclosure. Their more thorough and longer hiring process exposes candidates' emotional and relational capacities. On the other hand, Under-Resourced Churches rely heavily on candidates who have high self-awareness and self-disclosure. They lack the financial and human resources, and time, to conduct such a process. By posting their positions publicly, Under-Resourced Churches shift the burden of self-evaluation to the candidate, away from the committee and process.

Smaller, Under-Resourced Churches are not bad places to serve. I believe God has equipped someone (maybe you) to fill every available position, or else He is working to end the need for the position. The problem arises when candidates assume their only options are the jobs listed on a board. The position is not "best" because the candidates applying are not a good fit, and the committees evaluating them have not developed a reliable process. This doesn't stop those candidates from applying. Some candidates end up in these positions, and most will leave them in less than four years—frustrated, disappointed, and possibly burnt out.

Summary
If you approach job boards with an understanding of their limits, you will experience less discouragement in the process. You will be less inclined to take the impersonal nature of job boards and poor communication follow-up as a personal rejection.

Remember, a job board is just one of several ways to look for ministry positions. Jobs listed on boards require greater self-awareness and diligence on your part when evaluating these publicly posted positions.

Takeaways
- Do not let the impersonal nature of job boards frustrate your efforts. Job boards are impersonal.
- Do not let an organization's poor communication to job board inquiries frustrate your search.
- Remember that less focused jobs listed on a board are not a correct indication of the broader vocational ministry job market.

Action Steps
1. Write down one way you are thinking differently about interacting with churches whose job position is on a job board.
2. In your own words, write a short reminder to yourself on why job board applications are impersonal.
3. What steps will you take to prevent discouragement when applying for positions listed on a job board?
4. Spend 15 minutes familiarizing yourself with the structures of at least three different job boards. Try to find one hosted by a university or seminary (https://mycts.covenantseminary.edu/jobs), another hosted by a denomination or network (https://www.thegospelcoalition.org/jobs/), and another hosted by a marketplace company (https://www.churchstaffing.com/).

What Job Boards Can Do
There are many expectations that job boards can't meet, and there are ways that job boards don't serve you during the job search. Job boards still serve you in several essential ways when searching for ministry positions.

Job boards confirm that you are looking for a ministry position.

Job boards expose you to actual ministry positions. This may seem obvious, maybe even a little silly to state. But I remain surprised by how many ministerial candidates are not *actually* looking for ministry work. When asked to describe a "month in the life of" their ideal ministry job, they string together a list of activities that have little to do with the everyday responsibilities of vocational ministry. Some have a distorted view of ministry, hoping to spend 90% of their time reading, writing, and preaching. Go read 20 different ministry descriptions listed on a job board. If the duties and responsibilities of these positions do not excite you, then it is worth asking, "Am I pursuing vocational ministry?"

Every person is different. Consequently, every person embraces aspects of ministry in unique ways. Some write, others craft with wood,. and some create music. Others join neighborhood book clubs and community gyms. I am an advocate for these unique expressions of ministry. But these activities are secondary to the primary responsibilities of most ministers: prayer, the study and preaching of God's Word, pastoring people, counseling, organizational management, and administration. The reality is that most pastors spend far more time counseling people and administrating systems than their ministry training prepared them for. A significant gap exists between the expectations of future pastors and the reality of active pastors, as shown by an experiment by Dean R. Hoge and Jacqueline E. Wenger. They write:

> [The experiment] had to do with the gap between the ideal ministry position as these persons envisioned it and the real ones they were forced to live out. Ever since the earliest research on how Protestant ministers spend their time, done in the 1950s, it has been found repeatedly that ministers hope to devote themselves to preaching, teaching, and pastoral ministry but instead find that they need to spend the majority of their time on institutional tasks, administration, and program planning.[2]

Pastors were asked to report how much time they spent in four areas of ministry: 1) preaching or leading worship, 2) teaching or training people, 3) pastoral care and visitation, and 4) administration. Then they were asked how much time they would ideally spend in these areas. Hoge and Wenger report:

> [M]inisters commonly experienced a gap between the ideal and real expenditure of their time. In the areas of preaching and teaching, the actual time they spent was much less than their ideal: on preaching, 8 percent said that the actual time they spent was more than the ideal, while 49 percent said it was less. In the area of teaching, 10 percent said the actual time was more than the ideal and 50 percent said it was less. In the area of pastoral care, the gap was smaller: 24 percent said the time spent was more than the ideal, and 34 percent said it was less. The fourth area, administration, was just the opposite. Sixty-four percent said the actual time spent was more than the ideal, versus a percent who said it was less.[3]

The romanticism of vocational ministry is understandable. A young woman experiences relational healing through a counseling ministry, so she pursues a counseling degree. A college student embraces the Gospel through the preaching and care of a campus pastor, so he wants others to understand the same freedom. These people go to seminary to become *like* the best part of what they saw in the people who influenced them. But neither has a scope of ministry practice that is broad enough to close the gap between their ideal expectations and the reality of vocational ministry, which often includes long days of meetings, administration, organization, planning, budgets, bulletins, billing, and scheduling (in counseling practices), and building maintenance.

A romantic view of what it means to be a pastor or counselor—sermon preparation and preaching or caring for people—is a beautiful and powerful force to draw people into vocational ministry. But ministry is no more limited to these activities than marriage is limited to romantic dinners and long walks on the beach. If your experience has not exposed you to the manual labor of vocational ministry—meetings, administration, management, planning, set-up, clean-up, conflict resolution, and a thousand other tasks that stand over and against sermon preparation, preaching, teaching, and casting vision—looking at actual job descriptions helps close the gap between the real and the ideal.

On this point, Dr. J.D. Funyak found that "an essential role of leaders in the process of shepherding new talent is to define the terms, context, and setting of an organization, and then outline how the leadership functions...."[4] Even if you haven't had someone reorient you to the complex realities of ministry, looking at actual job descriptions can provide you with this kind of insight.

Should you find yourself uninterested in the core aspects of ministry as listed in the average job description, consider how the Lord may be leading you to another type of vocation. I know former seminarians who fell into bouts of depression and chemical dependence because others pressured them into vocational ministry when, in fact, the Lord had wired them for other vocations.

One seminarian sat across from a professor during office hours. The student did poorly in class, was disengaged, and emotionally despondent. The student wanted to focus the conversation on his academic performance and how to improve his grades, but the professor redirected the conversation.

"What kind of work are you most excited to do in the future?" he asked. The student looked out the window, down at his hands, then at the professor.

"I want to be a forest park ranger," he said.

The professor leaned toward him, touched the student's hand, smiled, and said, "Then go be the best forest park ranger possible for God and His kingdom. God loves forest rangers."

This student was not alone. I have sat across from students who borrowed heavily to attend seminary only to discover they had no real love for most common ministry duties. Freed from artificial expectations from within and without, these people found joy and fulfillment in other vocations for God and His kingdom. Charles Spurgeon, in his sermon "Christ's Pastoral Prayer for His People," said to those pondering a vocation in ministry:

> I think it exceedingly wrong when I hear exhortations made to young people, "Quit your service as domestics and come out into spiritual work. Business men, leave your shops. Workmen, give up your trades. You cannot serve Christ in that calling, come away from it altogether." I beg to say that nothing will be more pestilent than such advice as that. There are men called by the grace of God to separate themselves from every earthly occupation, and they have special gifts for the work of the ministry; but ever to imagine that the bulk of Christian people cannot serve God in their daily calling, is to think altogether contrary to the mind of the Spirit of God. If you are a servant, remain a servant. If you are a waiter, go on with your waiting. If you are a tradesman, go on with your trade. Let every man abide in the calling wherein he is called, unless there be to him some special call from God to devote himself to the ministry. Go on with your employment, dear Christian people, and do not imagine that you are to turn hermits, or monks, or nuns. You would not glorify God if you did so act.[5]

Job boards broaden candidate awareness of the types of available ministry positions.

The second thing job boards can do is broaden your awareness of what types of ministry opportunities exist. For most of us, our understanding of ministry is limited by our experience of those ministers we've observed. To say you are "called to ministry" is not saying much of anything, definitively.

In a 2008 Wall Street Journal editorial, Jonathan A. Knee made this observation about business school students:

> When business school students announce that they have narrowed down their career focus to investment banking, private equity or a high-growth start-up company, in reality they have not narrowed their options down at all. These three kinds of jobs are all distinct categories of occupations, each of which draws on different talents and in which different kinds of people are likely to thrive.... The odds that the same person would prosper equally in more than one of these environments are low.[6]

Similarly, ministry candidates have limited models of ministry in mind when starting out. Perhaps, an exceptionally caring youth minister or an insightful campus pastor comes to mind. Broadening this perspective guides you in the search process, especially as you learn to differentiate yourself from other candidates in personality and preferences. You may not have any of the skills, capacities, or traits of the person who had the most influence on your sense of calling. Unless you are free of that unrealistic comparison, your ministry trajectory will never entirely engage you, leaving you frustrated, discouraged, and disappointed.

Abby came to seminary because she wanted to care for people the way her Youth Pastor cared for her. She could articulate the desire to model life-on-life discipleship for young women, teach, and engage in community formation. These are tasks and duties, not job descriptions. Pursuing job boards allowed Abby to see other contexts where she could practice these skills. Initially, she thought she would end up in a youth ministry position. Instead, she pursued a hospital chaplaincy position that gave her the same opportunities but with a different group of people in quite different stages of life.

There are as many diverse types of ministry positions as there are ministers. While these may be clustered into a manageable set of titles—Senior/Solo, Assistant/Associate; Director of Youth, Worship, Women's Ministry, or Counseling; Missionary, Chaplain, Campus Minister, etc.—even two jobs with the same title require different capacities and allow for varied expressions of spiritual gifts. Where personality inventories are good at naming what is unique about an individual, job boards enable candidates to see more possibilities for ministry contexts than their limited experience can anticipate.

Job boards help you develop an Ideal Job Description

In the board game Settlers of Catan, players must acquire combinations of resources to expand their scope and reach. An ideal job description functions as a resource list to guide you in gaining the necessary experiences while developing essential skills. This is the third way job boards support you in your search. Building an Ideal Job Description using actual job descriptions is one way to turn a subjective sense of calling into a clear line of direction.

I often begin my time with candidates asking them to tell me what they expect a week in the life of ministry looks like. What are their duties? What tasks consume the most time? Are they more often with people or alone studying and praying? Who are they spending time with: adults or children, college students or older people, believers or unbelievers? Are they more often in their offices or out in the community? This exercise forces them (and you) to name specific settings, contexts, people, and tasks that naturally flow out of their unique personality, experience, and sense of call. Two hundred people said, "I want to pastor youth." That is generic language. One person said, "My ideal ministry will let me focus on the spiritual development of emerging adults, instructing them through one-on-one discipleship and praying with and for them." That is specific.

Here are examples of specific (unedited) language from actual job descriptions:

- Provide a balanced ministry of evangelism and discipleship by teaching the Bible with clarity, creativity, and conviction.
- Provide meaningful opportunities for students to connect with other students and build a healthy group identity.
- Serve as the ambassador and liaison between the women of the church, other ministries, and the church Session and staff.
- Develop annual ministry plans for worship, media, events, and ministry training.
- Be committed to the 5Ps of our church: Prayer, Plan, Privilege, Professional, and Promote.
- Inspire and guide the vision and overall ministry of the church in a way that is aligned with the Scriptures and the church's values and culture, in conjunction with a strong team approach to leadership.
- Perform general clerical and admin tasks, including typing, copying, filing, scanning, reserving rooms, etc.
- Shepherd women toward maturity in Christ, knowing that every woman needs care and has a calling.
- Function as a cohesive member of the Pastoral Care Team, providing care services for patients of other chaplains as needed.
- Commitment to establishing & growing a church plant while serving as Senior Pastor with emphasis on planting and developing a new church seed within the current church, preaching, teaching, and meeting the congregation's pastoral care needs.
- Recruit, train, and supervise adult volunteer staff to minister to students.
- Work with the Pastors and staff to recruit, audition and incorporate new vocalists, instrumentalists, and audio-visual media volunteers.
- Help ensure smooth Sunday services through administrative or logistical oversight (e.g., help ensure that child check-in or A/V systems are operational).
- Do the work of an evangelist by first engaging in personal evangelism and then making outreach and evangelism training and opportunities a visible and integral part of ministry to the congregation.
- Maintain up-to-date written missionary committee ministry policies and guidelines.
- Prepare and deliver Sunday messages tailored to each respective group within our Children's Ministry (Toddlers/Elementary) and lead Sunday morning praise with our children.
- Complete all cleaning duties as assigned, moving furniture and setting up for regular and special activities.
- Provide oversight of the Trustees & Finance Team, connection with, and follow-up in developing a sustainable church budget.
- Develop a comprehensive discipling ministry for Middle Schooler.

- Provide proactive administrative assistance to the Senior Director of Missions & Church Planting; exhibit a degree of independence and accountability for results.
- Engage the mission field of the University by serving with a consistent presence on campus – reaching out to students, staff, and faculty alike to share the love and grace of God through the Gospel of Jesus Christ.
- Ensure that crucial admin responsibilities are being completed in preparation for launch/sending.
- Serve as the first point of contact with visitors by following up on first-time visitor information cards collected.
- Provide theological oversight for Sunday school curricula and Men's and Women's ministries.
- Promote and multiply co-ed small groups/community groups.
- Develop a regional fund-raising network expanding the ministry's influence in select geographic areas and Reformed denominations.
- Actively lead classes and/or groups to help individuals become disciples of Jesus Christ.
- Lead the messaging and adoption of the church's Strategic Plan by overseeing that church publications are aligned with strategic initiatives and, where appropriate, provide special content.
- Shepherd, equip, challenge, and motivate church members and staff to participate in international, national, and global ministries.
- Manage the training, development, and evaluation of the Pastoral Staff along with the Senior Pastor.
- Work collaboratively with medical treatment teams.
- Lead weekly rehearsals with the worship band/team with a view to musical excellence.
- Make campus ministry opportunities visible and accessible to the congregation and actively find and offer opportunities for congregational engagement.
- Cultivate relationships with the un-churched in the target area.
- Change the fuses in the church phone system after an electrical storm.

What excites you? Which items are new concepts to you? Which should you put on your Ideal Job Description? An Ideal Job Description guides you in your vocational trajectory.

I deliberately did not include what job title went with each of these responsibilities because we get hung up by job titles. Put less focus on the job title and more on the actual duties. I think you would be surprised to know that the more mundane items (e.g., administration, management) above come from job descriptions for lead pastors, while the more traditional and "exciting" ministry responsibilities (e.g., teaching) come from support role job descriptions. Also, you can think about these ministry responsibilities individually by decoupling them from a job description.

How Job Descriptions are Created
Most job descriptions are created in a vacuum. They are designed to include as many duties as possible, designed by people who often know little about the job's requirements. When a church creates a new position, the job description is often a catch-all. Perhaps the church seeks a Youth Pastor who can also lead worship. (I see this type of job posted at least once a month but have only seen it filled twice in 20 years). The ideal candidate *could* also do small-group development *or* oversee the local and global missions' efforts No actual person is in mind when the job is composed, but the theoretical "someone out there." Even if another person held the position in the past, the job description is often an amalgamation of everything the last person did well, plus everything the previous person didn't do well, minus everything the last person did poorly.

I recommend you approach job descriptions assuming that what is on the page is just the beginning of a negotiable conversation. So long as you are interested in ten percent of what is described in the position, I encourage you to apply. The church needs the opportunity to engage real candidates who aren't excited about leading worship and youth as much as you need the chance to test your sense of calling against the present-reality needs of the church.

This process clarifies when you have a map charting your vocational direction. Candidates confess that they have not applied for or declined positions because of undesirable elements of the job description, the wrong title, the lack of opportunity for promotion, or the inability to pursue ordination. An Ideal Job Description serves as a lodestone pointing you in a vocational trajectory. Educators call this backward planning: structuring a class around the one or two skills the instructor wants students to come away with at the end of the course. An Ideal Job Description helps you start at the end. Where do you think you want to be in 20 years? What opportunities, experiences, skills, and competencies do you need to develop to reach the desired goal?

Consider that very few candidates secure the ideal job right out of seminary. I estimate most candidates are ten years into ministry before they predominantly function in areas of competency and passion—what Dr. Philip Douglass calls the "60/40 rule." That is, sixty percent of the work is in activities that give energy, while forty percent is in areas that drain energy. This doesn't mean a person is weak in areas that drain energy. Plenty of pastoral candidates can manage an organization or conduct administration but few find joy in the work, and many are exhausted by doing it often.

When you give substantial time to develop an Ideal Job Description, you come away with a vocational road map. Keep it dynamic: refine as necessary and reference as needed. The Ideal Job Description ensures you continue pursuing positions that allow you to develop critical skills while gaining essential experience.

Bradley mapped out his vocational trajectory. His 20-year goal was to be the primary preaching pastor of a church, spending substantial amounts of his time researching and writing. The types of churches structured to allow for this time allocation are either large—with competent staff and an executive pastor—or very small, having low expectations of their generalist pastor. (See the section on Church Personality in Chapter 7.) Bradley ignored positions involving youth, assuming that these jobs would not advance him in his vocational trajectory. By developing a robust Ideal Job Description, Bradley identified essential experiences and skills some youth positions would allow him to gain and develop. He applied for and eventually landed a youth ministry position. Within five years, he served as a medium-sized church's Solo Pastor.

Buy a LEGO set. Each set comes with a step-by-step manual to guide the building process. In some cases, you can take the manual into the LEGO store and construct the same model using the spare part bins in the store. An Ideal Job Description is like the last page of the LEGO manual. You know precisely what the finished product looks like. Unlike a Lego set, your vocational trajectory does not come with prepackaged elements or a step-by-step guide. You build it from scratch along a winding and circuitous route. A dynamic, Ideal Job Description keeps you on the right path. It lets you know if you are building with black and gray bricks or bright red, blue, and yellow bricks.

Job boards develop familiarity with how most churches manage the hiring process.

The final way job boards can help you in your search is by allowing you to develop familiarity with the hiring process. As mentioned in the introduction, applying for a job at a corporate firm is straightforward: quick, thorough, and efficient.

I often wish the non-profit sector was as efficient and straightforward. While many factors contribute to an extended evaluation process, non-profits regularly adopt ineffective practices for candidate evaluation. Churches post jobs with only general goals and responsibilities listed. More of the job description is dedicated to character traits and vocational qualifications than to outcomes, making it harder to figure out the grounds on which your effectiveness in the position will be evaluated. After sending the requested documents, an applicant may not hear back from the church. If you do, it might be a month later, or six months. The interaction may be personal, or it may be electronic. The applicant may or may not get an interview. After interviewing, an applicant may not hear anything for months as the search committee deliberates over the various candidates. On-site interviewing may involve one site visit or two. Even then, a candidate may not receive a concrete salary offer until the church decides to extend an offer.

Katie applied for a position. Seven months later, she received her first reply from the church. She had already accepted another job. Thomas never heard from a committee after an encouraging, two-hour phone interview. And when I interviewed for a youth position, the committee talked as though I had already been offered and had accepted the job: "We signed up for these summer trips. Are those the trips you would want to lead this summer?" Are you surprised I never heard back from the committee after our in-person meeting at the church?

Finding, applying and interviewing for, evaluating, and accepting a ministry job is marked by periods of slow progress and ineffective methods. You may experience frustration with the process and pace of many churches, especially if you expect them to hire the way corporations hire. Few give little insight into the application process. At a minimum, reading about and experimenting with how churches hire helps to normalize your expectations while minimizing frustration.

Why Non-Profit Jobs are Broad, Unspecific.

When you look for a new job, Bolles and Brooks recommend seeking a "job-description change." They mean you should find out which of your current skill sets are transferable to other positions. The marketplace does this better than non-profit and church settings. Public-sector job descriptions state definable qualifications, specific skills necessary for the work, and expected outcomes. This clarity allows you to identify the additional training, education, or certification you will need to be a viable candidate.

Small businesses can't be that focused. Most small businesses depend on utility players, generalists: people willing to take a job today that will change a month from now. Non-profits, including most churches, function like a family business. They are small organizations built around a combination of formal and informal hierarchies. They expect employees to flex, tack, and adjust to the demands of the season or the challenges of the context.

My dissertation research focused on seminary graduates whose Senior Pastor left within the graduate's first two years at the church. All my research participants experienced a substantial job description change within the first six months of ministry, some unrelated to the Senior Pastor's departure. Additionally, in ongoing interviews, most support role church staff report significant changes to their job requirements or expectations within a year of accepting the position. And in a recent discussion with seminary staff, members reported they "happened" into their current position—they did not seek or plan for it—after administrators recognized specific skills or gifts. Most of these adults were in their second or third unrelated position within their institutions, and all were responsible for multiple areas of oversight for which they had received little or no formal training. How you make sense of this pattern affects your capacity to navigate changes when they occur. Knowing why this pattern exists informs how you conduct your search.

Non-profits have more work than existing staff can do, and that leaves little slack for growth or new program development. Also, non-profits are still figuring out what they need in a new hire because there are so many needs. A specific job opening triggers a hiring cycle, but the job you accept will often look different—sometimes radically so—from the job you are doing a year later. Church search committees report putting every possible responsibility on a job description, hoping the final candidate will excel at some of them.

Turnover within non-profits means existing employees slide into other roles or responsibilities. Even without a turnover, this likely occurs when your gifts become more clearly demonstrated to senior leadership. Most non-profits hire people who reflect their values and culture first, and then they look at professionalism, education, and experience. Promotion from within is standard. Your gifts, skills, and capacities impact what opportunities you have within the organization.

Finally, and this is no small matter, hiring a new staff member is often the first opportunity for other staff members to rest. In addition to their regular duties, paid staff and volunteers often share the responsibilities of a vacant position. Like most small organizations, churches often need more staff before they have the funds to hire them. Existing staff regularly wear multiple hats, are stretched thin, and are often overworked. Hiring new staff finally provides space for other staff to breathe, rest, and feel emotions. This accounts for new staff members taking on more responsibility than previously outlined in their initial job description. It also explains why some Senior Pastors resign after their first sabbatical, coinciding with a new hire.

Knowing these realities can help you navigate the relational dynamics of the church. Most people think about a new job as an opportunity to gain new experiences and try out burgeoning skills. We get excited by vocational possibilities or the chance for mentoring by more experienced ministry leaders. Like a child learning to ride a bike, we want to hold the handlebars and sit in the seat but need the support of someone behind us. Do not squelch that desire or enthusiasm but expand your expectations of the first year to include a picture of yourself holding the bicycle seat for someone else. Your willingness to serve and support, even as you learn and acclimate, can be your greatest gift to existing staff and your new church.

Challenges of a Broad Job Description
Non-profit organizations make job descriptions broad to the pool of potential candidates and to fill as many organizational holes as possible. But this brings challenges for candidates. The most obvious challenges of a broad job description are determining whether you have the

necessary capacities or skills for the position and discerning whether you would be a viable candidate. Candidates must have a high degree of self-awareness in evaluating broad job descriptions. The burden of discovery lies on the candidate, which is why employing Behavioral Interviewing is so important (see Chapter 2).

Broad job descriptions communicate the expectation for candidates to excel in competing skill sets. People described as left-brained tend to be more logical, methodical, and rational. People who self-identify a preference for these values also tend to prefer *Sensing* and *Thinking* on the Myers Briggs Type Indicator (MBTI). They are more commonly D or C Types on the DISC Profile. People described as right brained tend to be more creative, curious, and intuitive. People who self-identify a preference for these values also prefer *Intuition* and *Feeling* on the Myers Briggs. They are more commonly I and S Types on the DISC profile. (See Chapter 4 for more on the MBTI.)

Some readers get hung up on the misapplication of the concept of brain laterality, and others will argue against the scientific propositions of personality tests. The fact remains that people are different, and all of us seek ways to understand these differences: relationally versus results-oriented, intuitive versus data-oriented, analytical versus value-driven, initiating versus receiving, externally-focused versus internally-minded, orderly versus flexible, accommodating versus asserting, verbal versus quiet, and the list goes on.

In short, people who reject models that account for differences in how people think, communicate, and relate, don't replace those models with an alternative, functional view of reality. Instead, they create their own rubric for assessing the actions of others against their values, beliefs, and preferences.

Where a position at a financial firm or medical practice requires specialized expertise, ministry jobs sprawl across multiple areas. Preaching requires different skills than teaching, but both differ from practicing human presence. Talking is distinct from listening, and instruction is distinct from inquiry. Managing is distinct from creating. Organizing is distinct from planning. Vision is different from implementation. Leadership is different from management. Shepherding is different from structuring.

When pastoral job descriptions are too broad, they fail to consider applicants' individuality and limited capacities. Most people can do anything within reason. Nobody can do everything. When a church or committee recognizes this, they can adjust their expectations. When they don't recognize these God-given limits, some candidates try to do it all and experience burnout.

This is why I recommend the creation of an Ideal Job Description. This allows you to name your strengths and capacities—who you are—before seeing in what way you may be able to serve in a specific context.

Action Steps
1. Get a sense of the process (and pace) most search committees adopt in hiring. To do this, you might need to apply to several positions you are only remotely interested in.
2. Grow your awareness of the process to make expectations more realistic, reducing frustration.
3. Read ten or more job descriptions focused on areas that interest you. Start with those that have compelling titles but also look at jobs that don't seem at all interesting. Use three highlighters to mark up several job descriptions: green for the parts that excite you, yellow for aspects you can do but may not give you energy, and red for the activities you can't or don't want to do.
4. Use the parts you highlighted develop an Ideal Job Description. Incorporate elements from your education and experience, the feedback others have given you, personality inventories you've taken, and your evaluation of job descriptions.
5. Revisit your Ideal Job Description weekly at the beginning of your search and after each conversation with a Network Partner. Later in the process, reread your Ideal Job Description at least every two weeks. This keeps your vocational goals in front of you as you continue the ministry job search process.

2

HOW TO BECOME AN INTENTIONAL NETWORKER

Chapter Summary

Traditional networking comes with the negative connotations of self-promotion. By comparison, *Intentional Networking* is a redemptive conversation in which you honor another person's wisdom, insights, ideas, and experiences. When you practice networking to learn and grow instead of just finding a job, you position yourself as an active learner, filling your knowledge gaps. You honor the experience of others when you ask them to teach you what they have learned. Inviting other practitioners to speak to areas of your proficiency reveals knowledge gaps of which you are unaware. In turn, you develop the skills and practical knowledge necessary to navigate interviews. Simultaneously, you strengthen your connection to the individuals most likely to hear about the jobs you seek. *Intentional Networking* involves asking the right people the right questions in the right way. By expressing humility, curiosity, and appreciation, you find Network Partners willing to advocate for your vocational ministry search.

Intentional Networking

Intentional Networking is the act of interviewing people—Network Partners—who are experts in vocational contexts similar to those in which you want to work. Being an *Intentional Networker* means you believe the most valuable gift these people offer you is stories of their experiences. These stories inform and instruct and even expose your knowledge gaps. An Ideal Job Description helps define your interests and desires: what type of work you want to do and what skills or knowledge you need. *Intentional Networking* exposes what you don't know that you don't know, what Donald Rumsfeld called "unknown unknowns,"[7] *Intentional Networking* is different from other networking approaches because it emphasizes the relationship between you and a ministry practitioner, focusing on preparing you for the job you seek.

This approach to networking is designed around elements borrowed from qualitative research and combined with principles of complex system theory, educational practices of memory and recollection, and what business calls strategic advantage. The approach doesn't come up in my research of best practices for finding a ministry job. Few candidates intuitively include elements of *Intentional Networking* in their job search. And yet, it is the most practical approach to finding and securing your Ideal Ministry Job.

Traditional Networking
Traditional networking prioritizes you: your knowledge, experience, and competency. In the process, you talk about yourself and what you bring to your next job. Your goal is to convey your credibility to networkers who, in turn, can recommend you for positions.

When candidates call me using a traditional networking approach, they start with a strong sales pitch: a summary of their education and employment history, their achievements, who their references are, and their enthusiasm about new opportunities. Most candidates talk about themselves for 30 minutes. Then, candidates shift to the ask: "Can you recommend me for any positions? Do you know people I should talk with?"

What can I say in response? I can affirm, or I can challenge. Ironically, my affirmation is ultimately worthless. In most cases, I need to learn more about the candidate to discern whether or not his self-assessment is accurate. Even if I know the candidate, I have been—at best—activated as an enthusiast whose mission is now to encourage.

Those few times when I challenged candidates, they responded as if in an interview. In an interview, people assume a position of strength. Even admitting weakness or deficiency is an opportunity to portray strength and discuss growth, collaboration, and capacity. There is often little space for self-reflection.

One seminary graduate called me, looking for his first ministry job. I started with my lead-in question: "Tell me more about what you'd like to talk about today." The candidate talked for twenty minutes about his background, experience, education, and readiness for senior leadership. When he finally paused, I said, "It sounds like you have been encouraged to use your gifts as a Senior Pastor. I'm curious, in what ways do you think such a role will challenge you?"

"I don't know all the challenges I'll face," he replied, "but when they arise, I'll draw on the approaches that have proved successful in the past." He then talked for another ten minutes about the challenges he'd overcome in other situations. Far from conveying maturity and wisdom, he communicated an unwillingness to be genuine, humble, and self-reflective. I would only recommend such a person for any ministry position if I had evidence of growth. I discovered months later that he had given up his search for a ministry position and returned to a marketplace job.

Knowledge Gaps

Traditional networking prioritizes your knowledge. *Intentional Networking* prioritizes your knowledge gaps: what you don't know. Your conversations with Network Partners focus on learning what you don't know about the position you eventually want to hold. While filling your knowledge gaps, you develop meaningful connections linking you to job opportunities that would otherwise never be available. *Intentional Networking* uses your knowledge gaps as an opportunity to gain insights from experts who can fill those gaps.

What is a knowledge gap? Knowledge gaps exist between the spheres of your personal education and practical experience. The scope of any knowledge gap changes depending on how much or little overlap exists between what you know (education) and what you have done (experience).

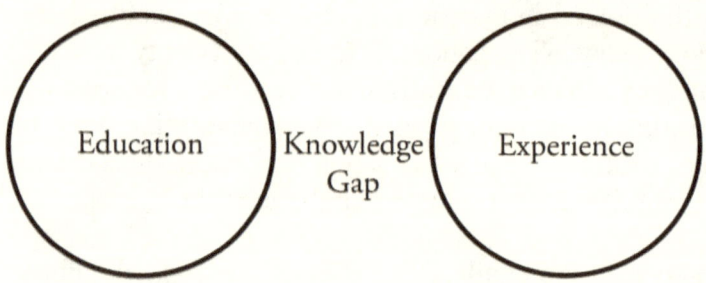

As a minister or ministry candidate, your knowledge gap between theology and ministry may be smaller than your knowledge gap between theology and quantum mechanics (different disciplines).

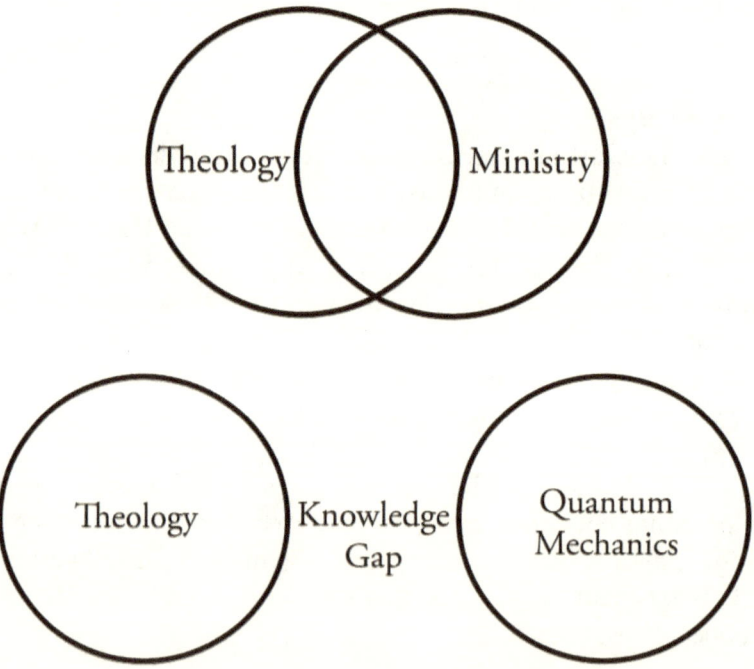

However, your knowledge gap between systematic theology and its influence on sermon preparation may be smaller than your knowledge gap between approaches to practical theology applied in counseling, even though both are forms of theology.

In my first ministry position, I worked as a Youth Director. I was 23 years old, fresh out of college, enthusiastic, and sufficiently ignorant about youth ministry. During my first week on the job, I rudely offended the local electronics store owner. The second week on the job, I had members of the Women's Auxiliary Committee frustrated that I'd removed a phone from the kitchen (to use in my office) and left wires dangling out of the wall. Over the next two and a half years, I bumbled through innumerable ministry situations. I caught a student looking at pornography and ignored it. The head Deacon was regularly frustrated with me for forgetting to turn down the air conditioner at night (guilty as charged). I inadvertently gave the treasurer erroneous information for a check that I later could not cash to rent a van for a youth trip that almost got canceled! I left a dozen 7-year-old kids running wild in the Fellowship Hall while trying to fulfill a conflicting appointment with the church directory committee. I struggled to communicate with my Senior Pastor, felt insecure with youth parents, and got angry with the students when they complained about the film choice for movie night. My knowledge gaps were wide.

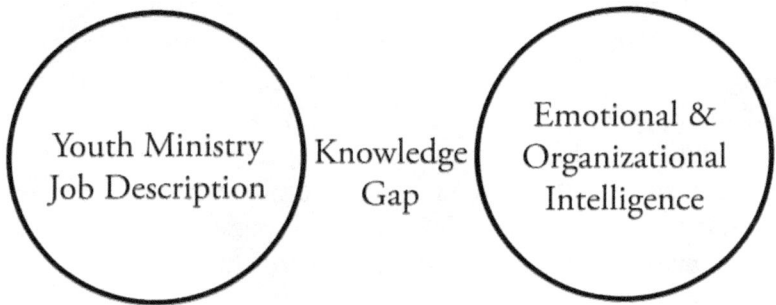

What should I have done differently? I should have picked up the phone and called a dozen youth ministers. I should have peppered them with case studies from my own experience. I should have asked about their experience navigating the various interests of their constituents: parents, students, the Pastor, Elders, Deacons, and the Women's Auxiliary Committee. Specifically, I should have picked up the phone and called these Youth Pastors before accepting the job. I didn't know what I didn't know. My knowledge gaps hindered my effectiveness in ministry.

Knowledge gaps are a natural part of development. They do not reflect a deficiency in character. They are not the fault of your parents, upbringing, college, or seminary. Active learners are people searching to expose new holes in their knowledge. I recently attended a presentation by a talent acquisition recruiter at a technology development conference. Addressing a group of college-aged students, he reminded them, "Learning comes from discomfort." Identifying your knowledge gaps involves practice, self-reflection, curiosity, and maturity. This is part of the active learning process.

People go to seminary for ministry preparation. Where they go to seminary reflects what skills and capacities, they believe are necessary to be an effective minister. Every seminary has unique foci. No seminary teaches you everything you need to know about every aspect of ministry; no seminary could. As R. Robert Creech put it, "[T]he territory of congregational life is so diverse and so unpredictable that no education could prepare one for every possibility."[8]

The best formal education teaches students the foundation of learning—the information necessary to build a solid base. Formal education should instill a framework of knowledge that supports life-long learning. Our ability to learn something new depends on our integration of prerequisite information. Using Bloom's Taxonomy, exposure to knowledge must lead to comprehension before we can apply that knowledge in proper situations, and so forth. Active learners constantly move up and down Bloom's taxonomic pyramid through the various stages. As an active learner, you need experts to walk you through their journey to the top of Bloom's Taxonomy in specific areas of knowledge where you have limited experience and exposure.

Candidates have two kinds of knowledge gaps: known and unknown. There exist aspects of ministry that you *know* you need to learn, areas of ministry outside your vocational experience or tasks at which you do not excel. If you have yet to be a lead minister, you don't know what it is like to preach to the same congregation week after week for years in a row. Weekly preaching to college students or at a nursing home is different. Itinerant preaching is different. Intrinsic organizational expectations in a church influence how a pastor prepares and delivers his sermons and how the congregation receives them. This is a known knowledge gap. But there are also unknown knowledge gaps: ministry aspects you *do not know* you need to be aware of (e.g., the Women's Ministry Committee). Often, these are positional and situational. They involve enmeshed or triangulated relationships, power dynamics, individual and group interests, undefined and unnamed values, unspoken expectations, ambiguous roles, and deep fears. If you haven't served in the specific job you seek, you have unknown knowledge gaps in areas of ministry competency.

How to Expose Your Knowledge Gaps
Intentional Networking fills your known and unknown knowledge gaps. When interviewing Network Partners, start with known knowledge gaps related to the position you seek (i.e., Ideal Job). This is where having an Ideal Job Description is helpful. A well-developed Ideal Job Description requires more of you than your experience and education have prepared you for. It should.

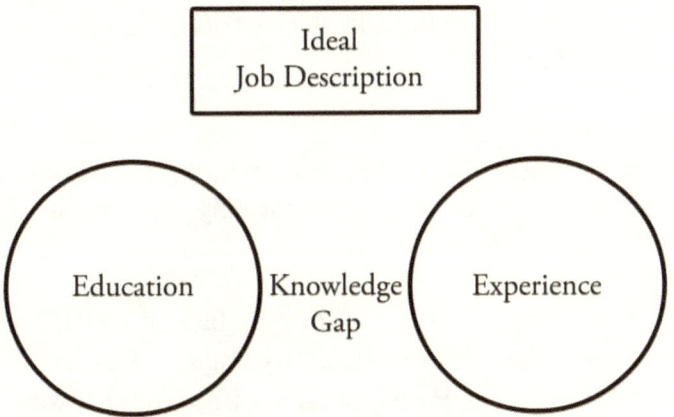

Ignorance isn't a flaw. It is a lack of information or experience. But our ignorance elicits feelings of inadequacy and insecurity. Candidates often need to secure the job to gain the necessary experience. But sometimes, you learn about those roles or duties by interviewing ministry practitioners: people with expertise in areas essential to your success in a specific position.

Take your Ideal Job Description. Interrogate it. What does the job expect that you have yet to experience? How might the job stretch you? What types of questions arise when you consider the position? What are situations the role may put you in and for which you have no context of assessment? What are areas of responsibility outlined in the job that you know you are not ready for? What areas of inexperience do you expect a search committee might or should ask you about?

The result of such an interrogation is a disorganized list of observations, questions, and concerns. Spend time finding the themes that arise out of that chaos. The themes emerging from this analysis clarify the specific areas of practical information and experience you need to explore.

Michael served as an Assistant Pastor for four years, supporting the work and ministry of the Pastor and church as a generalist. He began to feel a call to preach more and to practice more leadership than his current position allowed. Around the same time, his Senior Pastor went on a two-month sabbatical, allowing Michael to serve as the Interim Pastor. During that time, he had opportunities to preach and lead. He described it as a "season of thriving." When the Senior Pastor returned, Michael returned to his old duties, which he now found unsatisfying. He had functionally been the Senior Pastor, hadn't he? He felt the call to that position. Moreover, people in the congregation had affirmed his preaching and leadership.

Michael's Knowledge Gap Map
As we crafted his Ideal Job Description, we explored knowledge gaps specific to senior leadership. He eventually landed on these three research questions (R.Q.s):

- How does a Senior Pastor lead in the face of resistance?
- How does a Senior Pastor healthily engage conflict?
- How does a Senior Pastor preach with a mind toward personal, congregational, and organizational change?

While answering these questions, Michael realized that, as the Interim, he had not faced meaningful resistance or conflict. The congregation and Elders hadn't viewed him as the senior leader. This impacted how they heard Michael and changed how they responded to him—"with kid gloves," as he put it. Research substantiates Michael's experience, showing that Assistant Pastors most often have conflict with their lead pastor. In contrast, lead pastors most often have conflict with the Elder Board (Session) or the congregation. This doesn't mean that Elders or congregations don't get frustrated with an Assistant Pastor; instead, these parties convey their frustration to the Senior Pastor instead of directly to the Assistant Pastor. In this respect, Assistant Pastors experience conflict indirectly—in a triangulated way—while lead pastors are more likely to experience conflict directly.[9]

The more specific your research questions become, the more effective they draw out the information you need to fill your knowledge gaps. Michael's three questions are strategic or "big picture" questions. By framing questions in this way, Michael could elicit experience-focused narratives. Then again, they might send a Network Partner into a less helpful, esoteric monologue. By expanding these R.Q.s into behavioral-interviewing questions, you expose the information necessary to fill your knowledge gap.

Behavioral Interviewing
Behavioral interviewing, also known as behavior-based interviewing, is "an analysis of a candidate's potential abilities by examining skills used in past job performance. The main difference between this type of interviewing and a regular interview is that candidates are asked to give specific examples of how they acted in the past, instead of being asked to share their opinions or ideas."[10] Behavioral interviewing asks people to draw from their personal experience—not from what others have said or done. This is why it's necessary to interview people working in the job you eventually want to have. Your Network Partners must be ready to speak from personal experience about the areas of ministry you want to explore.

You will find that people tend to reveal more than they know when answering a behavioral interviewing question. Behavioral interviewing is a form of qualitative research that relies mainly on data collected from structured conversations around personal experience. A structured discussion has a particular purpose and often seeks a predetermined outcome.

Behavioral interviewing follows the STAR. acronym: Situation or Task, Action, and Results. I have adapted and expanded this rubric for ministry contexts to STARR.

Set the Stage (context)	Give context for the questions you ask. Context enables practitioner to answer genuinely. Questions that have no context often produce answers that are general, ambiguous, or abstract.
Situation or Task (story)	Ask the practitioner to describe a situation where the skill, competency, or expression of character is likely to be revealed. Look for specificity and concreteness. The narratives should be factual and historic with details about who was involved and their relationships, along with the goals or desired outcomes of the situation/task.
Action (taken)	Ask the practitioner to describe what actions he or she took in order to reach the desired outcomes or objectives, or to resolve and address the issue. Continue to encourage details on the specific activities, even while allowing the candidate to protect the identities of those involved in sensitive situations.
Results (achieved)	Ask about the outcomes of the situation, what were the results, and what was accomplished. Listen for who did the action, who received the credit, and who was at fault. Who is the hero and who is the villain?
Reflection (learning)	Ask what the practitioner learned or would have done differently next time. Listen for self-reflection, growth, development, and humility.

Setting the stage for your questions creates safety for an honest response; it shows curiosity as opposed to judgment. Asking for reflection at the back end gives space and grace for maturity. This form of question should be used by both search committees and candidates whenever possible. Applying this method, Michael reformulated his three R.Q.s as follows:

- Tell me about a time you experienced resistance while implementing a new program. What happened? How did people react? How did you respond to them? What did you feel about yourself? What was the understanding of those who were against the change? What was the outcome?
- Tell me about a time you experienced meaningful conflict with a key influencer within the congregation. What was the issue? How did it come to your attention? What did you do? How did they react? How did you resolve this conflict? What did you feel during this time? In retrospect, is there anything you would have done differently?

- Tell me about a time you saw a meaningful change within one or more congregation members after a particular sermon or sermon series. Who were they? How would they describe the change? How do you understand the change in the person? How does that change the way you prepare for and deliver your sermons?

As you interview Network Partners, you may tweak or adjust your Behavioral Interviewing questions to get at something more specific. Usually, this does not involve changing your R.Q.s. A change in the R.Q.s usually consists of a change in the knowledge gap you are exploring. Avoid trying to fill too many knowledge gaps at once, as this dilutes the quality of the information you gain from asking the same questions to multiple people. If there are different knowledge gaps you want to explore, generate a new set of R.Q.s and behavioral interviewing questions specific to that topic. Then, ask these questions of a new group of Network Partners.

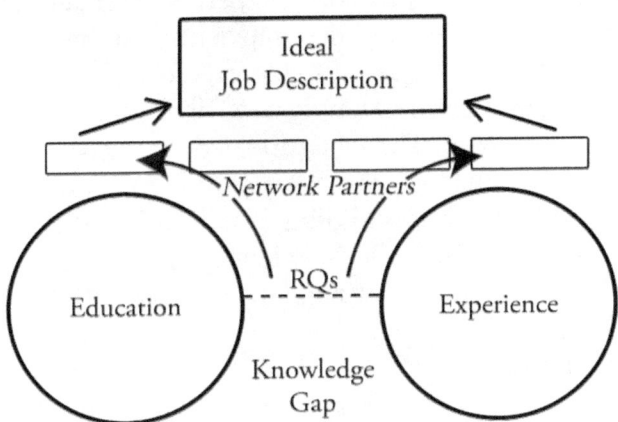

What you learn from your Network Partners during this exercise is more than helpful information. It's essential! You are not the only person who sees your knowledge gaps and inexperience. Search committees see them, too. If you have too many knowledge gaps in areas essential to a job, or the gap between your experience and the church's expectation is too wide, search committees won't even engage with you. Your preparation for interviewing with the committee depends on what you learn from people—Network Partners—with experience working in similar jobs.

Dustin interviewed for a youth position in New England. The church had a core group of 30 high school students and a space dedicated to youth activities. The church was located near the county high school. While the church had grown, the youth program had been stagnant. The search committee committed to finding a candidate who could build stronger connections with the high school administration and faculty to reach the students with the Gospel.

During the interview, a committee member asked, "It doesn't look like you have much experience starting new programs, so how would you help us reach the students at the local high school?" It is a poorly worded question, inviting speculation. Dustin needed more information. What had the church tried previously, and what had been the outcome of these efforts? What worked and why? What failed and why? What was the school's view of the church? Did the church have students at the school? Were there needs the school had that the church could help fill?

Because Dustin had spoken with a dozen experienced Youth Pastors, he could speak directly to his experience gap with insights gained from conversations with Network Partners. He talked about his ability to initiate and innovate, giving the example of a Bible study he started with fraternity brothers in college. Then, he reflected on the best practices he learned from conversations with the other Youth Pastors. He ended by summarizing his values when building a new ministry. This search committee was aware of Dustin's experience gap, but so was Dustin. And by learning from Network Partners, he addressed these gaps.

The Power of Listening
Candidates often express fear of imposing on a busy pastor or ministry leader for their own growth and development. It's true that many pastors are stretched thin, and now you want to take an hour of their time to ask questions. It can seem more respectful of a pastor's time to ask for only 15 minutes to talk about yourself.

You couldn't be more wrong.

Overworked ministry leaders will prioritize time with you because nobody schedules an hour to talk *to* them *about* them. Think about the last time you scheduled a meeting with a pastor, ministry leader, or professor. How much of the time did you spend talking about them, and how much of the time did you spend talking about yourself? Practitioners—pastors, counselors, and ministry leaders—rarely get to talk about themselves and, even more rarely, get to talk about what they have learned through experience. Other people want to speak to them for help, to share opinions or complain, to have someone listen, to be excused for their actions, to make demands, or even to argue a point, but not to talk about the practitioner. Congregants want to talk about their problems. Staff members want to talk about their challenges. Church leaders want to talk about their frustrations. Nobody asks to meet with the Pastor to talk about the Pastor.

Practitioners are dignified in their vocation when you—a younger, less experienced candidate—desire to learn from them. You encourage them by validating their experience when you listen. The technology recruiter I mentioned earlier also said, "Helping others has exponential returns."

When you ask ministry leaders for an hour of their time and commit to asking questions and listening to their responses, you regard them as worthy of instructing you. When you reflect on what you heard and how you're thinking differently about ministry because of these conversations, you honor their wisdom and discernment. Few pastors are invited to speak at conferences, and even fewer can teach at a seminary. Your desire to learn honors a group of people—pastors, ministry leaders, and counselors—who regularly feel under-appreciated.

Over the past 20 years, I've asked nearly 550 people (some of them twice) to serve as Network Partners for young ministry candidates. I've asked them to donate an hour to speak to ministerial candidates about their experience. Four people said no, and twelve said yes but never did. The other 534 were thankful for the opportunity. Dozens of Network Partners contacted me after the phone call, expressing their appreciation and desire for more opportunities to talk with young ministry candidates. You aren't inconveniencing pastors by asking for an hour to learn from them. You are encouraging them.

Ask, Don't Tell

There will come a time in the conversation with a Network Partner that you will be tempted to affirm or challenge a statement by telling what you know. Don't! Your efforts to show what you know through telling goes only so far. Credibility established *through* telling is only as convincing as the credentials behind our name or social media trends. Speaking authoritatively displays the boundaries of our knowledge and experience. Life is not simple or uniform. There are multiple perspectives on matters not central to the Christian faith. Our snapshot view of life can only be expanded by integrating other people's perspectives, to create a panorama of reality. Besides, you are in the role of the researcher at this point, gathering information more than interpreting it.

You show greater credibility through the questions you ask than through your statements. Questions reveal your appreciation for nuance. Questions demonstrate your scope of the topic. Questions convey discernment and a reluctance to rush to closure. Questions provide space for humility. You are more likely to prove your credibility in the eyes of a Network Partner and a search committee through questions than through statements.

Of course, there are churches looking for a hero leader. Hero leaders have answers to the questions asked. Hero leaders have the solutions to present challenges. Hero leaders have a vision for growth and a plan to implement it. Hero leaders make bold and decisive statements. Some churches are determined to hire that kind leader. Ultimately, those leaders burn out, get fired, or their churches split. Search committees looking for a hero leader, who will solve their problems and return them to a golden age, have set you the new pastor on a path littered with the wrecks of failure.

A low-context culture emphasizes *what* is said—the actual words—instead of *how* something is said.[11] When we believe that our desired outcomes are achieved through efficient information exchange, the solution to any failed endeavor is to adjust the message: use more words. We talk, explain, extrapolate, expound, exegete, revise, correct, and restate. This behavior is ubiquitous. You can hear it on talk radio, read it on social media feeds, listen to it in board meetings and the college classroom, and find it in many personal arguments and professional

42

disagreements. One of the downsides to a low-context culture is the need to talk, *a lot*.

There are two reasons people overuse the *tell* communication method. First, we conflate telling with teaching. This perspective assumes that you have taught somebody something if you communicated the information. By extension, if you have been told something, then you know how to respond accordingly. Failure to do so puts the burden of responsibility on the information receiver, rarely the communicator or the communication media.

Second, people *tell* to establish credibility. People attempt to establish their credibility as experts by telling others everything they know about a topic. Car sales associates tell me everything they know about a car, and boat salespeople tell me what they know about a boat. Over-eager mechanics tell me everything they know about the integration of systems and the breakdown that is causing my car issues. And theologically trained people use technical language to show their expertise on God and the human condition.

Five people in my life rarely tell me everything they know. They are my doctor, counselor, financial planner, executive coach, and patent lawyer. My conversations with these people are dominated by pointed and pertinent questions, proving their credibility. For example, here are the questions my doctor asked at my last physical:

> How are you feeling? Are you having any discomfort? When did the pain begin? Describe it for me. Where do you experience it now? On a scale of one-to-ten, rate the pain. Has anything changed since your last physical? What are you doing to stay active and fit? Tell me about your diet. What are you drinking?

Granted, I don't know what I don't know, but my doctor does. He rarely uses the didactic method; when he does, it only comes after asking quite a few questions. The information he presents is focused and intentional:

- As men approach 50, we want to start monitoring their digestive systems. How is your digestive health?
- Muscle deteriorates after the age of 45. You might feel this in your lower back, neck, arms, or joints. How is your back? How

are your joints? Do you experience regular discomfort anywhere? Are there motions you can't do? Are there motions that are limited?

My doctor never tries to divulge everything he knows about every health issue that threatens me. My doctor doesn't try to change my mind, perspective, or lifestyle by overwhelming me with his knowledge. His curiosity guides me to the logical outcomes of my choices. His brief statements of knowledge guide our conversation into areas where he can then ask more questions.

My doctor is an expert in both medicine and asking questions. My counselor is an expert in emotional and behavioral systems. My financial planner is an expert in financial planning. The patent lawyer I've consulted is an expert in patent law. Their expertise is first established in the scope and focus of the questions they ask and, only then, in the limited knowledge they share.

Telling Network Partners about yourself is not the remedy for an ineffective network. There are better solutions to disinterested looks or evidence of disengagement than inundating search committees with your knowledge. Research shows that most of us can listen to another person for only 20 minutes before we start to lose focus. This is why TED Talks are 18 minutes long. Even then, most listeners might only remember a key concept or a compelling image. But the majority of what we hear is lost to memory and recollection. We need activities that "interrupt the forgetting process."[12]

Why do so many ministry leaders believe their credibility is primarily proved by presenting knowledge, information, and perspective? Part of it grows out of a genuine commitment to the authoritative nature of the Scriptures. Most Christians believe that "all Scripture is God-breathed" (2 Tim. 3:16). Therefore, its interpretation and application derive from an external, divine source. Sound theological training prepares students for historical, cultural, and contextual interpretation and current application of the Scriptures. So, when asked, "What is your view of divorce?" theology students are quick to respond with a statement grounded in the Scriptures.

By default, when statements are our first response to questions, we sacrifice the opportunity to establish credibility in terms of pastoring, shepherding, and counseling in our rush to be the expert. The woman who asked the question, "What is your view of divorce?" served on the search committee of a small church. The candidate gave a clear, concise, and scripturally founded response. The candidate later found out that the last pastor had barred this woman's daughter from taking communion after she (the daughter) separated from her physically abusive husband. When the woman asked, "What is your view of divorce?" The committee member really asked, "Will you care for my daughter?" Only open-ended questions would have revealed that desire.

Questions help us discern where other people are coming from. I may not like it when someone says, "I don't like your shirt." But I won't know where that dislike comes from unless I ask questions. Likely it has nothing to do with me. Most visceral statements like this come from places of big emotion or pastor hurts in the other person's life. Learning why people say, behave, and believe what they do, positions you to know how to respond. It enables you to affirm And, in the process, good questions allow us to respond wisely while affirming the good in others.

Good and Better Questions
Open questions invite the best answers, leading to rich conversation. "Open questions have two key benefits: they let [your interviewee] direct the conversation (because they can be answered in many ways) and they make [your interviewee] think by eliciting longer answers."[13]

What is the difference between open and closed questions? Closed questions allow for single-word answers: yes or no. Closed questions typically start with these words: can, will, do/does, are, could, would, is.

- Is that a good church to work for?
- Will you stay in your current position?
- You don't like your Senior Pastor, do you?
- Does the leadership understand the pressure you are under?

Open questions start with traditional interviewing words: who, what, when, where, why, and how.

- How would you assess that church?
- When will you know to look for a new ministry position?
- What kind of pressure are you under?
- Who are the people you can talk with about these challenges?
- Do you like your current position?

Open questions can also start with inquisitive statements. I prefer to start these statements with "Tell me about a time."

- Tell me about a time you dealt with a difficult staff person.
- Tell me about a time you launched a new program.

There are ways to misuse open questions. Leading questions aim to elicit specific responses. Leading questions emerge from our pre-formed conclusions rather than curiosity about the situation. We have all been on the receiving end of leading questions and know the feeling of being trapped. Leading questions take freedom away from the people you are interviewing and puts them on the defensive.

The Changing Landscape of Vocation
Something happens to most people when they get to a place of curiosity. Wonder replaces judgment. Listening replaces talking. And there is possibility in the silence. This is a mental space as much as it is an emotional reality. It is an ability we all have. The child and the child in us perpetually wonder. This is like poetry when every feature of Western culture drives us to the prosaic of propositional truth.

This may seem a tangential and pedantic retrospective, but the cultivation of non-judgmental curiosity is central to your pursuit of finding fulfilling employment. It may even lead you into a new and unexpected vocation. Since the first Industrial Revolution, vocation has been a fluid reality for most people in developed countries. Wars destroy old jobs, and technology creates new ones. Economic crises lead to unemployment, and new frontiers lead to new opportunities.

You believe you are called to pursue ministry. Good! But do not replace your grip on grace with clinging to vocation. There are lifelong pastors

46

whose effectiveness has dwindled over the decades, doing disservice to the individuals, families, and organizations they serve. Others cannot find a suitable ministry position. Some have been physically, mentally, or emotionally injured and cannot meet the demands of full-time ministry. And others have obligations that keep them geographically limited. One seminary friend had to limit his ministry search to large metropolitan areas because his daughter had a heart defect and needed to be within 15 minutes of a specialist. I know of men and women who fervently believed the Lord was directing them into vocational ministry, only for those doors to close.

The Lord redirects these people to other work. They have started businesses, written deeply personal reflections, entered roles in other non-profits, created art, and designed products. They found vocational fulfillment as financial planners, bankers, in real estate, as authors and teachers, mechanics, carpenters, and engineers.

I know of seminary-trained men and women who influence large nations' political and economic systems using their ministry training. These vocations serve to open doors for gospel engagement and evangelism. And sometimes, these vocations help to make houses safe and automobiles dependable, support financial stability, and make retirement possible.

The same curiosity that enabled me to learn to build bicycles as a kid led me to two unrelated conversations with patent lawyers. The combination of problem-solving and patent law led me to develop and sell a product concept to *Audi*. Like many people, I am regularly renewed for ministry by my non-ministry interests and hobbies. These outlets provide a sense of accomplishment and completion in seasons when ministry has left me drained and discouraged.

A threat to ministerial vocational stability is progressive secularization. As a nation drifts from tenets of the Christian faith, there are more ministry opportunities and fewer full-time, fully funded ministry positions. In most parts of the world, vocational ministry is conducted by leaders who are part-time at best. Like the Apostle Paul, many are paid nothing and depend on a marketplace job for material provision. Many current and prospective ministry leaders—and maybe you—will be, at some point, bi-vocational.

Even if your unique skills and abilities don't lead you into other areas of ministry, the nature of your ministry will change. In many ways, seminary graduates from 1957 were not prepared to respond to the sexual revolution and the civil rights movement. The sermons, letters, articles, and writings of pastors of that period reveal as much. Few seminary graduates from 1999 were trained in how to think about the social concepts of gender fluidity or Internet technology. These cultural phenomena were not on the map at the turn of the century. The ways these students were primarily trained to preach—emphasizing propositional truth rooted in orthodox interpretations of historical documents—are dismissed by a society that rejects concepts of truth, viewing the Bible as a product of oppressive patriarchy.

I graduated with my Master of Divinity in 2004. We had one lecture on homosexuality in my Christian Ethics course. On the other hand, I read an entire book on openness theology. My key homiletics text was Bryan Chapell's *Christ-Centered Preaching*. Counseling courses focused primarily on models and methodologies. We were trained to proclaim what was true (indicatives) and in response what to do (imperatives). We were "trained for a world that is disappearing…"[14]

In 2020, students at the same seminary read multiple books on engaging issues of sexual orientation and confusion but read nothing on the openness of God. *Christ-Centered Preaching* is still used, but so is Zack Eswine's *Preaching to a Post-Everything World*. The new preaching methodology emphasizes earning the right to speak: relationship and reflection alongside the indicatives and the imperatives.

Most of your congregants work in industries that didn't exist 30 years ago. In that time, we have seen incredible technological advances in artificial intelligence, medicine, investments and currency, corporate governance, and the geopolitical landscape. Congregants are challenged by ethical and moral dilemmas that weren't matters of consideration 30 years ago. You can't be an expert in all these disciplines, but your thoughtful engagement with them helps the people in your church think about and respond to the issues they face.

Even educational institutions recognize the need to train for specific technical and relational *skills* more than for jobs. This refocusing means that institutions see people as "students of problems, not disciplines."[15]

Meanwhile, businesses are recruiting high-school graduates away from college altogether, promising to teach them the necessary skills to succeed without the exorbitant cost of higher education. What Hoge and Wenger found in their 2005 research, namely that "Protestant ministers serve a more educated laity than they did a half-century ago," may not be true in the coming years.[16] I don't mean congregants will be less-educated so much as they will be educated in non-traditional ways. When most congregants share a liberal arts foundation, pastors can make assumptions. Students going directly from high school into an industry-specific workforce will not have that shared foundation. This changes how pastors teach, preach, and minister.

Exploring Curiosity
You are talking with Network Partners to explore your knowledge gaps. These are specific to the areas of ministry you want to fill, and Network Partners are the best people to help you think about your vocation. Listen when they mention other areas where they get to use their skills. Be willing to let them go off-script to talk about book writing, watercolor painting, or making model train parts. My interests today in investing, product design, and brand development grew out of conversations in which I explicitly sought information about ministry.

Be willing to ask what other work you can do. When I ask ministry leaders this question, it sounds like a challenge—as if their ministry skills and capacities are not enough. I mean the question as an acknowledgment of dignity. You will still be creators and contributors long after you (and others) have given up weekly preaching, church administration, classroom instruction, and institutional leadership. There is no retirement from active participation in the work of God's kingdom—good works, which God prepared beforehand that you should walk in them (Eph. 2:10).

If you need additional inspiration, the United Nations has identified 17 Sustainable Development Goals that provide a blueprint for peace and prosperity for people and the planet: https://sdgs.un.org/goals. Lay aside any objections you may have for governmental institutions. To varying degrees, these goals can be aligned with Kingdom values.

49

Who to Prioritize in Your Network

Who you prioritize as Network Partners depends on the type of jobs you seek. Who is most likely to hear about open solo pastorates? Other Solo Pastors. Who is most likely to hear about open youth ministry positions? A youth minister. People serving in a job are most likely to hear about other lateral—or similar—ministry jobs, especially when the job is in another region of the country.

This is a point that I want to drive home. Otherwise, you may struggle to stay engaged with Network Partners in parts of the country you don't want to live in. I am describing a complex system in which the participants (nodes) of the system change as they interact. In complex systems, two things are true about the nodes. First, no node has all the information. Second, all nodes are connected. The alternative to thinking about the ministry job search process in terms of a complex system is to assume the system is merely complicated and disorganized—a mass of disjointed relationships in disconnected regions bound by weak affiliations. Candidates who think in terms of difficulty emphasize geographic proximity over other forms of connectivity to their detriment. In a complex system, geographic proximity has no greater value—and may have less—than other forms of connectivity.

There are three primary reasons a Solo Pastor is more likely to hear about other solo pastorates and a Youth Pastor is more likely to hear about other Youth Pastor jobs. First, people spend time with other people who do what they do. This is true in most industries. Youth ministers attend youth ministry conferences more often than other types of pastors. In a review of 20 years of events hosted by Covenant Seminary, we found that Senior Pastors are more likely to take part in gatherings when the other members are all Senior Pastors. In every job, aspects are only fully understood and appreciated by people in similar positions with similar experiences.

Second, committees regularly initiate with ministers serving in similar positions during the Pastoral search process. A committee may engage a Worship Minister at a sister church for a list of names of other potential Worship Ministers, or a committee may ask the Worship Minister to come and do the same work he is already doing for another church. Lateral moves are not uncommon. The reasons ministry leaders move from one position to another similar position are the same reasons they initially take a job: the people, the place, and the position.

I once recommended a committee talk with my church's Assistant Pastor of Youth. The committee represented a church in need of a new youth minister. I believed the Youth Pastor at my church would guide this other church in best practices while also giving them additional names. Instead, the committee extended a call to him. He accepted. The church was larger, the scope of the position broader, and there were more opportunities to take part in other aspects of church life. For many reasons, I think churches should talk with, and even look to recruit, ministry leaders from other churches, one being the opportunity for the committee to develop the necessary muscle memory to evaluate all their candidates.

Third, we pay attention to information when it is relevant to our lives. This has to do with the Reticular Activating System: the part of the brain that helps filter out information, allowing us to focus on what matters to us. Recently, I returned from a business trip. The terminal was noisy with people and gate announcements. Thirty yards away, an airline attendant spoke my name to another employee, and I heard it clearly. Without effort or my focused attention, my Reticular Activating System allowed me to pick out my name from the din of background noise.

Similarly, an Assistant Pastor is more likely to pay attention to details about an open assistant position than a worship position. He may want to know the impetus for a fellow Assistant Pastor's transition, the scope of the vacated position, and the nature of the new job, or he may wish to learn how to transition effectively when the time comes to do so himself. He may even know of friends who could fill the vacated position.

For these reasons, I recommend prioritizing Network Partners serving in, or who have recently served in, a similar position to the one you seek, even when those Network Partners live in different geographic regions. Prioritize these Network Partners over people who may live where you want to live but work in unrelated positions.

Look back at your Ideal Job Description. Who is the best person for that position? What experience, skills, competencies, and character does she have? Who can you interview that fits your profile? Who are the people most likely to hear about the job you ultimately want to land?

The Different Types of Network Partners

Not all Network Partners are equally efficient at making connections. Certain people are uniquely adept at creating and maintaining broad relational networks across geographic and ideological perspectives. Malcolm Gladwell calls these people Connectors: people uniquely talented at making and sustaining meaningful relationships across various sectors of society. "These people who link us up with the world, who…introduce us to our social circles—these people on whom we rely more heavily than we realize—are Connectors, people with a special gift for bringing the world together."[17]

The first mark of Connectors is that they "are the kinds of people who know everyone."[18] Connectors collect people like others collect stamps and have a penchant for cultivating acquaintances.[19] The second mark of a Connector is "the kinds of people they know."[20] Connectors "are the people whom all of us can reach in only a few steps because, for one reason or another, they manage to occupy many different worlds and subcultures and niches."[21]

When I ask candidates to describe an ideal Network Partner, most start with big-name pastors, professors, and business leaders. The assumption is that prominent people know lots of people. This assumption is often wrong. The skills necessary for people to become experts in their field are often at odds with the skill and disposition necessary to be a Connector. People become well-known as ministry leaders by growing extensive ministries, publishing books, speaking publicly, and gaining an audience of followers across different strata of church life. The duties, activities, and responsibilities that demand their time are at odds with building a vast network of meaningful relationships. The public abilities that propelled these men and women to prominence differ significantly from those necessary to be a gifted counselor or mentor. Most well-known ministry leaders are just too busy to be effective Connectors. This is not a critique or a criticism. Healthy organizations need people with different abilities. The point is, having well-known people in your network isn't as important as it may seem. It is fine to have them as Network Partners, but you aren't at a loss if you don't.

The second group of people described by candidates as ideal Network Partners are those from their sphere of relationship and vocation: close ties, not weak ties, friends more than acquaintances. Historically, close relationships played a significant role in finding a spouse but an insignificant role when getting a job:

> Sociologist Mark Granovetter provides a brilliant example of how Connectors function. In his 1974 study *Getting a Job*, Granovetter looked at several hundred professional and technical workers from the Boston suburb of Newton, interviewing them in some detail on their employment history. He found that 56 percent of those he talked to found their job through a personal connection. Another 18.8 percent used formal means—advertisements, headhunters—and roughly 20 percent applied directly. This is unsurprising; personal contact is the best way to enter the door. But, curiously, Granovetter found that of those personal connections, the majority were "weak ties." Of those who used a contact to find a job, only 16.7 percent saw that contact "often"—as they would if the contact were a good friend—and 55.6 percent saw their contact only "occasionally." Twenty-eight percent saw the contact "rarely."[22]

People weren't finding jobs through friends. They found them through acquaintances. When it comes to finding out about new jobs—or, for that matter, gaining new information or new ideas—"weak ties" are always more important than strong ties. Your friends occupy the same world that you do. They might work with or live near you, attend the same church, school, play on the same sports teams, and go to the same parties. They talk about their interests, promoting products or services they use. How much do they really know that you don't know?

On the other hand, your weak-tie acquaintances occupy a different world than you. They are more likely to know something that you don't. Granovetter coined a marvelous phrase to capture this apparent paradox: the strength of weak ties. Acquaintances, in short, represent a source of social power, and the more acquaintances you have, the more powerful you are.[23]

What does this mean for you? Just as having well-known people in your network isn't that important, you should not lean too heavily upon close relationships—friends and family—in the job search. Friends and family members suffer from cognitive bias. The more they know or think they know about you, the more they make assumptions. They make assumptions about your current skills, capacity, and character. These assumptions are often based on long-term interactions with you. Close acquaintances are hindered by how they have experienced us in the past. They become less curious and more settled in their disposition toward us. They assume behaviors and extrapolate actions. And they can be affected by conflicting motives. Instead, emphasize weak ties: Network Partners you connect with through a mutual acquaintance.

Erin pursued positions focused on building relationships with women. She wasn't actively looking at youth ministry positions, but hadn't dismissed them entirely. Eventually, she found and accepted a new job. Two months later, she learned about a position at another church in another part of the country that was a better fit. She mentioned this disappointment to a former seminary classmate, who responded, "I knew about that job, but I didn't think you wanted to do youth. And I knew you hated cold-weather areas." Erin's friend allowed what he knew of Erin to affect his decision not to tell her about the other job.

Sometimes close-tie friends and family members overemphasize or underreport information when it benefits them, even if it harms the candidate. Weston's father pulled me aside at graduation and urged me to pressure his son to return to the mission field. "God gave my son the ability to speak Spanish for a reason!" Weston's father wanted something for his son that Weston did not want for himself or his newlywed wife.

One way family and friends can support you better in the job search process is through prayer. Close-tie relationships are more likely to pray for you: for God's provision, direction, and wisdom. Don't exclude close-tie connections from your network; but emphasize weak-tie acquaintances as you seek your next job.

Prioritizing Weak-Tie Relationships
Which "weak ties" should you prioritize? Someone working in a job like the one you want is most likely to hear about similar lateral positions. An Assistant Pastor learns about other vacant Assistant Pastor positions more often than his Senior Pastor. The next person most likely

to hear about a particular job is someone in another organization to whom the Assistant Pastor reports. That is, Senior Pastors at other churches are the next most likely group to hear about Assistant Pastor positions.

As stated above, people tend to associate with other people at similar levels of organizational hierarchy. This trend increases as someone moves higher up within organizational hierarchy. Early literature on the burgeoning field of executive management recognized the imbalance of power dynamics in management-employee relationships. In 1926, Edwin Schell wrote, "I don't favor the developing of a personal interest and friendship with workmen."[24] And in 1936, T.N. Whitehead wrote, "[T]he executive is himself a social being and his general attitudes are oriented by his society, but this society is *not the group is he directing...*" (emphasis added).[25]

This isn't an antiquated concept of socialization among employees and employers. In a 2006 book, Shri L. Henkel writes, "The department manager shouldn't socialize with his or her employees. This isn't meant to be cruel, just practical."[26] And in 2018, Slate Magazine declared, "The power dynamics in a boss-employee relationship make true friendship impossible."[27]

While social stratification today is more collaborative and less hierarchical, the outcomes are little changed. Doctors still associate primarily with doctors, not orderlies. Business executives primarily associate with other executives, not administrative staff.

Youth Directors tend to connect naturally and more often with other Youth Directors, though they are glad for the opportunity to "rub shoulders" with Senior Pastors. On the other hand, Senior Pastors opt out of egalitarian gatherings of ministry leaders that also include Assistant Pastors and Youth Ministers. Instead, Senior Pastors choose to take part in groups dominated by other Senior Pastors: people who understand their world. Senior Pastors decide to spend time with other Senior Pastors. Youth pastors spend time with other Youth Pastors locally or at large national conferences. And when they do, they hear about lateral job opportunities.

Ideally, you will interact with Network Partners who have moved from a position like your current position and into the kind of position you seek. These people should be able to provide a road map of the transition—in what ways they were ready, in what ways they were not, and how they could have prepared better for the change. Hindsight may be 20/20, but when someone is further ahead in the journey than you are, their hindsight is your foresight.

If you seek a ministry position different from the one you are currently in, I recommend you create a new Ideal Job Description, as described in Chapter 1. Next, identify your knowledge gaps specific to that job. Then, build a new list of Network Partners currently working in your desired jobs. Finally, interview these people. Interviewing techniques and protocol are covered in Chapter 8.

Here is a possible networking map for an Assistant Pastor looking to move into a Senior Pastor position:

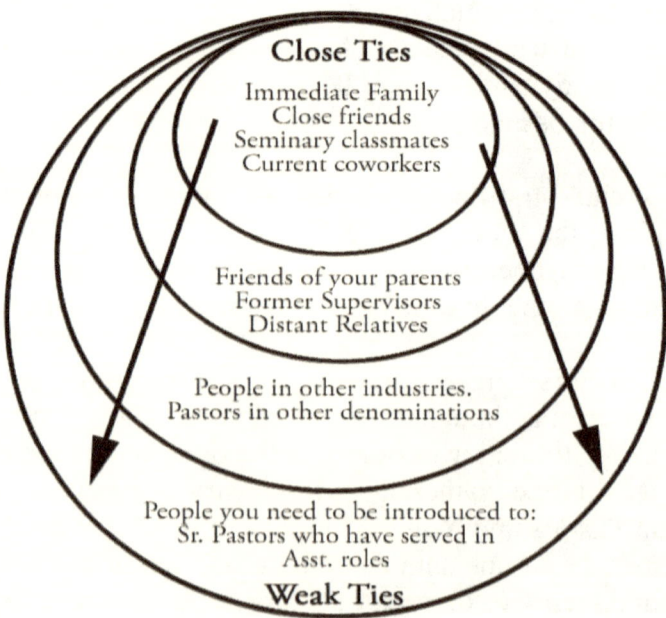

Profile of a Networker

I mentioned asking almost 550 people to serve as Network Partners for young ministry candidates. While 16 people weren't willing or able, 534 were and did. This first step is the easiest for Network Partners to commit to: one hour talking about their own experience. A large drop-off occurs at the next step. Fewer than half of the Network Partners ever respond to a networking email (discussed later in this chapter). And fewer than half of those who responded made connections for the ministry candidate. You can't know the relative importance of any single person in finding your ideal job. Still, you can be confident that individuals gifted at networking will connect you to more people and job opportunities.

What types of people make good Connectors? Gladwell notes something "intrinsic in their personality, some combination of curiosity, self-confidence, sociability, and energy."[28] In my experience, Connectors tend to be first *Extroverted*, then *Feeling*, and finally *Judging* on the Myers Briggs. These personalities tend to be warm, empathetic, responsive, and responsible, "highly attuned to the emotions, need, and motivations of others [who] want to help others fulfill their potential." As such, they may "act as catalysts for individual and group growth."[29]

How do you identify Connectors? Watch who they interact with and listen to who they talk about. Connectors are drawn to people regardless of social status. Their conversation is populated with stories of human interaction: Johnny, the man with special needs who bags groceries but is excited to find a new job and go on his first date in over a year; or Donna, the college freshman who is transferring this fall so she can study secondary education and math. This isn't the posture of a name-dropper but the disposition of someone who delights in helping people connect with other people. Gladwell writes, "Success of any kind of social epidemic is heavily dependent on the involvement of people with a particular and rare set of social gifts."[30]

Part of making this less daunting is learning to be a connector yourself. I recommend the book *The Seven Levels of Communication* by Michael Maher.[31] Maher tells the fictitious story of Rick, a struggling real estate agent living on the cusp of bankruptcy. Rick is introduced to Michelle, an advocate for a positive, structured communication approach to engaging people. The charts on pages 37-40 give the book a visual synopsis, but you need the context presented in Chapters 3-7 to understand the framework. Maher's method is an instructional guide to connecting for those of us who struggle with *Intentional Networking*.

Monitoring your network is crucial in finding how effective it is, who the active members are, and whether you need to grow it. I will address network follow-up later in this chapter.

The Power of Stories
Speeches, lectures, legal briefs, syllabi, presentations, to-do lists, and instruction manuals convey details: facts, rules, laws, and schedules. The Ten Commandments give a list of accepted beliefs and behaviors. The United States Constitution details a corpus of fundamental laws. Ikea furniture manuals illustrate steps for construction.

Narratives are categorically different. Narratives have a unique power to give meaning to the world. Narratives define our reality and explain our role in it. They make meaning of information. Narratives are stories: an account told with detail in an order that conveys a plot leading to resolution. Biology describes what life exists; stories tell why life exists. Physics tells how light travels; stories tell what happens when light travels.

Narratives are universally present in life. Principles convey truth. Story brings truth to life. My daughter's math problems are stories—who has how much money and how many items can she buy with it at an expressed price. After any tragedy, news reporters run through "what we currently know"—a list of facts: who, what, when, and where. This usually takes only two or three minutes. The rest of the time is spent pursuing the question of why, often leading with a statement, "Authorities do not yet know why…." I believe humans are ultimately unsatisfied with information that is anti-narrative, and few people actively remember anti-narrative information.

H. Porter Abbot writes:

> We make narratives many times a day, every day of our lives. It so permeates our lives that Nick Davis could write that when we try to understand the nature of narrative, we are like "fish trying to discuss the nature of water." In fact, we start making narratives almost from the moment we begin putting words together. As soon as we follow a subject with a verb, there is a good chance we are engaged in narrative discourse.[32]

Why make such a fuss about narratives? Because narratives and stories are at the heart of meaning and understanding in pastoral leadership as much as anywhere. Narrative is the foundation of your theological training. Dan Doriani writes, "In an important sense, the Bible is one long narrative."[33] Your study of the Bible is a study of God's story of initiation in history toward the redemption of His creation.

The second reason understanding narratives is so essential is because stories are how we make meaning of events. Here is a list of facts:

- The woman yelled at you.
- The man cursed at the doctor.
- The child cried to his teacher.
- The car hit the tree.

Immediately, our minds try to make meaning of these facts. Why the woman yelled at you changes the way you feel and respond. Did she yell "Merry Christmas!" across the parking lot, or did she yell, "Watch out!" as you crossed the street? Did she yell "NO!" when you delivered the news of her son's death or, "You are a terrible pastor!" after you preached something she disagreed with? We can't make meaning of this life without the narratives that link facts. Facts alone are not enough to make meaning. Without the ability to make meaning, we cannot discern the necessary patterns to guide us in life.

Where the Ten Commandments are instructions through proposition, the Book of Proverbs is instruction through practical situations. The eighth commandment instructs, "Do not steal." The Book of Proverbs says, "Wealth gained quickly will dwindle, but whoever gathers little by little will increase it" (Prov. 13:11), and "Whoever robs his father or his mother and says, 'That is no transgression,' is a companion to a man who destroys" (Prov. 28:24), and "Do not say to your neighbor, 'Go, and come again, tomorrow I will give it'—when you have it with you" (Prov. 3:28). The eighth commandment is more efficient. The proverbs are more profound, require greater discernment, and provide guideposts for what is included in the command not to steal.

Without the ability to discern meaning, we make our own interpretations of events. In the book *Crucial Conversations*, Kerry Patterson and team write, "[T]here is an intermediate step between what others do and how we feel. That's why, when faced with the same circumstance, ten people may have ten different emotional responses…. What is this intermediate step? Just after we observe what others do and just before we feel some emotion about it, we tell ourselves a story. That is, we add meaning to the action we observed."[34]

Your interactions with Network Partners should provide you with narratives, stories of their experiences, observations, actions, and interactions. These narratives are embedded with truths and principles. Discernment draws them out. This practice has a technical term: Qualitative Research. Sharan B. Merriam writes,

> Education, health, social work, administration, and other arenas of social activity are considered applied social sciences or fields of practice precisely because practitioners in those fields deal with everyday concerns of people's lives.[35]

This applies to the ministry as well. None of these fields—education, health, administration, or ministry—is without factual basis and quantified approaches. Yet all of them are more than that; they need technical and often tactical knowledge that grows in scope and significance as your understanding of the narrative deepens.

The Importance of Story
The Behavioral Interviewing questions you ask your Network Partners should elicit stories, and these stories serve you in multiple ways throughout your job search process.

First, you need to understand systems. Daniel H. Kim defines a system as "any group of interacting, interrelated, or interdependent parts that form a complex and unified whole that has a specific purpose."[36] People in relationships comprise a human system, and the more people in the system, the more complex the system is. A family system may have just two people, a husband and a wife, or hundreds, as in the case of extended family ethnic groups in Africa. Your Network Partners are part of the emotional, human systems comprised of their own family, church leadership, church membership and, to some degree, the community outside the church.

While you ask questions primarily to explore your knowledge gaps, questions also function to expose your Network Partners' perspectives of their emotional and relational systems. If you can listen to these stories without choosing sides—without cheering on the hero or chanting down the villain—you gain a perspective of critical distance on system behavior.

Drew, a ministry candidate, interviewed Jessie: a single, 30-something working as a Youth Director. Drew asked Jessie to elaborate on the challenges she had experienced with parents. Jessie told Drew that several youth parents were disgruntled with youth group events. The parents had expressed their frustration to the Senior Pastor. The Senior Pastor turned that anxiety onto Jessie, expressing serious concerns about her ability to lead youth events effectively. The Senior Pastor never talked with Jessie directly about the situation, opting to outline his new expectations for Jessie via email.

Jessie explained how she experienced the email: "It was extremely impersonal and intensely critical." She perceived the Senior Pastor as an ineffective leader who capitulated to every perceived concern: "He never stands up for me, even when I do exactly what he asks of me."

The candidate interviewing Jessie felt drawn to her cause as the victim of the situation until Jessie answered his next question: "Tell me about a time you tried something new and failed." Jessie laughed and began telling story after story of innovative programs she started but abandoned within a few weeks, showing her struggle with finishing what she started. Jessie regularly did not follow through on tasks. She began with great enthusiasm but gave up at the first sign of resistance, boredom, or the excitement of "something new."

At that moment, the candidate later told me, he could see the first situation—poorly managed youth events—through the lens of these other events. Instead of seeing Jessie either as the perpetrator or the victim of the case, he simply saw her as a participant in the system.

It takes maturity to gain the necessary perspective to see ourselves in the system. Ronald Heifetz and Marty Linksy, in their book *Leadership on the Line*, call this "getting off the dance floor going to the balcony."[37] I find Behavioral Interviewing the most effective way to get on the balcony to see individuals and their roles in a system. And in time, this helps us see our own roles.

Behavioral Interviewing reveals how people interpret events, situations, and data within the system. Jessie perceived herself as the victim and the Senior Pastor as conflict averse. Youth families perceived Jessie as unreliable. Her Senior Pastor perceived her as lacking basic executive skills. "People interpret a story in light of their world knowledge, imposing order where none had been present so as to make a more logical story"[38] and in so doing, "we are readily misled by illusions, cognitive biases, and the stories we construct to explain the world around us and our place within it."[39]

I said earlier that qualitative research offers a unique ability to see reality more clearly through the stories of expert practitioners. Now I'm saying that stories enable us to create and maintain competing views of reality. Which is it?

Both. We make meaning—story, narrative—from facts, details, data, and events. And we sometimes construe inaccurate and incomplete narratives. One camp proposes separating historical facts from any interpretation, but this is impossible. The better approach is to seek more stories, constantly comparing the details, information, and perspectives of each. This "constant-comparative method" exposes deficiencies and errors, expanding a limited perspective.

As Christians, this is what happens when we read the Bible. Because the Bible is the most accurate story, constantly comparing every other human story to this grand narrative provides a fuller understanding—though always limited—of reality.

This requires relationship. The more stories you hear from more people, the greater your capacity to see how people view their role within a system. Critical distance is necessary for you to understand your role within a system. Your behavior patterns within any system reflect the patterns of interaction you experienced in your family of origin. The book *Generation to Generation* by Edwin Friedman is an excellent resource for exploring your role in your family of origin and, to a further extent, your role in the other systems you take part in.

Stories and the Interviewing Process

If I have yet to convince you of your need to listen to the stories of others' experiences, let me make one final case. You need the stories of others to develop answers to questions search committees ask. A good search committee digs in with questions about your knowledge gaps. You can dismiss these questions as irrelevant, or you can engage them. Even better, you can anticipate them, and plan thoughtful responses based on the research you have conducted through the *Intentional Networking* process. Your research may not meet the criteria of formal research methodology, but it is still valid research. Your *Intentional Networking* research provides the foundation for answers to challenging questions when experience and education cannot.

Darius served six years as an Assistant Pastor. His areas of responsibility grew to include oversight of adult Christian Education, visitor follow-up, new member assimilation, and counseling. But there were limited opportunities to preach, so Darius had only preached four times each year.

Darius wrote RQs and developed a Behavioral Interviewing protocol around his knowledge gaps—specifically how to develop the skill and capacity to preach weekly as a senior leader. He interviewed ten pastors, six of whom had made similar vocational shifts from support staff to senior leader. He wanted to know how they became more efficient in sermon preparation and more concise in sermon delivery. He asked Network Partners about the challenges of weekly preaching and the blessings.

Darius incorporated what he learned into his interview protocol when applying for Solo Pastor positions. In time, he became one of two finalists for a solo pastorate. The committee was divided; half were enthusiastic about Darius because of his history leading adults, while the other members preferred the other candidate. And the committee was transparent about their concerns.

"Darius, we've communicated our confidence in your ability to lead adults, but we have questions about your ability to preach weekly. Talk to us about preaching. What are your concerns? What gives you confidence that you can do it?"

Darius paused, took a deep breath, and replied, "I acknowledge I haven't yet been in a position to write and deliver sermons regularly. It's the question I asked my Network Partners. In anticipation of this question, I interviewed ten pastors to learn how they grew in sermon efficiency and effectiveness—going from a job where they rarely preached to a job where they preached weekly."

He went on, "All the pastors admitted to a learning curve. Like many skills, growth came naturally with practice. Growth also involved learning about the people. Only as these pastors developed relationships with their congregants—learned where they worked and spent their time and money, what they hoped for and prayed for—did sermons become more relevant. They said it took about two years to develop their homiletic voice. So, I think time, practice, and life-on-life ministry are keys to growth as a preacher."

Darius addressed the committee's concerns by providing concrete data from pastors who successfully transitioned from assistant to Senior Pastor, from preaching only occasionally to preaching weekly. Even if Darius knew these data points to be correct, he gained credibility by affirming their concern and citing the experience of other Senior Pastors. You need this level of credibility when speaking about your knowledge gaps. Researching the experience of others provides that credibility.

In the end, the search committee hired Darius. He is in his fifth year as the congregation's Solo Pastor.

Here is a sample email to your Network Partners with the purpose of scheduling a phone call or personal visit.

Dear Monica,

My name is Joel Hathaway. I am the Director of Youth and Family at Covenant Presbyterian Church in Waynesboro, MS. Reflecting on the past three years, I see areas where I want to learn and grow. Specifically, I want to learn how to navigate the challenges of competing interests. You were recommended to me.

Here are the questions I would like to ask:

- Tell me about a time you were under competing expectations from different people. What was the situation, and how did it develop? What was the outcome, and what did you learn?
- Tell me about a time your church dealt with significant conflict.
- Tell me about a time you were expected to do a task for which you needed to be trained or prepared.

I believe I can only fill my knowledge gaps by learning from your experience, insight, and wisdom. Also, you serve in the type of position I ultimately want to work in, which makes your perspective more valuable.

Will you please donate an hour for me to learn about your work and experience?

Thank you for your time and consideration,

Joel Hathaway

How to Follow Up with Your Network Partners
Good follow-up with Network Partners has two parts. Within two days of your interview, mail a handwritten note thanking your Network Partners for their time. State something you learned from them and how that knowledge benefits your ministry. The art of note-writing has been lost in the age of digital communication.

I've worked with over 600 individuals and 100 teams. I pray with most of these people and write about 50 notes annually. Occasionally someone remembers my prayer or an email. But regularly, sometimes decades later, people remark on handwritten notes I sent. A handwritten note is not an optional follow-up with Network Partners. It is at the heart of meaningful, lasting interaction.

Why are handwritten notes so impactful? They convey the commitment of time and thoughtfulness from the sender to the receiver. Handwritten notes make the recipient slow down when reading. And emotions can be conveyed in handwritten notes in a way that they cannot be in typed or printed messages.

Ongoing follow-up includes a regular email at least once a month. I recommend sending emails more regularly—but not more than once a week—as you near a critical date: graduation or a decision about a particular job. Emails should be concise, actionable, and relevant: C.A.R. for short. The recipient should be able to read and act on these emails quickly.

Emails should be concise because your Network Partners are busy. I am on the email lists of 60 ministry leaders, including campus ministers, church planters, and missionaries. Most of these emails have over 800 words, and few have pictures. They regularly start with a lengthy story and wrap up with prayer and financial requests. That format is loosely based on the Associated Press writing style I learned in college, emphasizing narrative journalism. It does not work when contacting Network Partners.

Leave the colorful narrative for your last email when you announce your new position. A good, concise email should have at most 100 words. After the greeting, one sentence should remind the recipient what you need—what specific jobs you seek—and one sentence should share an important detail. Here are three samples:

- As you know, I am seeking a Solo Pastor position allowing me to minister to a community of faithful believers. Recently, I preached at a local church, and you can listen to the sermon here.
- I am sharing my updated resume with you as I continue my search for a ministry position focused on young adults.
- Last semester, I taught a Sunday school series on neighboring. You can view my PowerPoint presentation here. I seek a ministry position that will let me teach, preach, and reach people outside the church.

The lead sentence/paragraph changes monthly depending on where you are in the process. Keep these sentences relevant and on topic. Our desire to connect with people through stories leads us to share information that isn't essential for this mode of communication. Save stories about your weekend or family updates for another time. Keep the content of these emails relevant to the single purpose for writing. You want your

Network Partners to remember you whenever they learn of available ministry positions. Any personal information that doesn't equip them to do this is a distraction from your primary purpose in writing.

Marketing research suggests consumers must be exposed to a message seven times before it sticks. In his book *The Tipping Point*, Malcolm Gladwell calls this the "stickiness factor." Make your emails sticky by repeating key terminology from one month to the next. Be concrete and specific. You don't just want to soak them with data but to saturate them with memorable information.

There is an agricultural analogy that captures this concept. When a tree is replanted, it needs constant watering. An arborist could dump 20 gallons around the roots, but much water is lost in runoff. The ground can't retain it fast enough. The other option is to use an irrigation bag— a water-filled sack with tiny holes. Once full, the irrigation bag is placed on top of the root ball, slowly releasing water at a rate the ground can absorb.

By sending information in smaller segments over an extended period, you expose your Network Partners to the message that you need a job, and they can help you find it. This is called, in technical terms, "interrupting the forgetting process."[40] Networking emails that are concise and relevant are also memorable. When you send smaller packets more regularly, you help your Network Partners remember information about you for longer periods.

The Big Ask
Finally, emails should be actionable. You must ask your Network Partners for *something*. Remind them what you want them to do for you. I recommend making these three requests from your Network Partners in every email:

- Take one minute to pray for you.
- Take one minute to tell you about *any* jobs they may know.
- Take one minute to connect you to others they think you should be speaking with.

One Minute of Prayer

Ask Network Partners to spend one minute praying for you. I presume you and your Network Partners believe in prayer and its effectiveness. Discussions about prayer often elicit other emotions as well. People can experience feelings of failure for not praying enough, fear of praying the wrong thing, or guilt for not praying for people who asked for it.

We don't always know what we are committing to when people ask us, "Will you pray for me?" Do they mean to pray one time right then or once a day, or every day, or all the time, forever? And when we agree to pray, how do others know we kept our word to do so? Making a bounded request—one minute—gives your Network Partners a manageable task. They may pray for you more and longer, but when they do, it won't be with a sense of guilt or obligation but with joy and freedom.

New Job Opportunities

Ask Network Partners to tell you about *any* jobs they may know of. If you ask them to tell you only about jobs that fit your criteria, silence may mean they don't know about those types of positions. Then again, silence may mean they aren't actively engaged in your networking efforts at all. The more reasons to be in touch with you, the greater your opportunity to engage with them.

Many candidates have discovered their ideal ministry role is a job they had not previously considered. The job title didn't make the cut, but further engagement revealed a job where these candidates flourished. Eighteen-year-old Joel would never have considered a seminary the ideal workplace. Yet, as I have grown in knowledge and interests, the needs of the Seminary have become the perfect place to engage my passion and employ my gifts.

When you learn about jobs that aren't interesting, you become a networker, helping others find the jobs they seek. Be part of the networking process and become a Connector.

Connection to Others

Finally, ask your Network Partners to put you in touch with people they think you should be speaking with. Complex systems assume that no node has all the information. Your Network Partners don't know everything. Expanding your network to friends of friends brings you into closer proximity to other people (acquaintances) who can further fill your knowledge gaps and help you look for employment opportunities.

When initially building a network, we default to people we like or have known for a long time. Remember, these people do less work on your behalf than casual acquaintances. This is not for lack of desire. The most effective network includes more people separated by two or three degrees than one. As Gladwell states, "Six degrees of separation doesn't mean that everyone is linked to everyone else in just six steps. It means that an exceedingly small number of people are linked to everyone else in a few steps, and the rest of us are linked to the world through these special few."[41]

Action Steps
1. Make a working list of the knowledge gaps you want to explore.
2. Write three or four RQs about each knowledge gap. What do you want to learn about each topic?
3. Expand your RQs and convert them into Behavioral Interviewing questions. Write out the follow up questions you'll ask and each Behavioral Interviewing question to keep it focused on your knowledge gap.
4. Repeat the above process for each if you've identified more than one knowledge gap.
5. Make an initial list of people you want to interview for each knowledge gap.
6. Practice listening to stories. Look for meaning. As you listen, write down the follow up questions you would ask to direct or redirect the conversation toward greater clarity and relevance.
7. Draft an initial introductory email to your Network Partners.
8. Secure blank envelopes and note cards to use when sending thank you follow-ups and buy postage stamps.
9. Email Network Partners asking them for an hour of their time.

3

HOW TO THINK ABOUT STAYING
AND LEAVING

Chapter Summary
Seasons of vocational ministry follow repeatable cycles. These common patterns contribute to the validity of what statisticians call group wisdom. This chapter introduces the six phases of the ministry cycle. As you find yourself facing a "new chapter" of ministry, you need landmarks to help orient you to where you are and billboards where you may be headed. Elements of the six phases clarify what is happening around you, with the people in your church, the organization you serve, and inside of you. This information equips you to assess whether or not a period of conflict, decline, or spiritual disease is a legitimate reason to look for another position or double down on your current position. The ministry hiring cycle has its distinct phases: when positions open and when they are filled. Your desire to transition and the availability of jobs only sometimes coincide. Understanding these two cycles and the points at which they intersect frees you from unnecessary frustration and distraction. This allows you to engage faithfully in your current church in the interim.

Considering a Move
The decision to leave a position usually comes after deep thought and extended prayer. Most candidates accepted their current ministry position with the hopes—naïve or otherwise—they would be in the job for a long time, maybe forever. The decision to leave elicits questions such as:

- Am I leaving for the right reasons?
- Am I ready for a position with more responsibility?
- How do I know when it is time to leave these people?
- How do I decide what I'm looking for in my next position?
- What if the next position has greater challenges?

Candidates regularly report self-doubt, including these limiting beliefs:

- I am not ready to be a lead pastor.
- I haven't preached enough to be a Senior Pastor.
- My experience has not prepared me for what I want to do in the long term.
- Search committees have told me I'm not _____ (e.g., experienced, energetic, dynamic, etc.) enough for their congregation.

I encourage you to consider two realities as you consider a vocational change. First, there are "lifetime of ministry" reasons not to leave too soon. And second, don't be afraid to look.

Six Phases of Ministry Life Cycle
Sleep has a natural cycle that lasts approximately 90 minutes. During this cycle, the brain moves through five distinct stages, after which it starts over. The seasons change in patterns, affecting the weather predictably and cyclically. The Western linear approach to causality means we often miss that aspects of life are more cyclical than causal. Ministry also has a natural cycle. This cycle includes six phases.

Phase One: New Pastor (Historical)
This stage of a ministry career happens at the beginning of a new position. It is sometimes called the honeymoon stage, but I find that language confusing. "Honeymoon" implies something wonderful and sweet, while the New Pastor stage may be full of challenges. The New Pastor stage is marked by curiosity on the Pastor's part and lowered expectations on the part of the congregation. During this season of ministry, the Pastor leans heavily on recent history. (In fact, some congregants expect a new pastor to bring back the "glory days" of the past.) New Pastors just out of seminary quote heavily from seminary professors. When preaching, they imitate preachers who have influenced them. If this is a second ministry position, pastors draw

heavily from what worked and didn't work in the last job. They may even preach through a series of sermons they preached in their old context. This is called the historical phase because pastors rely upon the recent past to inform how they do ministry in the present. This stage of ministry typically lasts between six months and two years.

Phase Two: Confusion (Technical)
Eventually, pastors enter a season of turmoil. Their sermons don't have the same impact or aren't well received. Issues with congregants or fellow staff grow in regularity and intensity. Conflict arises and seems to go away, only to surface again. Pastors face challenges that seminary didn't seem to prepare them for. They have used up quotes from seminary professors and can no longer recycle older sermons. In response, pastors resort to technical solutions: sound exegesis of the Scriptures to guide preaching, new models for counseling, or new structures for church programs. Pastors read books, attend a conference, or pursue continuing education. These approaches originate from a place of technical confidence: I have a seminary degree. Or it may come from a position of functional authority: I am the minister of this church. But the results are mixed, muted, and temporary at best. This leads to confusion. This stage of ministry typically lasts one to two years.

Phase Three: Active Learning (Adaptive)
Pastors become discouraged after a year or more of throwing everything at the problems—changes in programs, adjustments to the length of their sermons, augmentation to the worship style. Confused, often frustrated, and likely reevaluating their call to ministry, pastors at this stage have two options. They can leave, or they can learn. Which do you think is easier? I get more phone calls from pastors in this phase of the ministry cycle than any other. They say a great deal, both positive and negative:

- I've done everything I can here. I need to make room for the next person who can take the church to the next level.
- I never wanted to do this kind of ministry (e.g., youth ministry, worship directing, Assistant Pastor) long term, and I'm ready for the next challenge of ministry.
- People don't respect me, but they would if I were the Senior Pastor.

- I've done everything a lead pastor does, so I'm ready to pursue that type of position.

Few pastors ask me outright, "Should I leave this church now?" Instead, the tone is one of determination: "I am leaving. Help me find my next job." Beneath these declarations is a request for affirmation: Don't you agree with me?

Whether or not I agree, the data does not agree. There is extensive research on the first five years of ministry post-seminary. In summary, ministers who stay in their first ministry position between 48 and 60 months are—throughout their ongoing ministry career—more confident in their calling, less anxious about their ministries, and more satisfied in their vocation. They believe they need to earn the right to speak in people's lives instead of assuming their credentials and experience automatically grant them the right. They have seen and can tell stories about ways they have influenced people for the better. When these pastors transition to a new role, they move into roles of greater responsibility, staying in these later ministry positions longer.

On the other hand, ministers who leave their first ministry position before 36 months are less confident in their ministerial calling, often say they have not influenced people, are less satisfied with their ministry and believe the most significant problem is that people don't respect their functional authority. They often move laterally into similar positions with similar responsibilities and stay at subsequent ministry positions for shorter periods of time. Many of the Pastors I've tracked through this process have changed ministry positions every three years or less.

Ministers who leave their current ministry position at this stage have several advantages. They can regurgitate the last three years of ministry in their new role. They can re-preach their old sermons. They can quote seminary professors for the first time again. They are less burdened by skill development, which gives them the freedom to focus on the emotional and relational aspects of the new congregation.

But all this comes with a hefty price tag. What they miss is the opportunity to become active learners. Active learning is essential for vocational longevity and effectiveness. Active learning requires the

74

right conversation partners, experimentation, personal reflection, processing and reprocessing, and re-experimentation. As I stated in Chapter 2, conversation partners broaden our perspectives in crucial areas. Ronald Heifetz and Marty Linksy, in their book *Leadership on the Line*, describe leadership as a two-scene act. First, leaders are engaged in the action and activity of leading. This is called the dance floor. But leaders must also gain a global perspective on the action to assess the situation accurately. This is called the balcony.[42] When you lack the necessary perspective for proper assessment, conversation partners can, in essence, get on the balcony for you. Conversation partners are to ministry development what Network Partners are to network development.

Conversation partners can help guide personal reflection. Stress, tension, and trauma hinder the ability to be reflective. A driver in rush hour doesn't have the cognitive space that a hiker does resting on a river bluff. The best conversation partners have weathered similar situations and challenges that you are facing, and they function as coaches— asking more than telling. Coaching helps people clarify their thoughts, values, and aspirations—helping them build and implement a plan around those ideals.

Recently, a pastor, Nathan, confessed he was contemplating leaving vocational ministry to become a teacher. Conflict in the church exposed his leadership deficiencies and renewed his desire to go into teaching. The conflict brought confusion. He shared, "I feel like I'm running away from a hard situation even to consider going into teaching." He confessed to experiencing feelings of inadequacy and shame.

When invited to explore the desire to teach, Nathan reflected on his choice of college major and seminary studies to become a schoolteacher. Providence (or serendipity) led him into vocational ministry, first as an assistant and later as a Solo Pastor.

Conversation partners gave Nathan the space and inquiry essential for him to name his core values and aspirations, apart from the confusing noise of conflict. For Nathan, conversation partners provided insights from their experiences and curiosity into his aspiration, freeing him to see teaching as something he ran toward instead of seeing ministry challenges as something he ran from.

Guided by conversation partners into learning and reflection, other pastors have come away excited to experiment. The nature of an adaptive challenge is that it doesn't respond to technical solutions. Heifetz and Linsky describe the difference between technical and adaptive solutions as follows:

> "Every day, people have problems for which they do, in fact, have the necessary know-how and procedures. We call these technical problems. But there is a whole host of problems that are not amenable to authoritative expertise or standard operating procedures. They cannot be solved by someone who provides answers from on high. We call these adaptive challenges because they require experiments, new discoveries, and adjustments from numerous places in the organization or community. Without learning new ways—changing attitudes, values, and behaviors—people cannot make the adaptive leap necessary to thrive in the new environment. The sustainability of change depends on having the people with the problem internalize the change itself."[43]

I describe the difference between technical problems and adaptive challenges as the difference between sending a rocket to the moon and mapping a black hole. The moon has a fixed mass and moves at a constant speed in a prescribed trajectory. Its telemetry to other objects is calculable. Getting to the moon is a technical challenge.

By comparison, a black hole has a changing mass moving at incalculable speeds. The mass of a black hole warps space, altering the trajectory of neighboring objects. This makes it challenging to chart accurately. We identify the moon by looking at the moon. We identify a black hole by looking at how everything else behaves around it. This is an adaptive challenge.

Experimentation is a way to identify the parameters of an adaptive challenge—like mapping the edges of a black hole. Experimentation may include a slight change to the order of worship, a new model for small-group ministry, or a change in your schedule and availability. Experimentation likely involves giving the work back—another concept from Heifetz and Linsky—in which you are present with others in their anxiety but leave them to seek solutions for their problems.

For one pastor, experimentation involved turning off his phone at 9:00 PM. every night. Congregants who had grown accustomed to quick replies to late texts were disappointed, leading to good conversations and, eventually, healthier boundaries. Experimentation asks, "What would happen if I...." and then identifies a slight adjustment. The goal is to determine the resilience of an organization to change.

Experimentation does not require large or significant changes. There comes a time for that in any organization. Usually, that degree of change comes after a series of iterative adjustments—experimentations—transforming the shape of an organization and its members: the tipping point. A potter working clay on a wheel uses a slight touch to produce substantial transformation in the image of the vessel. Water, speed, and patience multiply the effect of the soft touch. That is the effect of experimentation.

Phase Four: Growth (Progression)
A pastor who weathers the adaptive season of ministry often describes a period of internal growth and external impact. These pastors tend to be more confident in their abilities, more honest about their limits, and more inclusive of others in the art of leadership. In such an environment, there is often numerical and spiritual growth. More people participate in the act of ministry implementation, no longer fulfilled by only 20% of the congregation. People are excited about being part of a healthy organization guided by healthy leaders, where the pastor has learned to pastor, and the congregation has learned to minister.[44]

One church grew from 190 to 250 over 11 months during such a season. In another, the church launched new ministries engaging with the local community. And in another tiny church, the growth was evidenced spiritually, where members began to pray for opportunities to share the Gospel with their neighbors. One Pastor reflected on this season of ministry, saying, "The church changed so quickly in so many different ways, I became excited again about being their Pastor."

Phase Five: Challenge (Conflictual)
Progress doesn't last forever. The exciting changes that occur in a congregation also bring new challenges. A church with a lot of visitors finds parking an issue. New groups may inhabit old spaces. The narthex may smell like cigarette smoke or the body odor of newcomers. A

member may find their "regular seat" taken. The church may need to revisit policies about who can volunteer in the children's ministries. Significant issues like divorce, remarriage, sexuality, and politics arise. So do minor problems: how is the budget spent? Is it more important to start on time or give grace to latecomers? Is the Pastor expected to continue mainly meeting with long-time members, or is he free to focus on visitors and guests? All these issues have the potential to create conflict.

A church I attended had the vision to start a Christian school. The school began with 30 preschoolers and kindergarteners, all from church families. These small classes took over the nursery space during the week but otherwise had negligible impact on the church organization. Twenty years later, the school had 159 students, of which only 25% were from church families. The school filled every space available between Sundays. Weekly Bible studies had to move into another building. Volunteers rearranged rooms to accommodate Sunday School activities, leaving teachers scrambling to reset their classrooms on Monday morning. Growth produced new challenges, including conflict.

Sometimes, the challenge seems random. In one situation, following the installation of a new pastor, a sharp increase in visitors and new members followed. Within a few months, two church leaders had public character failings, leading to church discipline. The congregation was confused, even a little frustrated. The church entered a period of sober reflection with hopes dulled and joy muted. While this situation seems utterly unrelated to the growth and progression of the church, I believe a family-system approach to organizational thinking provides one way to understand these situations.

The family-system approach to organizations was developed by Edwin Friedman, expanding on the seminal work of Murray Bowen. (Friedman is author of *A Failure of Nerve* and *Generation to Generation*.) In short, a family-system approach to organizational thinking sees all members in a group—whether a family, a club, a church, a business, or a league of nations—as emotionally interconnected contributors to the overall emotional process that binds them together. Friedman believed that "All processes are emotional processes."

In the case of the two leaders mentioned above, the situation's complexity shrouds complete understanding. Here are a few contributing factors. The church had lost a long-term Senior Pastor a few years earlier, followed by two years of an Interim Pastor. Two staff members resigned to take other ministry positions during the interim period. While the transitions were healthy and sound, these additional changes increased pressure on church leaders to maintain the caliber and quality of church management. The organization and leadership styles of the church valued order, proficiency, excellence, a classical aesthetic, and professionalism. The weight of these expectations rested on the congregationally elected leaders who remained. The cracks of weakness only appeared once the pressure was lifted.

It is natural to assume that failures in leadership would occur during the season of increased pressure. Not so. Take, for example, the cascading failure of a water main pipe. A segment of the line may be cracked for years, but the high pressure within the pipe keeps it from failing. A sudden drop in pressure—such as when workers turn off the water to repair a breach farther down the line—allows weakened areas to collapse. The line that seemed fine under pressure collapses when the water is turned back on. This summer, I watched the water company chase cascading failures of this sort along my road. Workers repaired the first breach, only to have another explosion a dozen yards down when the water turned back on. This happened four times over the length of a quarter mile. The cracks that caused these failures didn't suddenly appear. Many had been there for years. Changes in pressure exposed them.

We see an example of this in Acts 6:1: "Now in these days when the disciples were increasing in number, a complaint by the Hellenists arose against the Hebrews because their widows were being neglected in the daily distribution." Expansion of the church through growth brought new challenges from an unexpected, unrelated area.

Whatever the nature of conflict or challenge, this phase strains pastors' capacities and wears on their commitments. Pastors can hold on to the sense of accomplishment from the last phase (growth) for a while, but eventually, the challenge or conflict takes its toll. Pastors begin to experience doubt, frustration, anger, and vocational burnout. Many, out of concern for their families and personal health, completely reconsider their call to ministry. Others seek to escape into addictive behaviors and sinful proclivities. Most feel the burden of "seeing it through," but some pastors leave if the challenge isn't addressed, and the conflict remains unresolved.

Phase Six: Plateau (Consolidation)

The new building is finished, the dissertation is defended, the daughter church plant is launched, the conflict is resolved, and problematic people have changed or left the church. Following a season of heightened engagement, pastors—and often their congregations—enter a lull. Energy is low. Worship feels rote. Attendance declines, and the congregants who remain seem less engaged.

This is normal. More than that, it should be expected. College students are most likely to fall into depression after finals are over. Soldiers tend to be at their lowest after a tour of duty. Writers experience the worst creative blocks after the publication of a work. Some men and women experience deep sadness in the months after their joyful wedding as they come to terms with losses associated with marriage. Post-partum depression usually comes after the baby is born, after the joyful months of planning and preparation.

According to psychiatrist Marc Schoen, "It's a phenomenon that's often referred to as 'the let-down effect,' a pattern in which people come down with an illness or develop flare-ups of a chronic condition not *during* a concentrated period of stress but *after* it dissipates."[45]

Our dispositions sag after extended periods of focus and exertion. We cannot remain perpetually at emotional highs. And yet, most of us seem surprised by this natural plateau. The relief of a job well done is conflated with the belief that this should result in energetic excitement. What if the weariness and discouragement of Elijah in 1 Kings 17 is a normal emotional and physiological response to intense seasons?

Pastors in the plateau stage often consolidate their energy. They can become self-reflective, even moody. They can experience listlessness and longing. The best antidote for these periods is intentional self-care: spiritual engagement, healthy eating, physical (cardiovascular) exercise, good sleep, mental rest, and relational support. Self-care is not self-indulgence. Self-indulgence is marked by excess, misuse, abuse, and excuse. Self-care is marked by acknowledging weakness, accepting limits, seeking guidance, and asking for help.

Here again, pastors ask, "Is there something else out there for me to do?" Fear is one of the driving emotions behind that question: fear that this period of weariness, disengagement, and discouragement will continue indefinitely. It doesn't! This period often lasts six months, sometimes a year. Rarely does it continue indefinitely, though an individual's propensity to a melancholy disposition or depression can extend these difficult seasons.

Having acknowledged this emotional reality, the best thing a pastor and his family can do in such a season—after the self-care listed above—is look at other ministry jobs. I'm not suggesting he leave. But something transformational happens when pastors become open to and explore new vocational opportunities.

Several years ago, I interviewed ministers who served in one church for at least 25 years. I asked them all the same questions. Later, I applied the same questions to dozens of pastors who stayed at least ten years but less than 25 in a ministry position. I entered this research looking for differences. I suspected I would find that pastors who stayed 25 years had something the other cohort of pastors lacked: maybe depth of character, caliber of skill, leadership capacity, clarity of vision, strength of character, relational integrity, emotional maturity, or spiritual vibrancy. I found none of those things.

The two groups of pastors were almost identical. During a plateau period, both groups asked, "Is there something else out there for me to do?" Both groups pursued other positions and entertained positions offered to them. Both groups prayed about leaving, asking the Lord to open a door. In fact, there was only one difference between the two groups. For those who left, the Lord opened the door for them to go. In the case of those who stayed, He didn't. That's it. Humanly speaking, all these pastors did the same thing: they knocked on a door. Utterly beyond their control, sometimes it opened, and sometimes it didn't.

Knock on doors. Engage in redemptive conversations. Dream about vocational opportunities. Envision where you would thrive. Read other job descriptions. Learn from the experience of others. Only God knows if this process prepares you for your next position or equips you to serve longer where you are currently planted.

One word of advice: Don't take a sabbatical during this stage in the cycle. That is akin to a pastor taking Monday as his day off. Far from being a day of rest, Sunday is the busiest day for pastors. Monday tends to be the day when pastors experience the most discouragement and self-doubt. The careless comments of members and the complaining emails or calls from disgruntled members clunk around in the Pastor's head. Pastors are most critical of and, simultaneously, least objective about their own effectiveness. One pastor quipped, "Monday is the day I am most likely to consider being a garbage man." Another group of pastors dubbed it "Melancholy Monday."

Many pastors save their day off for Wednesday or Thursday. They are more rested and have more critical distance from the exhaustion of the previous Sunday. Also, they can be emotionally present with their spouse and children.

In the same way, pastors who take sabbaticals during a plateau exhibit many of the same characteristics as "Melancholy Monday." Time away finally gives them the space to see just how weary they are. Without going into further detail here, consider saving your sabbatical for another stage of the Ministry Life Cycle.

The Plateau is the last stage in the Ministry Life Cycle, after which the cycle repeats, or the Pastor leaves for another position.

The Ministry Hiring Cycle
There are industries that have perpetual hiring cycles. Ministry is not one of them. Like schoolteacher and administrative positions, the ministry hiring cycle follows a predictable—even seasonal—pattern. Understanding this pattern frees you from the fatigue of perpetually engaging in the search process. Few people have the mental and emotional energy (or the time) to serve their current employer faithfully *and* constantly look for a new ministry position. This section offers guidance on how to stay engaged in the search for a new job without completely neglecting your current ministry obligations while, at the same time, avoiding emotional fatigue.

Most ministry positions are vacated during the summer. Most of these positions are subsequently filled the following summer. This isn't apparent from just looking at data from job boards. Here are the average quarterly job postings that churches submitted over ten years, categorized by position type and when they were submitted.

Job Board Data	JAN-MAR	APR-JUNE	JUL-SEPT	OCT-DEC
Senior/Solo	26.40%	2.00%	47.17%	24.42%
Asst./Assoc/	25.82%	29.85%	13.43%	20.89%
Youth	31.48%	20.37%	27.77%	20.37%
Other	28.71%	25.64%	12.82%	12.82%

This data shows that only 2.00% of Senior/Solo positions are posted on job boards in Q2 (April-June). Here is the same data in chart form:

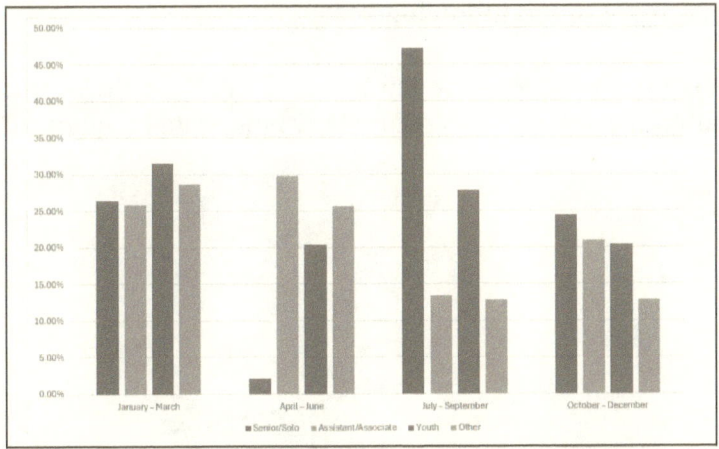

Looking only at this chart, a candidate seeking a senior or solo position should put the most effort and energy into the latter half of the year. Someone seeking an assistant or associate position should put more effort into the first half of the year.

The problem with this data is it only shows when a ministry position is *posted*; it doesn't show when the committee responsible for finding the candidate *does its work*. In the case of search committees looking for a Senior or a Solo Pastor, the typical process is as follows

Month	Activity
April – June	Previous candidate resigns.
July – August	Search Committee is formed.
August – November	Committee reviews and posts job description. Initial evaluation of candidates.
Late November – December	Committee on hiatus for holidays.
January – April	Committee evaluates candidates.
April – June	New pastor is hired.
June – August	New pastor moves.

Back to the data above. Even though almost 75% of senior and solo positions are placed on a job board in the second half of the year (Q3 & Q4), these committees do most of their work—evaluation, interview, reference checks, sermon evaluation, and the initial visit—between January and April of the following year.

When consulting with search committees, I track the time-on-task that they spend on the search. This chart shows that data by quarter:

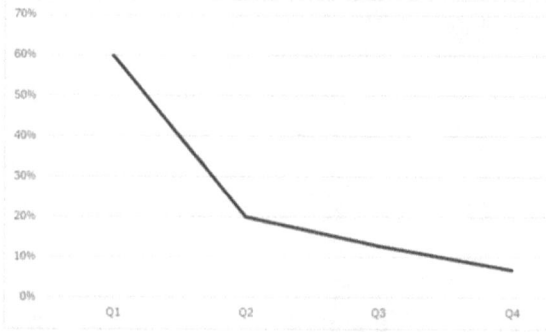

Now, let's overlay only the Senior/Solo job board data with the chart showing when search committees spend their time. The columns represent the number of positions posted by quarter. The line represents the amount of time committees report spending in each quarter.

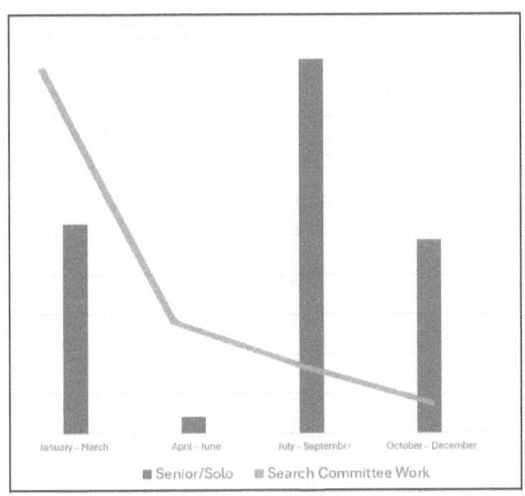

According to this last chart, senior and solo candidates who focus more of their energy on the first five months of the year are more efficient and effective than those who focus their energies primarily at the end of the year. And rightly so. Search committees often collect names of potential candidates in Q4 (October - December), but most of their engagement, vetting, and evaluation process takes place in Q1 (January - March).

With respect to assistant positions, there are two types: newly budgeted and recently vacated. For most churches, the fiscal calendar runs from January to December. Next year's budget is presented and approved in Q4. When a church budgets for a new Assistant Pastor, the person or committee responsible for filling the position spends the spring evaluating candidates. Ideally, they identify and hire the new person by Q2 (April - June) with a late-summer Q3 (July - September) start date. This allows the committee time to consider candidates who are just finishing seminary as well as those seeking a transition. A summer start date provides the church several months of financial cushion, in the event there are unforeseen expenses with hiring the new pastor.

In the case of a recently vacated position, the majority of these open up in Q1. These are usually second or third pastoral staff positions at larger churches. Committees actively engaged with candidates in Q1 and Q2, with the goal of hiring by Q3. This means that the assistant who accepts a new position in Q1 announces his intended departure by summer. In most cases, the church refills this position by August, doing all candidate evaluations in the spring and early summer.

Youth ministry jobs are the exception. Because these are often non-ordained ministry positions, churches can hire from a much broader pool of candidates: college students, recent college graduates, part-time seminary students, and recent seminary graduates. These are the only positions that can become vacant at any time and be filled within four months of when they are posted, regardless of the time of year.

When & How to Work Your Search Process

	Activity	Time Spent / Week
AUG - OCT	Update resume packet. Spend most of your energy developing your network. Check job boards weekly.	4 – 5 hrs.
NOV-DEC	A period of low activity for committees and Network Partners. Focus your energy on your current job. Check job boards infrequently.	3 – 4 hrs.
JAN-MAY	Look and apply for jobs. This is a period of high activity for committees.	15 – 25 hrs.
JUNE-JUL	Continue engaging with open positions. Very few new jobs are available during this period.	4 – 5 hrs.

Example Timeline for Senior / Solo Positions

Typically, a Senior Pastor is offered another position in the spring. He announces his intentions to leave and goes through the process of ending well. Over the next month, the church celebrates with a going away party, and the ministry family spends focused time with significant people in the community. The Pastor may even seek to reconcile differences or restore damaged relationships. The leaving process usually lasts four to eight weeks but can run longer when celebrating a long-time pastor.

The Pastor leaves in the summer. This is a natural break in the cycle of life and ministry. It is easier to sell a home. Younger children are on summer break, while older children are transitioning to college. Summer provides a natural break in the rhythms of life and ministry.

After his departure, the leadership spends the next few months managing the church. Church leadership recruits preachers to fill the pulpit, and the congregation forms a search committee. The committee is presented with a straightforward task—finding the next pastor— without clear training or direction. Search committees are usually a collection of volunteer individuals (not a "group") elected to a task (not a process) for which they have not been trained: to determine the fitness of one candidate (among many) for a position about which the committee members have minimal experience, limited understanding, and almost no organizational knowledge. Committees spend most of August, September, and October determining steps for evaluating candidates, guided predominantly by the individual hopes of committee members for the next pastor and elements from the last pastor's job description. During this time, committees update the job description and list the job publicly. They entertain cursory conversations with early applicants. One almost universal expectation is that the committee will identify, evaluate, and hire a new Senior Pastor within 12 months of the last pastor's departure. This is rarely the case.

In November and December, search committee work is interrupted by the holidays, during which many committees stop their work altogether as families travel or host others and the regular church calendar is full of special events.

In January, committees "wake up" to the realization they have six months, according to their timetable, to find their next pastor. They re-engage the search process with vigor, focusing on candidates who applied for the open position. The spring is filled with candidacy trips and guest preachers, followed by the announcement of the new pastor who moves to the community the following summer.

Example Timeline Assistant/Associate Positions
The process for support staff is generally truncated compared to searches for senior leadership. Support staff positions are often filled within six months.

A church looks to hire its first Assistant Pastor. This newly budgeted position is approved at the end of the fiscal year (December). Another church is losing its Assistant Pastor, who announced he has taken another position and is leaving in May.

In both cases, a person (usually the Senior Pastor) or committee is tasked with filling these positions. They spend part of Q1 creating a new or revising an existing job description. By April, committees actively look for candidates, often reviewing those recommended by trusted people. By summer, a candidate has been identified, evaluated, and hired, with an anticipated start of August.

When to Wait
Candidates seeking a new position never stop looking, but how they use their energy should change based on where you are in the hiring process. Candidates have less opportunity to engage with committees between August 1 and December 31. It doesn't make sense to keep working as hard. Statistically, there aren't as many jobs available. Continuing to spend 10-15 hours a week during this period looking for your next job leads to frustration and discouragement. You can be intent on finding a ministry job; but if few are out there, that fervency can quickly become a frenetic, anxious energy. Working harder won't generate more job opportunities. It's like trying to find a date for the April prom just after the September start of school.

Ronald, a Youth Pastor, decided it to look for a new position focused on counseling and outreach. He spent the fall semester engaged in *Intentional Networking* and resume building. In the winter (Q1) and spring (Q2), he looked at job boards daily, talked with Network Partners multiple times a week, and interviewed with two churches. But for one reason or another, he either did not get or declined the positions.

August (Q3) came back around, and he had no strong leads, but he continued to work as hard, beating the bushes for new job leads. He dedicated at least 15 weekly hours to pursuing every possible ministry opportunity. He found out about several outlier positions and had one meaningful conversation. But there weren't enough jobs to apply for or committees to interact with. By February of the next year, he shared how discouraged he was.

"I've been looking for a new job for 19 months. I had twenty phone calls, a dozen interviews, and two callbacks. I don't have the energy to keep looking, and my wife is tired of living in perpetual transition." Just at the point in the hiring cycle when Ronald needed to be energetic and engaged (Q1), he was tired and discouraged.

Ronald's wife isn't alone. Few people can live in perpetual transition. Candidates who spend as much time on the job search in the last six months of the year as they did in the first six months are likely to have worse results. Moreover, they come into the first half of the following year depleted of the energy and enthusiasm necessary to engage the search process well. This low-energy mode can sour your interactions with committees, undermining your vocational goals.

The second downside of working just as hard in the last half of the year on the job search is vocational unfaithfulness. It is hard to be faithful to your current ministry position when spending a third of your time looking for a new job.

So then, how should you use the second half of the year? Focus this time on creating or expanding your network using the *Intentional Networking* method described in Chapter 2. Refine your Ideal Job Description and resume packet, especially if there are developments in ministry proficiencies. Look at job boards but less frequently.

I encourage candidates to focus their energy and attention on their current ministry position from August to December, using the Five Ps:

- People: Who are the people you believe the Lord wants you to invest in over the coming year, especially if this is to be your last year? How will you invest in them: meeting together, writing notes of encouragement, talking on the phone, inviting them to a small group, or something else? When you are gone, what will be the holes in the organization and ministries of the church, and who are the people you can help train to fill those needs? Are there young leaders who need to be developed? Are there estranged members who need to be pursued?
- Programs: What programs should you help the church start, improve, or grow? If the church is without a person in your role for 6-18 months, what structures can you implement to ensure a smooth transition during the interim period?
- Passages: What are the books of the Bible on which you should teach and preach over the next year? Pastors already spend part of the summer planning their preaching schedule for the coming year. Giving attention here blesses your current congregation even as it helps take your mind off the search process.

- Proficiencies: What ministry skills or competencies should you look to develop? Inevitably, one reason candidates don't progress through the interview process is a skill deficiency, real or perceived. There is never a downside to exploring your vocational gaps—in areas of relationship, leadership, organization, communication, management, administration, conflict management, or theology—and improving your capacities by reading a book, attending a conference, taking a class, finding a coach, or asking someone to mentor you.
- Prayer: Make a detailed list of specific prayers for your current ministry situation and the next one to which the Lord may lead you. Use a book like *Pray for Me* to let the depths of the Psalms guide you in specific prayers for specific people. One of the significant deficiencies of the modern church is the narrow range of what we ask God for, with an over-representation of requests for "help and healing."

What if you are looking for your first call out of seminary and don't have a current ministry to invest time and energy into between August and December? You may need to continue the job search more intensely than your employed counterparts. But even you cannot be in perpetual search mode without growing frustrated and cynical. Take regular breaks to focus on other areas of life: your family, self-care, and your church community.

There may come a time when you need to take a non-ministry job to provide for yourself. You may find it easier to take a marketplace position in August, knowing that in five to six months, a new slate of ministry positions will come online.

Women's, Youth, Children's Ministry, and Other Support Roles
Non-ordained ministry support roles follow a different pattern than Senior/Solo or Assistant/Associate roles. A Youth Director may decide in November to move and start seminary in the Spring term. A Women's Ministry Director needs to transition out when a new baby is born. A Children's Ministry Director may need to move when their spouse works in another city.

Churches often post these jobs publicly. Still, because these positions can be part-time—and many do not require a degree or credentials—these positions are most likely filled by someone already in the congregation or community. Proportionally, fewer candidates move to take these positions.

If you seek these types of positions, you should put even more focus on the *Intentional Networking* process over job boards. The people most likely to learn about these positions are the women and men already serving in them. Focus on developing your network with people in the type of positions you seek. Be consistent in your communication with your Network Partners. Look for established networks or conferences focused on this type of ministry leader. As of this writing, the Gospel Coalition has a biennial conference for women, and the Presbyterian Church in America's Committee on Discipleship Ministries (PCA-CDM) has regional conferences for people serving in Children's Ministry, and there are dozens of youth ministry leader conferences.

Leaving Wisely
You made the decision to leave your current position. How much trust and equity you have with people in your current context determines who you should tell, what you should share, and when you should share it.

Trust changes in different contexts with different people. I trust my financial planner to make prudent investment decisions, but I would not ask him to watch my children. I trust my neighbors to call me if my house is on fire, but I don't know them well enough to give them a key to my house. I am in two men's groups. With one group, I share everything indiscriminately. I know and trust them enough to keep in confidence what I share, to encourage me when I'm discouraged, to remind me what is true, and to rebuke me when I am in the wrong. In turn, these men are equally vulnerable. The other group does not have that level of trust, mainly because some of the men are private and disinclined to transparency.

Sometimes, we set limits on our trust because of discrepancies between areas of competence and character. For example, I have been treated medically by competent doctors who were maritally unfaithful. They have a skill or competency I can trust but a questionable character. Other times, the disconnect is because of someone's capacity. Ronald Heifetz and Martin Linksy call these two groups of people allies and confidants. Confidants are people you can trust with everything, all the time. Allies are people you can trust only until you can't.

I know a story about a young man in ministry, call him Jim, who broke his hand after punching a wall in anger. He confessed his sin and shame to a church Elder. This young man and the Elder worked in the same office building. Some weeks later, the Elder saw the young man in their building and called loudly across an open space, "Hey, Jim, punched any walls lately?" Dozens of people heard him. The young man felt terrible shame. He lost respect for the Elder and never confided in him again. What's more, he learned the painful lesson that being in a position of shepherding care does not guarantee somebody is a confidant.

Time and experience are the only markers for figuring out if someone is a confidant and not just an ally. How do those people react to your moments of transparency? In what settings do they bring those matters up again? How do they speak about other people and situations that do not involve you? If someone lets other people's secrets slip to me, I am reasonably confident they are letting my secrets slip to other people. It takes years for someone to earn your trust; it takes seconds for them to break it.

Seeking to grow as a confidant is one of the best ways to evaluate others in this area. How do you treat the sensitive information you know about—regardless of whether it was shared with you, or you stumbled upon it? Do you find yourself telling other people's stories? Moments of indiscretion happen when we try to connect with someone by sharing vulnerable details about a third person. Murray Bowen wrote that one sign of a healthy relationship is how long two people can talk together before they start talking about a third person.

One of the challenges is that the number of confidants people have is falling. A 2006 study published in American Sociological Review found that people today have fewer confidants than people in 1984.[46] A growing number of people reported having no one in whom to confide. Who are your confidants, and who is on the way to becoming a confidant? How do you know they are more than allies?

Be a Student of Your People

Your current organization already has rules when it comes to matters of loss, disappointment, change, and disruption. You can anticipate how your supervisor, the Session, congregational leadership, and friends in the church respond to news of your planned departure by how these people have dealt with previous losses. This pattern gives you an indication of who has the capacity to hear about and absorb the anxiety of your anticipated departure. A surprising number of leaders respond poorly to news of a staff member's departure, even leaders believed (by others) to be emotionally healthy and mature.

When Mandy cheerfully told her supervisor she was leaving her position at the church to teach, her supervisor responded, "I'm not surprised. You haven't lived up to my expectations. I expected so much more from you." Dryden confided in fellow staff member Barrett that he intended to pursue another position. Barrett urged Dryden not to tell the Senior Pastor until he had to. When Dryden finally broke the news to his Senior Pastor, the man responded, "I can't believe you would betray me that way." Dryden and his Senior Pastor barely spoke again in the two months that followed before Dryden left for his new position.

Both Mandy and Dryden said they had great relationships with their supervisors before they announced their departures. Both believed their supervisors were confidants with whom they could share anything. They had shared many ministry challenges and successes, joys and sorrows. Only later, Mandy remembered how her supervisor relationally cut off another staff person who had left. And when Dryden asked a trusted congregant about his Senior Pastor's reaction, she responded, "He does that with everyone who leaves."

In another case, Chong shared that he had accepted another position, the rest of the Leadership Team began meeting without him. He was no longer welcome. Bevan's Senior Pastor wouldn't meet with him again after he shared his intentions to go into campus ministry. And Lauretta's supervisor waited until Lauretta's last day before making her departure public—no celebration or going away party, just an after-hours email "thanking her" for her five years' of service.

Let me be clear. Not all organizations or supervisors respond poorly. These are the worst examples I've come across. I know more situations in which the departure went smoothly. When it does, praise the Lord. But candidates should not be caught off guard when broken people and systems in a post-Genesis 3 world don't live in pre-Genesis 3 ways. The point is this: the people in your organization have a history and a pattern. Become a student of *both* in order to discern how they are likely to respond to news of your departure.

The Need for Triangulation in a Season of Uncertainty
Emotional triangulation isn't intrinsically bad. What do I mean by triangulation? Gerald Juhnke put it this way:

> Triangulation suggests that when excessive anxiety or stressors arise within a relationship, often one person triangulates or seeks a third person to confide in. Or, in some cases, instead of triangulation to a third person, one of the partners turns to something such as an addiction to escape the relationship tension. Although such triangulation may initially reduce anxiety or stress within the problematic relationship, there is no final resolution. Instead, the triangulation merely dilutes the presenting anxiety or stress and inhibits the persons from actually resolving the problems that initially engendered the anxiety or stressors.[47]

The authors of *The Leader's Journey* write, "[T]riangles, like anxiety or the togetherness force, are an aspect of human behavior that is neither good nor bad. They just are. Triangles are in themselves neutral; they exist as a part of human behavior."[48]

And there are many ways a relational triangle offers support when a two-person relationship is strained. Grieving parents consult a pastor. Couples struggling in their marriage see a counselor. A troubled parent may bring in a youth leader, teacher, or principal when dealing with a difficult child. These third parties balance the instability of a two-person relationship, help navigate challenging situations, and enable the development of new patterns of interaction. The relational triangle becomes an issue when it functions primarily to enable two people to avoid dealing with their relational anxieties.

Your departure from a church will trigger several predictable responses, and others that could not be predicted. These are the most common statements people make when hearing their pastor is leaving:

- Why didn't I know sooner?
- I knew you wouldn't stay.
- What did we do wrong?
- I guess it's time for me to look for another church.
- We need to find a pastor just like him.
- We need to find a pastor *not* like him.
- The Assistant Pastor should be our next pastor.
- All we need is a good preacher.
- Let's get [previous staff person] back.

Understand, no matter how you break the news, who you tell, and when, there are people who feel hurt. Others get angry. Some people might try to convince you to stay. And a few may cut you off. These reactions are not an indictment of your service. Many of these people still love you, but at that moment, their incapacity to deal with loss is greater than their care for you.

Your decision to pursue or take another job is difficult *for you* before making the decision. Your decision is hard *for others* after you make the decision. Your resolve comes at the cusp of their sadness, frustration, fear, and uncertainty. Uncertainty generates anxiety. Anxiety is a powerful force. I am inclined to think we give anxiety more power than it deserves. To that end, Murray Bowen wrote, "When anxiety increases, one has to decide whether to give in and retreat or carry on in spite of it. Anxiety does not harm people. It only makes them uncomfortable. It can cause you to shake, or lose sleep, or become confused, or develop physical symptoms, but it will not kill you and it will subside. People can even grow and become more mature by having to face and deal with anxiety."[49]

Whatever you and I believe about the power of anxiety, we still live in a world where our choices create anxiety in other people, just as their actions do in us. Exceptionally few people in your current congregation can listen to you talk about leaving, walk with you through that process while remaining non-anxious, *and* maintain the necessary degree of confidentiality. They will be prone to seek out other people—a relational triangle—with whom to process their own emotions.

I can sit calmly and listen to pastors talk about their frustration with ministry, financial needs, unemployment, disagreement with their spouse, unrealistic family expectations, and even spiritual unbelief. When these situations involve my immediate family, I struggle (and regularly fail) to remain non-anxious.

You need people with whom to process your decision. Seek those confidants outside of your immediate context. Be prayerful about who, from your current ministry context, you can confide in and when to do so. The more you expect support and encouragement from another person, the greater their need will be to process with someone else.

Elements of an Ideal Departure

My children had a Matchbox Car book with a yellow bus. In the story, a student rushes to the bus stop, gets on the bus, and makes it to school. Throughout the book, the phrase "just in time" recurs on every page.

Ideally, just in time, you share your intention to leave with key leaders. They listen well and support your decision. Just in time, they announce your departure to the congregation. You neither stay too long nor leave too quickly and, just in time, the church celebrates your service. Just in time, the leadership gives you a formal exit interview and can hear and receive your feedback. In turn, you can hear and receive their feedback affirming areas of strength and encouraging areas for growth.

Reality looks different. Not all leaders celebrate your departure. Confidants prove to be allies, breaking your trust as your intentions to leave slowly leak out into the community. Not all supervisors give exit interviews, and fewer want honest feedback. And not all churches celebrate you before you leave.

In one of my positions, my supervisor approached me and asked, "What are you thinking about for next year?" The question caught me off guard. I had to stop and think. I conveyed my impressions of the previous year, recounted several successes, and reflected on my relationship with people in the organization. I finished by saying, "Overall, I think I'm doing a good job. I connect well with the people I'm serving, and I think they like me."

He replied, "I don't know that they do." The conversation ended there with me mumbling that I would get back to him in a couple of weeks. In my mind, I had already decided that I needed to look for a new position. This was the only time this supervisor had debriefed with me about my work effectiveness and vocational aspirations. I had no exit interview and no opportunity for feedback.

When you finally share your intentions to leave, give people space to process. Don't expect your Senior Pastor or the Session members to dive into the details of your departure immediately. People need the opportunity to think, reflect, and grieve. After sharing your plan to leave, ask for a follow-up meeting to discuss further details.

Ask when the news should be shared with the congregation at your second meeting. Ask if there are other considerations you should have in mind. And, when the time is right, ask if the church will have a going away event. Ask if there will be a formal exit interview and who will be included in it. If an exit interview is not planned, ask if you could have one with representatives of the Session—if you think it is safe to do so.

Relational tensions with his Senior Pastor were one of the main reasons Landry looked for another position. Landry described his Senior Pastor as emotionally distant, easily frustrated, dismissive, and sometimes belittling of others. These personality traits affected church health, and many of the younger families had left or considered leaving the church. While talking with an Elder about the youth program, Landry expressed disappointment at having his ideas dismissed by the Senior Pastor. The Elder laughed and patted Landry on the arm: "Son, you got to have thick skin. That's Bill, and he's not going to change."

Alyssa asked if she would be given an exit interview. The Chair of the Elder Board responded, "If you want one, but remember that the Pastor's family and my family are best friends. I don't think we'll take kindly to any criticism." In both situations, the Senior Pastor and leadership were unwilling or unable to hear honest, loving feedback. It is better not to push for an exit interview in such situations.

As a positive example, Drew felt a call away from youth ministry. He and his Senior Pastor, Frank, met regularly to process life and ministry. When Drew decided to look for another position, he confided in Frank, who kept the news to himself. Frank offered support and encouragement. After Drew was offered a position, he and Frank planned how to announce it to the church. Frank asked the Session to conduct a formal interview with Drew before he left. Drew recounts, "Frank told me and the Session that he had personal and vocational blind spots that would only be exposed through systems of high trust and accountability."

If, like Drew, you have good relationships with the church and staff you are leaving and are given an exit interview—where should you focus your feedback? Every organization has areas for growth, for leaders to be more reflective, or for ineffective processes to change. How do you prepare for loving but difficult conversation before you leave?

Start with Affirmation
You have been given space to grow and learn. There were times when you received support, encouragement, and protection from the irrational attacks of others. You have fallen short or failed; the church has helped you back up. You've received physical gifts and acts of hospitality. You made memories, laughed, cried, and deepened the bond of friendship.

Start with these affirmations. What are you grateful for? Who can you thank for their actions or words of kindness? Where did you find encouragement and support? What can you affirm in the character and skills of those in leadership? Starting with gratitude is not just a political move to grease the tracks. Reflecting on gratitude helps you broaden the narrow view of dysfunction that can creep into our subconscious and hijack our best intentions. If you cannot think of five points of gratitude, you have let criticism and correction shadow God's good work in others' lives. Until you can name at least five things for which you are thankful, I suspect you are not ready to have an exit interview.

Evaluate the Realities of Your Expectations
When I ask ministry candidates what they want in their first or next position, at the top of the list is a desire for their supervisor to be a mentor and friend. Close friendships can develop among fellow staff. When they do, the departure of one—often the senior leader—results in vocational turnover of other key staff.

But close friendship between a supervisor and a direct report—a Senior Pastor and an Assistant Pastor—is rare. There are just too many confounding variables. A Senior Pastor must direct, redirect, and sometimes correct support staff. Shared camaraderie usually takes second place to managerial expectations. When there are issues, congregation members more often complain to the Senior Pastor about the Assistant Pastor, putting relational pressure on all points of the relational triangle.

Meanwhile, the Senior Pastor tries to navigate his own one-legged stool. The one-legged stool is what pastors experience when all areas of life conflate, personally and professionally. One pastor described the one-legged stool phenomenon this way:

> Most people in our church have a life that is like a stool with three legs. They've got their spiritual life, their professional life and their family life. If one of these legs wobbles, they've got two others they can lean on. For [ministry leaders], those three things can merge into one leg. You're sitting on a one-legged stool, and it takes a lot more concentration and energy...[50]

The point is this. Senior leaders are challenged to extend solidarity to support staff over their obligations and commitments to their leadership, congregation, role in the organization, and family.

If close friendship (confidant) is unrealistic, should Assistant Pastors at least expect to be mentored? This depends significantly on both parties' personality, maturity, and experience. Most Senior Pastors hire people with different abilities and skills from their own. An Assistant Pastor is not a lesser version of a Senior Pastor in areas of responsibility. Functionally, they are more like apples to oranges. To meet a complex organization's disparate and varied needs, staff members complement one another more than replicate.

Usually, areas of personal interest and individual ability reflect aspects of one's unique personality. At my church, the Senior Pastor is a *Thinking-Judging* Type (MBTI), while the Associate Pastor is a *Feeling-Perceiving* Type (MBTI). The Senior Pastor is more oriented to structure and vision. He approaches situations objectively and regularly seeks closure. The Associate Pastor is oriented to relational connection, leisure, and flexibility. This is why they work well together, and why they sometimes experience tension.

The commonality of these personality differences means that few Assistant Pastors report experiencing mentorship in the forms they expected. In a data set of 1,390 pastors, there are fewer than 50 situations in which both the Senior *and* Associate Minister said of the other that they were confidants *and* where the Associate Minister viewed the Senior Pastor as a mentor.

Peyton is an ESTJ on the MBTI, described as extroverted, meticulous, rational and logical in his decision making, and quick to come to closure. He was hired as an Assistant Pastor to bring structure to a growing church plant in the city center. His Senior Pastor is an INTP: creative, innovative, and an internal processor prone to last-minute decisions, redirections, and changes. In short, they were opposites.

Peyton went into most meetings ready to talk about the steps he'd taken to implement decisions from their last meeting, only to be confounded. The Senior Pastor typically wanted to skip over what he called "updates" and jump to his newest ideas. Those ideas regularly contradicted decisions made in earlier meetings. Peyton supported the sudden changes, but he pressed the Senior Pastor to help him understand the
process of redirection. The Senior Pastor—an internal, intuitive processor—grew frustrated by what he experienced as "demands to explain." The breakdown in their professional relationship arose from differences in leadership, relationship, and communication styles.

Another young pastor (ISFJ) asked to meet weekly for mentorship with his Senior Pastor (ISTJ). The Senior Pastor said, "I didn't need it. I don't know why you do." Another ministry leader (ENFJ) looked to her supervisor (ESFP) for mentorship in crucial areas of leadership and management. Instead, she left meetings with a litany of personal stories that had no bearing on their current ministry context or her ministry responsibilities. In all these cases, personality played a substantial role in these relationships, contributing to the practical realities of supervision, including management, oversight, and evaluation.

Your expectations of the kind of relationship you'll have with your supervisor are just one of the many expectations you'll have. I suspect you will experience more disappointment—or at least more "dis-ease"—than satisfaction throughout your life and ministry. I do not mean to be negative, but let's be honest. Looking back ten years, I had unrealistic expectations of my job, marriage, children, extended family, and myself. Disappointment showed me my idolatry, to appreciate a more comprehensive view of reality and, in time, to find joy amidst complexity.

An exit interview is not the time to dump all your unmet expectations on your supervisor or your organization's leaders. Evaluate your expectations against a more expansive view of reality. Then, decide to share only what you can quantify.

Don't Try to Say Everything
Is your critique of leadership longer than your list of gratitude? Shorten it. The tendency is to try and say everything about every moment of poor (or no) leadership, broken promises, misspoken words, dropped balls, no support, carelessness, forgetfulness, tension, frustration, and anxiety. The more you say, the less is heard.

When we try to say everything, we erode our credibility. Even admonishments spoken in love become just noise after about ten minutes. And the more you challenge or correct, the more you show your own limitations. None of us has the whole story, and it is arrogant to assume we do.

One of my supervisors told me I had enormous potential but was young and inexperienced. "A wife will help with that," he remarked. I grinned because I was dating a girl seriously (my future wife). He didn't know that and read my smile as a smirk, saying. "That's what I'm talking about. Cocky immaturity." It was a moment that seemed straightforward to him—a young man smirking at his advice—but he lacked the necessary information to make sense of the situation.

Another time, I led a team event. One member was distracted by two others who were talking. He told me how much he disapproved, then headed to the bathroom. I immediately went over to ask the disruptive members to stop talking over the speaker.

"We will," they agreed, "after we finish this story." I then went back to my seat. The first member was frustrated when he returned to find me sitting in the same spot while the two women continued talking. From his perspective, I had done nothing and ignored his concern. "You never take me seriously," he said loudly enough for all the other participants to hear. In these two situations, others did not have the full picture of me or my actions, but I have been on the other side just as often.

Assume you don't have the whole picture. Say what you know to be true. Avoid speculation or assigning motives. Focus on the three (at most) areas of change that would most impact on the organization's health—including its leaders and members.

- What is the best possible outcome for the organization and leadership from what you share?
- What is the most likely outcome for the organization and leadership from what you share?
- What needs to be addressed first or what needs to change first?

Change is like a series of dominoes. Pick any random domino out of a line. That domino isn't going to fall until the one before it does, and so forth. The area we most want to see change often requires precursors of change. Someone who has neglected her body and developed chronic back issues doesn't start the journey toward health by running three miles a day. She begins by walking a little and changing her diet.

After my family moved, my wife and I spent months organizing our new home. There were repairs, walls to paint, and rooms to remodel. We wanted to organize the basement so we could update the bathroom. But we needed the kitchen shelving system to organize the basement. And we needed the pantry remodeled before we could clean off the shelving system. Dominoes.

The organization you leave won't change overnight. Your words aren't likely to bring about massive transformation. But that doesn't mean your words are powerless. Focus on the area you think is most likely to be a catalyst for change in other areas. As you prepare for your exit interview, write down what you plan to say. It's easy to get muddled when the stakes are high and say things we regret.

Don't Theologize, Do Personalize
No, that isn't backward. When hurt and frustrated, we tend to seek out a clinical diagnosis or label for the issue and then find a Bible verse to

condemn that specific behavior. The biggest problem is conflating your perspective and judgment of the situation with God's. Here are several examples to illustrate:

- Jae, a *Perceiving* Type (P), found his supervisor's promises often empty. Frustrated by the supervisor's lack of follow-through, Jae accused him of lying and questioned his pastoral qualifications, citing Exodus 20:16.
- Alyssa's supervisor's socially awkward requests, often perceived as unkind, led her to label him a narcissistic misogynist. She cited Ephesians 5:21 in support of her assessment.
- Barrett, frustrated with his 20-something Youth Director's consistent failure to complete tasks, gave him two months' notice. Barrett labeled the director immature, unteachable, and a fool, citing Proverbs 12:15.
- Darwin's supervisor, avoiding direct confrontation, emailed him after congregants complained about his leadership. Darwin accused his supervisor of passive-aggression and violating the Matthew 18 principle.

In these examples, both sides have merit. Jae's expectations were reasonable, *and* the Pastor's oversights were minor. Alyssa's supervisor's comments could be perceived as harsh *and* understandable in context. Barrett, young and inexperienced, needed more support from his pastor.

When we theologize our perspective, we create relational scenarios in which we are *all* in the right and the other person or group is *all* in the wrong. Life and the Scriptures show that there is enough blame to go around. None of us lives in such a way that our character, behavior, and perspective overlap entirely with God's heart, will, and viewpoint.

Most of the time, you don't need to use the Bible to make your case. It detracts from your purpose. How could the people discussed above have responded differently in their exit interviews?

- Jae: "I need clear expectations. The Pastor's inconsistent follow-through often confused me. I think he would benefit from a scheduling assistant."

103

- Alyssa: "My supervisor's comments made me feel insignificant. Women in our church often lack leadership roles, so I'm sensitive to gendered remarks. I hope he'll consider how his words impact others."
- Barrett: "I apologize for not providing enough structure. Please forgive me. Also, it's important to know when to ask for help, and I encourage you to do so more frequently in your next role."
- Darwin: "Your email felt critical. I prefer direct feedback, including positive aspects. Sharing both strengths and weaknesses is important for my own personal growth."

Don't theologize. Rather, speak directly about what you wanted or needed and how those desires went unmet. Be specific. Focus on facts and your personal experience, not the broader stories of similar situations within the church. When you speak clearly about your own experience, the leadership is better equipped to know how to respond.

Summary
When preparing to leave, be selective with whom you tell and when. This requires you to be a student of your people. Be aware of the propensity for triangulation, good and bad. Remember the elements of an ideal departure during your exit interview. Affirm what you can. Evaluate the reality of your expectations. Don't try to say everything. Do not theologize but be specific to your personal experience.

Action Steps
1. What are your hopes for the next season of ministry?
2. How does the ministry hiring cycle inform when and where to direct your energy, and when to rest?
3. Draft a plan to navigate the ministry hiring cycle to prevent frustration and discouragement?
4. If you are in a ministry position, where in the Six-Phases of the Ministry Life Cycle are you now? Describe this stage.
5. What are practical steps you can take to prepare your current community for your transition? Think about the 5 Ps. Make a list of where you need to invest time and energy.
6. Reflect on a situation where you had a disagreement with someone. Write how your preferences came into tension with preferences that were different from yours. How would you change your response or reaction in a comparable situation?

4

How to Understand Your Unique Ministry Style

Chapter Summary
You need to understand the personality of the organizations you are considering. It is equally important for you to understand *your* personality and preferences. Understanding one of these realities is a matter of curiosity. A refined nuance of difference begins when you know and appreciate both yourself and others. This is why when somebody states their preferences—whether speaking in terms of the Enneagram, Myers Briggs, or another metric—I quickly ask, "With respect to who and what?" While I believe our personality preferences are intrinsic at birth, I also think their expression is shaped by the context in which they develop. They are refined over time. This chapter offers a high-level view of personality and how it will play into your search for and service in a ministry position, focusing primarily on the Myers Briggs Type Indicator. As you grow in self-awareness and differentiation from others, you grow in confidence and motivation.

How Does Personality Impact the Job Hunt?
Personality preferences are a factor in every interaction we have. That means personality also plays a significant role in your search for a ministry job. You need to understand your own personality and how it is experienced by others. I prefer the Myers Briggs Type Indicator (MBTI), and not simply because I am a licensed facilitator of the metric. The MBTI provides a model that is understandable and applicable without being overly complex.

Other metrics offer tremendous insight into your personality, preferences, motivations, and fears. I see value in the Enneagram and

Strength Finders. But when I talk with people who are assessed by these metrics, many struggle to articulate the implications of the results for their own life, much less the impact of these results on their relationships and vocation. Many people have a harder time connecting individual results to organizational dynamics: How does a church function as an Enneagram Type 1? At best, these individuals can say *what*, but rarely not *why* or *how*. The MBTI applies to individuals but can be expanded to explain interactions within family units and organizations of all sizes.

Your personality affects how you approach the ministry job search. Every Type has strengths and struggles. Some Types struggle with over-confidence, others with insecurity. Some convey warmth easily, others intelligence. Some Types overshare, while others are perceived guarded even when sharing from the most vulnerable places in their lives. Others are perceived as aloof, distant, friendly, dominant, passive, strong, intense, disengaged, emotional, tender, or tough, respectively. Your personality affects how you engage in the search process and how others in the process receive your interaction.

The following chart outlines the behaviors and tendencies of each MBTI dichotomy. If you do not know your MBTI Type, you can pay to be assessed online or in person. I see value in having a licensed facilitator interpret and apply your results. However, if you don't want to pay but want to explore your Type, you can also find free versions of the Jung/Myers-Briggs typology inventory online.

This chart is not intended to be comprehensive, but rather a summary of behaviors and perceptions based on Type.

Candidate Preference	Candidate Engagement	Growth Opportunity
Extroversion	Prefers to communicate through talking. Initiates through short email but prefers verbal communication. Often gregarious, looking for back-and-forth conversation. May be perceived as pushy, talkative, inflexible (with *Judging*), or scatterbrained (with *Perceiving*).	Ask more open-ended questions. Use the rubric, "Tell me about a time…" Give space to the other person for reflection. Practice reflective listening. Respect the value of written communication. Affirm before adding to or challenging.
Introversion	Prefers to communicate in writing. Receives engagement rather than initiates, waiting for others to respond. Often thoughtful or reflective. Can be perceived as flat, passive, better-than ("stuck up"), aloof, or bored and disengaged.	Invite people into your reflective process. Name what is happening inside or what you are thinking. Say, "Let me think about that a moment…" before a period of quiet. Process more out loud with qualification, "I need to think about that more, but my initial response is…." Take more risks initiating.

Candidate Preference	Candidate Analysis	Growth Opportunity
Sensing	Oriented to the present moment; practical, detailed, principled. Prioritizes concrete information available on job description, church profile, or website. Remembers specific words or phrases. Can miss or devalue big picture or systemic, organizational dynamics.	Ask questions that invite dialogue around the big-picture aspects of the organization. Seek out people who make broad observations. Ask the opinion of trusted global thinkers (*Intuitive* Types) to help you to make connections and associations that are not obvious to you.
Intuition	Oriented to possibilities and patterns. Prioritizes details that fit a pattern of association. Can make logical leaps or connections between seemingly unrelated data. Can overlook or dismiss important specifics or actualities that do not fit a chosen pattern. May not ask practical questions or clarify ambiguous answers.	Ask questions that focus on details and history, anchoring responses in actual events. Explore present-moment realities within the organization. Ask for speakers to expound on earlier comments. Be patient to let *Sensing* Types share their detailed narratives, even if the information seems extraneous.

Candidate Preference	Candidate Expression	Growth Opportunity
Thinking	Thoughtful and analytical. Oriented to logical processes or systems. Views information objectively. Focuses on analysis. Asks cause-and-effect questions, often at the exclusion of emotional and relational realities. May generalize their own experience, extrapolating into unrelated areas. May struggle to share vulnerable information, missing opportunities to connect with people relationally.	Look to make space for the relational values of emotional processes. Ask more emotional-based questions, "How did that make you feel?" Listen for the human and relational dynamics in a situation, not simply the facts. Remember, "every process is an emotional process." Practice sharing personal stories, with emphasis on the appropriate levels of vulnerability you want to share during an interview.
Feeling	Relational and connectional. Prioritizes narrative information gained through interaction. Makes decisions based on core values to achieve harmony. Can miss or underemphasize pragmatic aspects or make decisions based on internal sense rather than concrete specifics. May overshare vulnerable aspects of themselves to connect relationally. May soften direct speech or avoid asking tough questions. Can miss pragmatic aspects of the engagement process.	Practice emotional differentiation. Seek objectivity when analyzing information. Write down firm statements you want to make or direct questions you want to ask. Your goal is not to avoid anxiety or emotional discomfort. State your preferences even if they are unpopular. Seek input from trusted mentors on how much information to share, in what detail, and when.

Candidate Preference	Candidate Closure / Decision	Growth Opportunity
Judging	Structured and planning. Speaks decisively. Seeks to move processes toward closure. Wants decisions settled. Can struggle with the waiting involved in a job search. Frustrated by the lack of structure or professionalism. May push too hard to come to closure, souring relationships. Can come across intense, controlling, or inflexible.	Pray for patience. Examine your pursuit of needing matters settled. Look for places where you can practice flexibility. Prior to speaking, ask what other perspectives or options there may be. Caveat statements with, "I am open to other ideas on this," or "This is just one idea…"
Perceiving	Flexible and open to last-minute information. Conveys an openness to change or redirection, even if internally settled on a course of action. Unwilling to commit too early to a decision. May speak in a meandering way, sharing too much unrelated information (*Sensing*) or analogies/metaphors (*Intuition*) that are not clearly linked. Can be perceived as scatter-brained or easily distracted. Can struggle with follow-through.	Develop structures for task completion and follow-through. Be respectful of others' resources of time, attention, and energy. Practice keeping commitments promptly. Take initiative in the process. Look for ways to substantiate the structures you've developed and consistently use.

Additional Resources

Here are additional resources I use and recommend for people interested in exploring their personality and preferences further:

- *Gifts Differing*, by Isabela Briggs Myers and Peter Myers (1995), CPP, 2nd edition, 248 pages. This classic work is written by the co-creator of the Myers Briggs Type Indicator. This book uses a narrative approach to explain the four dichotomies of the MBTI and the concept of dynamic personality theory. This is a useful resource for someone who wants to give dedicated time to understanding the history, evolution, development, and application of the assessment.

- *Introduction to Myers-Briggs Type*, by Isabela Myers (2015), CPP, 7th edition. This 55-page booklet is a brief introduction to the MBTI. It includes a one-page history of the development and evolution of the assessment. Several pages are dedicated to a self-test. The rest of the book applies the results to each of the 16 Types. I use this section when trying to understand another person's type. This book is usually included in your paid MBTI assessment, but you can find used copies at many online retailers.

- *Becoming Us*, by Beth McCord and Jeff McCord (2019), Morgan James Publisher, 264 pages. This book has quickly become one of the leading texts explaining and applying the Enneagram. I particularly like the quick guide on each type (144-215).

- *Paid MBTI Assessment.* Those interested in the revised and expanded Steps I and II of the current MBTI should consider taking the paid assessment. The current cost is $49 for the assessment and results. This does not include an interpretive consultation with a facilitator. https://www.mbtionline.com/

- *Free Jung/Myers-Briggs Typology Assessment.* There are several free copycat versions of the MBTI online. Be selective, as these metrics range in quality. My favorite for people who want quick, free personality results can be found at: https://www.humanmetrics.com/. This 64-question assessment generally renders accurate results, assuming a moderate degree of self-awareness in the assessed.

Finding Your Motivation

Your motivation in the job search is going to wane. With few exceptions, the process is more convoluted, demanding, and slower than expected and desired. A sense of urgency can give way to frustration. Frustration can lead to anxiety and worry. And eventually, discouragement sets in. Discouragement is the antithesis of motivation.

You must prepare for disappointment, the way people in Florida prepare for hurricanes, people in California prepare for drought, and people in Kansas prepare for tornadoes. Disappointment may never come. You might be one of the few who never experience the agony of silence as you wait for word that you are still a candidate. But if you come upon disappointment without preparation, you may be derailed.

Here, at the beginning, capture your motivation. Why put yourself through this process—scouring job boards, networking with connectors, applying for jobs, answering initial questionnaires, preparing for interviews, and waiting in uncertainty for confirmation you are still being considered? Why face inevitable frustration and potential rejection? What beliefs are driving your commitment? What do you want to be remembered for at the end of your life and career?

How you answer these questions is your defense to frustration, discouragement, rejection, and resentment. What you write in response to these questions is your light of Eärendil: a vial of light shining in dark places at dark times. In the book *The Lord of the Rings*, the elf princess Galadriel presents Frodo with a glass vial of light from the most favored star of the elves. Frodo uses it against the deadly spider, Shelob.

Your enemy isn't a fictional spider but is no less dark. This list of motivations for staying in this costly endeavor *is* your light of Eärendil: something to hold up when the way forward seems hopeless. This record of your commitments is like the rocks of remembrance taken from the riverbed of the Jordan by the Israelites (Joshua 4). Your motivations will be tested in the dark, but you must bring them into the light.

Another helpful image comes from author Jim Collins in Good to Great. He calls it the Hedgehog Principle. The principle states that the engine of our motivation drives strongest at the place where three realities intersect:

- What are you deeply passionate about?
- What can you be the best in the world at?
- What drives your economic and resource engine?

Does this sound ambitious? Yes. And there is nothing wrong with godly ambition. Ambition is the energy to look for shalom in places of *dis-ease*. I believe God delights in our kingdom ambitions.

Where should you start? Don't just state that you need to preach, teach, lead, or support. State why and what happens to you in this redemptive moment if you give up that pursuit. Motivation meets the fruit of commitment at the end of our vocational journey. For what do you want to be remembered?

Rejection and Disappointment

High hopes and crushing disappointment mark the ministry job search. As with most job hunts, there are practical realities, like the need for income, the uncertainty of the transition period, and the exhaustion of applying and interviewing for jobs. Aspects unique to the ministry job search amplify the highs and lows.

Because the life of a pastor involves making a community with a group of people, rejection can feel more personal than professional. When committees turn a candidate away, sometimes a specific skill or capacity is the reason. Maybe a candidate doesn't have enough experience or isn't ready for the challenges in the church. More often, the sentiments expressed are more subjective and intensely personal. Here are some comments that candidates have been given and committees have made:

- We just didn't connect with her on a relational level.
- He didn't seem warm or empathetic.
- She was too enthusiastic for our church.
- He seemed too emotional.
- She seemed guarded.

A candidate can grow as a preacher, counselor, speaker, listener, manager, leader, and visionary. There are classes, sometimes entire degrees, focused on these skills. However, the above statements emphasize personality traits more than professional skills. A *Thinking*

Type on the Myers Briggs tends to be less empathetic and warm than a *Feeling* Type. The Enneagram Type 1 is perceived as more focused on results than relationships. Ministry is absolutely an informational vocation, but never exclusively. We might tolerate emotionally flat accountants and emotionally reactive administrators. But ministry leaders who are either of these things are short-lived for the ministry.

The relational nature of ministry means that the job search is more like dating than looking for a paycheck. Ministers' personal and professional lives are conflated in ways unfamiliar to lawyers, doctors, mechanics, and teachers. Most ministry leaders spend more vocational hours being with and caring for people—or preparing to be with and care for people—than at technical and administrative tasks. The rare candidate who expects otherwise will be disappointed with the hiring process. The rest, expecting this, must engage their hearts in the process: *Can I live with, serve, and grow to love these people?* A candidate who answers no to this question should not continue in the process with a specific church. Everybody else answering yes will experience hurt and feel personal rejection when they are turned down for a job.

Preparing for Rejection
You will be turned down for a ministry job. You can't avoid it. All you can do is prepare for it.

Koji began searching for a ministry position the summer before his senior year. As a result, he was ahead of his classmates. He progressed quickly with one of the first churches he applied to. The church wasn't ideal. It was further away from his desired geographic region. He would be allowed to teach regularly—overseeing Christian Education and Spiritual Formation—but he would not have much opportunity to preach. Still, the further he went through the process, the more he genuinely liked the search committee members. To his surprise and disappointment, Koji was cut from the candidate list in the last round.

Disappointed, frustrated, and more than a little hurt, Koji engaged with other ministry opportunities. One of the positions he applied for was ideal, located where his family wanted to live. The position allowed Koji to preach, teach, and oversee outreach. The Senior Pastor was slated to go on sabbatical within a year, at which point Koji would fill the pulpit three times a month.

The committee brought Koji and his wife to the church on a site visit as part of the final round of interviews. A few days after the trip ended, the Senior Pastor called. He communicated how much the Session and search committee liked Koji. But he added, "You seemed closed off, even a little guarded."

Koji thought about it. "I was guarded," he said. "I think I was scared of being turned down again." The Senior Pastor thanked Koji for his honesty, but said the church could not move forward with him. In the end, Koji's fear of further disappointment became a self-fulling prophecy, closing the door to a terrific opportunity.

When you experience rejection, how will you respond? Some people shut down and withdraw. Some put on a smiling face but, inside, they boil with resentment. Others cry, get angry, or act out. Knowing how you usually respond is the first step in preparing for disappointment.

On whom will you lean during these times? God intended the church to be a community, an organization of diverse personalities and preferences bound together with a shared belief: "one Lord, one faith, one baptism, one God and Father of all" (Eph. 4:5). You may be able to weather one or two disappointments alone, but you need a community to weather a lifetime of disappointments.

What do you do about your disappointment? The practices of self-care you establish before you face disappointment serve you well afterward. These include prayer, meditation, journaling, physical exercise, adequate sleep, and healthy fellowship. I practice the discipline of journaling and, in recent years, have read about and practiced Christian meditation. Another friend goes on a ten-mile run when he receives disappointing news. One pastor I know immediately texts a group of close friends who text back prayers and words of encouragement.

How do you break cycles of rumination? Rumination can be a destructive pattern of anxiously replaying events or situations in your mind. Even if you are an internal processor, you must find outlets to bring the situation into the outside world. I recommend prayer and sharing your concerns with confidants: trusted friends who have the capacity to listen, ask questions, and empathize.

Write Down Your Rejection Plan

Write down your rejection plan with a pen to paper. People who write down their action plan are more likely to follow through with it. Writing for the *Harvard Business Review*, Vasundhara Sawhney states, "Essentially, when we create a roadmap to help us reach a goal, we are more likely to attain it *and* more likely to focus better on other areas of our work or lives in the interim."[51] Make it tactile. A task list on your phone doesn't make the same cognitive or physiological connections between the body and the brain.

At the top of the plan, write one or two sentences about your core motivation from the last section. Why are you putting yourself through this process? What is so important that it's worth risking disappointment? We all need to be reminded of our deepest values and life-long goals. Let your unique motivation set the framework for your rejection plan. Here are three examples:

- God has called me to minister. Now I'm just looking for where He wants me to do that.
- Vocationally, I've never been more satisfied than when doing ministry.
- Ministry: I love it, am good at it, and get results. Ministry makes me feel alive. Let's go!

After you write it:

1. Post it where you can see it.
2. Look at it regularly.
3. Practice your plan before you experience disappointment.
4. Share your rejection plan with the people supporting you in this process. When others know about it, they can hold you accountable: "Are you working your rejection plan?" Dr. Gail Matthews, Psychologist and Career Coach at the Dominican University of California, found that people who consistently made and achieved goals formulated action commitments first and then—don't miss this essential step—"sent their goals, action commitments, and weekly progress reports to a supportive friend." You need encouragement, but you also need accountability.

A sample rejection plan includes four elements:

- <u>Your core motivations, commitments, and goals:</u> This is the constant reminder of why you do what you do. You must own this. It can't be about a mentor, spouse, parent (living or dead), or any other person. Only as you identify the beliefs at the core of your motivation can you rely on them as a source of drive.
- <u>The practical steps you will take when facing disappointment:</u> Be specific. General concepts are not actionable.
- <u>The time constraints for each element:</u> There is your time to grieve *and* a time to move on. Don't shortchange either of these processes. Author Chris Tuff sets boundaries for how long he can wallow in disappointment: "Success doesn't come from never facing challenges; it comes from being resilient in the face of challenges. I then remembered a rule I have. I call it my two-hour rule: when something doesn't go my way, I can dwell on it for two hours, but then I have to come up with a plan to bounce back."[52]
- <u>The names of the people you will regularly update on your progress:</u> For encouragement, accountability, and, when you need it, a kick in the butt.

<u>Sample Rejection Plans</u>
We are often stuck in our own narrow perspective of reality. Exposure to different settings, situations, disciplines, industries, and markets provides space to discover new responses to old problems. Here are two sample rejection plans. The first has nothing to do with ministry. Read it anyway because it may help you think differently about the nature of rejection you'll experience and how to respond to it.

As a Writer
1. I am a good writer. When I write, people tell me they are encouraged, inspired, and challenged to think differently about the world and their lives in it. I want to change the world through words. I am committed to writing every week, creating long and short works of fiction, poetry, and non-fiction. My goal is to write 300 words a day.
2. When rejected, I will journal about my frustration and disappointment. I'll write down my negative thoughts and feelings. After a disappointment, I get one hour to be sad, angry,

or disappointed. After that, I will close the journal and put it away. When those negative thoughts come up again (rumination), I'll remind myself I already wrote them down before the Lord and don't need to think about them again.

3. With major or ongoing disappointments, journaling may not help. I will seek out confidants and invite them into my disappointment. I'll ask them to remind me what is true about myself, who I am, and what they have observed in my life.

4. When talking with a confidant doesn't help, I'll schedule time with a counselor to explore why I'm unable to shake the negative emotions and experience.

5. As I pursue my goals, I'll keep these people up to date about my progress and setbacks: _____.

As a Pastor

1. I am a shepherd first and a communicator of truth second. When I preach, teach, and write to people, they experience blessing, encouragement, and inspiration. Some have grown. A few have shared how they feel free to live differently. I want to take part in the work of God by bringing peace to troubled hearts, reconciliation to troubled relationships, and restoration to broken situations. My goal is to become a shepherd-preacher ordained in the _____ denomination.

2. When rejected, I will text my men's group immediately. I'll explain the situation, how I received the news, and where I'm struggling. I won't cultivate feelings of rejection, hurt, disappointment, and judgment. I will ask confidants to text me words of encouragement followed by prayers (also by text).

3. When I feel stuck, I'll schedule a meeting with my counselor.

4. As I pursue my goals, I'll keep these people up to date about my progress and setbacks: _____.

Action Steps

1. Learn about several personality inventories. Settle on one that resonates with you. Take the inventory and make a note of your results. What bearing do those results have on your understanding of yourself and the churches to which you apply?

2. List the specific ways your personality affects how you engage the ministry search process. What are your strengths? Where might you struggle? How can you prepare for both?

3. Write a prayer asking the Lord to sustain you through your ministry vocation search. Put it where you can regularly see it.

4. Write three to five sentences about your motivation: why you do all this, even at the risk of disappointment and rejection. Put it where you will see it often. Be practical: one candidate taped it to his bathroom mirror and read it as he brushed his teeth. Or be creative: the wife of another candidate painted her husband's motivation in calligraphy on wood and hung it on the den wall.

5. Make a rejection plan. What does rejection feel like for you? Do research on ways to cope with rejection and disappointment. Develop a rejection plan. What is true about you that you need to document now before you are facing stress, frustration, or discouragement?

5

HOW TO BUILD YOUR RESUME PACKET

Chapter Summary
Each element of your resume packet has a purpose, a role. The resume packet includes a cover letter, resume, profile page, references, denominational form, and web presence. These elements work collectively to achieve a single outcome: to help you stand out from other candidates. I call this *differentiation*. With search committees giving less time to written documents, candidates with focused clarity stand out. In this chapter, you will learn the purpose of each element in your resume packet. You will discover different approaches to your documents' content, structure, and formatting. You will review your references and how to prepare them for that task. When finished, you will avoid common pitfalls made by other candidates by building a cohesive resume packet.

Elements of the Resume Packet
The elements in your resume packet serve a specific and unique purpose. There should be no redundancies. Here is how you should think about the task of each element in your resume packet:

Element	Purpose is to...
Cover Letter	To get a committee to read your resume.
Resume	To get a job interview.
Profile Page	To present the "human" side of who you are as a candidate.
Denominational Data Form	To present a summary of your theological commitments and reduce ambiguity around controversial topics.
Web Presence	To invite further interaction with the personal and professional aspects of your life.

The Cover Letter

The purpose of the cover letter is to compel people to read your resume. Too many candidates dismiss the importance of a well-crafted cover letter. Most candidates default to a generic cover letter that they send with every job application. A well-crafted cover letter differentiates you from other candidates.

Imagine a father receiving this note, "Dear Mr. Smith. I am a boy, and your daughter is a girl. I want to marry a girl and think I would make a great husband for your daughter. Please contact me at your convenience to discuss this matter further." A generic cover letter, though maybe not as bombastic or absurd, is about the same. It lacks relevance and conviction, focusing on the wrong things.

Research shows that public job postings can receive 70 unsolicited applications. In the corporate world, this number is closer to 250.[53] Often, applicants do not know anyone in the church. Applicants opt-in to the evaluation process. If a search committee member spends only five minutes on your resume packet, that equates to almost six hours reviewing resumes. A job receiving only 20 resumes still consumes an hour and a half of time. A typical committee member dedicates less than one minute to the cover letter.

There are several ways to draw attention to your cover letter. Just like your networking email, cover letters should follow the C.A.R. rubric: Concise, Actionable, and Relevant. Your cover letter should engage committee members quickly. Here is a sample cover letter:

Covenant Community Church
Attn: Pastoral Search Committee
12345 Hudson Lane
Marieville, AL 12345

Dear Pastoral Search Committee:

My name is Joel Hathaway, and I want to apply for the assistant pastor position at your church. I learned about this position from your job description. After reading your website, I knew I had to apply.

Yours is a church where people are encouraged to confess and admit their brokenness. That excites me because I believe personal transformation depends on this approach. **Thank you for your clear commitment to the Gospel of grace.** I can tell from the images on your website, your description of yourself, and the ministry values of your congregation that Christ is at the center of everything you do.

I look forward to discussing further how my ministry experience discipling adults addresses the needs of your church, your community, and this assistant pastor position. I will follow up with you in a week to see if I can clarify anything.

Your servant,

Joel Hathaway

Concise

Your cover letter should be short and to the point. I recommend three paragraphs. The first paragraph says who you are and why you are writing. The third paragraph calls the reader to action. Notice in the example that these two paragraphs are only two sentences long. The middle paragraph should be expanded to three sentences.

Employ the XO factor. Look at this series of letters: XOXOOXOXO. Our eyes slow down where the pattern breaks. We can skim only so long as the data matches an expected pattern, but we slow down when the pattern changes. The most straightforward way to break the expected pattern of your text is by using **bold**. Marketing research shows that when people scan written text—junk mail, web articles, or bulletin announcements—the use of bold text slows down the reader. The eye is drawn to the darkest part of a white page, and vice versa. The eye is also drawn to the break where the bold text interrupts the standard text. If readers are intrigued by the bolded sentence, they often read the sentence before and after it.

Look at the sample again. Committee members who only read the bold sentences get the most important details of the cover letter. If the bold sentence in the second paragraph is compelling enough, committee members may slow down to read the sentences immediately before and after. Whether or not the members read the entire cover letter, the use of bold breaks the pattern in the text, allowing for an engaged scan of the information, highlighting the essential elements.

Actionable

The last paragraph is a call to action. This is where you present your *ask*. Many applicants forget to include any call-to-action. Others make an open-ended request. Here is a bad example of an ask: "When it's convenient, please let me know what your next steps are." It may never be convenient, and the next steps may be to ignore applications that don't include something specific the committee is looking for. Instead, tell the committee what you want from them:

- Please call me within the next week to let me know you received my application.
- Please email to set up a time when we can talk further about this opportunity.
- I will check back with you in two weeks to see if I can provide other resources to help you know me better.

Notice the last call-to-action doesn't put responsibility on the committee. It keeps the responsibility on you. In a phrase, "Keep the ball in your court." Once you give up the ball—the opportunity to check in or follow up—you can't get it back. Take the initiative to reach out when appropriate; don't wait for the church to contact you. Experiment to see which call-to-action generates your desired outcome.

Relevant
The cover letter should be free from secondary topics of conversation. There are better places to talk about why you want to live in Michigan, how you love hiking, or why you love the city. Remember, you have about 60 seconds to catch a reader's eye and convince them to read your resume.

Specifically, in the middle paragraph, use the organization's language back at them. This is conversational mirroring. Ask yourself why you are applying for this job. Find descriptions or phrases from the church website, organizational profile, or job description that capture those connections. Then, incorporate that specific language into your middle paragraph.

In his book *Christ-Centered Preaching*, Dr. Bryan Chapell calls this "expositional rain." This intentional repetition of key terminology resonates with the reader. It is doubtful committee members have memorized all the documents they've put together. Many may not even realize you borrowed language from their job description or website. Whether they do or not, they are drawn to it.

These edits to your generic cover letter take less than a few minutes. By mirroring the church's key terminology back to them, you increase the likelihood that a committee member reads your resume—which is the purpose of the cover letter. Even if committee members don't read your cover letter, you've only lost a few minutes. On the other hand, a generic cover letter—read or ignored—communicates nothing of substance to the readers.

The Resume
The purpose of the resume is to get an interview. Resumes rarely secure you a job. In the corporate world, "...of the 250 resumes going out for every corporate job, the initial screening typically eliminates 98 percent of job seekers, and only two percent will even get an interview."[54] In the church world, the odds are little better. Churches that get 70 unsolicited resume packets report less than ten percent are seriously considered. Differentiation in this area is vital.

No resume can capture and communicate everything. You must be selective. Put more pointedly, candidates often view the resume as their one chance to show off everything they have ever done. Don't do that. Howard Gardner, an American developmental psychologist, said, "The greatest enemy of understanding is coverage." This means the best way to confuse your readers is to say too much. When you write everything, your readers remember nothing.

Generally, candidates get one resume page for every ten years of experience. Younger applicants may feel unfairly limited by this rule but be encouraged. Search committee members spend less time on the second page of longer resumes anyway, and most committee members ignore the third page. Regardless of your age or level of experience, the first page of your resume is your most valuable real estate.

In the board game *Monopoly*, Boardwalk and Park Place are the most valuable real estate. Baltic Avenue is the least valuable. The top of the first page of your resume is Park Place. The bottom of your last page is Baltic Avenue.

The purpose of the resume is to get the job interview. Any content that distracts from this purpose is superfluous. Remove it, no matter how proud you are of the accomplishment or position. A focused job description tells you exactly what skills, competencies, and capacities the employer wants from the ideal candidate. You don't have to guess. Let the job description guide the content of your resume. Search committees should be able to see *their* ideal candidate in your resume.

There are two standard resume formats: traditional and functional. (Samples of both can be found at the end of this chapter.) I recommend you read this entire section before your rush to edit your resume. Both formats have their strengths and shortfalls. Knowing when and how to employ each format is a critical point of differentiation between you and other candidates.

Traditional Resume
The Traditional Resume follows this structure:
- Name, Address block: Put at the top center or top left.
- Qualifying (or Objective) Statement: A brief description about you or the nature of skills that you bring to a job.
- Education: Include the name of the institution, degree conferred, and date received.

- Work Experience: Usually listed in reverse chronological order, with bullet points substantiating evidence of skills, experience, or capacity.
- Other Experience and Interests: Hobbies, awards, and nominations. Might include a short statement of faith, or a picture.

The Traditional Resume works best when you have applicable experience relevant to the specific job you apply to. Are you applying for a worship position and have experience serving on worship teams? Are you a Senior Pastor applying for a different Senior Pastor position? In both cases, use the Traditional Resume format. Either your job titles or the areas of responsibility, ideally both, resonate with the central features of the job to which you are applying. Search committees ask, "Can this person function in the role and do the work we need him or her to do?" When your experience aligns with the job description, the committee can see the answer to that question in a Traditional Resume.

Functional Resume
But what if your work experience doesn't demonstrate that you are qualified for the job you apply for? What if your vocational history includes a stint in youth ministry, a few years in the marketplace, a couple of unrelated internships, and a smattering of preaching opportunities? For example, I worked in the seminary's maintenance department while many of my fellow seminarians worked at Starbucks, Home Depot, and UPS. These vocational positions do not arguably demonstrate excellence in a specific role or success in particular duties. In this case, the Functional Resume works better.

The Functional Resume follows this structure:
- Name, Address block: Put at the top center or top left.
- Categories of Skill "Buckets:" You should have at least three but not more than four.
- Location of Relevant Employment: This list should include your job title, the place you worked, and the years of employment.
- Education: Include the name of the institution, degree conferred, and date received.
- Other Experience and Interests: Include relevant hobbies, awards, nominations, and preferences *not* already mentioned.

Where the Traditional Resume says, "Here are my abilities as demonstrated by my previous jobs," the Functional Resume says, "Here are my abilities as demonstrated by the skills I have and the tasks I've completed." Instead of listing your previous jobs in reverse chronological order (as you would on a Traditional Resume format), list every task and responsibility for *every* job you had and the role you filled—paid and unpaid. Then, look for consistent themes where specific skills were used: leadership, administration, communication, relational development, strategic planning, advancement, community engagement, etc. Each skill goes in its own category. Most people have more categories of skills than can fit on a resume. Choose the categories that best align with the responsibilities outlined in the job description to which you apply.

The greatest strength of a Functional Resume is the ability to move relevant personal experience from the "Other Experience and Interests" category (in the Traditional Resume) into the prime real estate of your resume. Most of us actively pursue what we are passionate about, even if these activities don't pay. After reviewing hundreds of resumes, I can usually tell what type of job people want based on where they volunteer. We often pour ourselves into those goals we are most dedicated to, in hopes that someday we might receive compensation for doing what we love most. These unpaid passions are usually listed at the very end of a Traditional Resume. The Functional Resume lets you move these items to the top of your resume.

Phil wanted to be a preaching pastor. He completed several ministry internships, but none demonstrated his communication skills. For two years, while in seminary, he preached weekly at a retirement home. This wasn't an official internship: no documentation, no job title, and he wasn't paid. This experience goes to the bottom of the page on a Traditional Resume. On a Functional Resume, it moves up into the Preaching "bucket" at the top of the resume.

I recommend you move the section on education to the bottom of the Functional Resume for a few reasons. Remember, the prime real estate is at the top of the page, and the resume's goal is to get the job interview. In a job search that may include 70 applications, it is essential to stand out from other candidates. When a position requires a specific degree, such as a Master of Divinity, you don't stand out by putting that information at the top. Every qualified candidate will have a similar degree. Moving education down enables you to move other elements higher up on the page, helping you stand out from the crowd.

There may be unique situations in which it makes sense to move education higher up, such as if you attended the same seminary as someone else on staff or if your training is uniquely relevant. You might also move education further up on the resume when applying for a position that doesn't require specific credentialing—when a master's degree is desired but not required—and your credentialing helps you stand out. Regardless of where you place the educational component or any element of the resume, always ask these questions: Does this element differentiate me from other applicants? Does this element add to or distract from the resume's goal: to get the job interview?

For both formats, the name block goes at the top left or center. We read left to right. When skimming, our eyes make a zig-zag pattern across a page. If you put your name block at the top right, there is a good chance someone skimming the page misses elements of the first paragraph.

Combination Resume
For applicants with more experience, there is value in blending the formats into what is called a Combination Resume. A Combination Resume borrows from both formats and usually follows this structure:

- Name block
- Qualifying Statement (if you include one)
- Functional Resume components
- Traditional Resume components
- Education
- Other

The Combination Resume is handy when your vocational history demonstrates your ability to serve in a desired role *and* your skills demonstrate an expanded capacity into new areas.

William served as an Associate Minister at one church for 15 years, during which time his responsibilities constantly changed. For two years he oversaw the youth program. He managed the youth staff for the next three years while also developing and expanding the church's small-group ministry. For six years, he developed and managed the development of lay leaders for the small-group ministry. He served as the Interim Pastor for nine months, preaching weekly and leading the Session meetings. In the process, he learned he was most energized supervising staff and overseeing church operations.

The Combination Resume served him well when applying for an Executive Pastor position at another church. While never having the title "Executive Pastor," his categories of skill—Leadership Development, Management, and Administration—captured the new position's responsibilities as described in the job description. At the same time, his reverse-chronological vocational history demonstrated experiences and achievements central to the desired outcomes. And, with 15 years of vocational history, he expanded his resume to two pages.

Master Resume

Whether applying for your first job or your fifth, many candidates feel overwhelmed revising their resume to address the specifics of each job. This is where a Master Resume helps. A Master Resume is a detailed explanation of every item you want to include on any future resume. Every time you preach, teach, disciple someone, participate in outreach or evangelism, publish a written work, lead a team or committee—paid and unpaid, vocational or volunteer—put it on your Master Resume. Use the Combination Resume. Have a vocational history section and a skill summary section. Expand your list of skill categories (buckets) to as many as you need and update it every two or three months.

A Master Resume keeps you from forgetting significant details. We think we will remember what we did, with whom, and when. In fact, our memories are faulty, and the demand on our present cognition is so great that we regularly forget essential aspects of our vocational careers. Updating your Master Resume at least quarterly helps you stop forgetting. I regularly consult with candidates looking to transition from one ministry position to another. Some have been in their current role for five years or more. Those who haven't updated their resumes along the way spend hours culling through Outlook calendar events, emails, sermon files, and meeting minutes to rebuild a realistic snapshot of their ministry outcomes and experience.

My Master Resume runs seven pages with 2,700 words. It lists five Skill Buckets and detailed information about eight jobs. There are sections on continuing education, professional development and certifications, publications, presentations, lectures and sermons, achievements, awards, volunteer events, and a catchall titled "Other, not sure where to put." I would never mail this resume to an employer, but by using the stated outcomes of a job description as a guide, I can create a resume specific to any job within minutes. It's much easier to cut irrelevant material from a Master Resume than trying to remember and create content to fit the description of a new job.

Qualifying Statement
I am ambivalent about a Qualifying Statement, sometimes labeled Objective Statement. When I was taught to create a resume, there was no Qualifying Statement. Then, someone thought a Qualifying Statement was an innovative idea. In time, it became standard. I'm seeing more resumes without this leading paragraph. The problem with most Qualifying Statements is they eat up two or three lines of prime real estate with little return. Most Qualifying Statements I read are so generic that they could describe every candidate in a stack of resumes: "I want to serve God by loving His people and proclaiming His word."

If you are determined to use a Qualifying Statement, *Show, Don't Tell!* Most Qualifying Statements tell something that the rest of the resume should show. Don't say you want to be a preacher; show when and where you preached. Don't say you want to minister to children; show what you've done when working with children. Show, don't tell.

When you include a Qualifying Statement, make it specific to you. One woman wrote, "At the end of my life, I desire to hear adults say Jesus first met them through my faithful ministry when they were just children." Another person wrote, "I want my ministry to be marked by marriages strengthened, children nurtured, the young encouraged, the elderly honored, and Christ glorified." Those statements are powerful, specific, and unique.

Pictures

There was a time when including a photo on your resume was considered unprofessional. However, social media has altered the way we look at printed material. Many of the newer resume formats incorporate features from social media layouts including a profile picture and a left-navigation bar. Whether or not you include a photo on your resume, I recommend including a picture of yourself on a profile page covered in the next section.

A Profile Page

The cover letter's job is to get committees to read your resume. The resume's job is to get an interview. A Profile Page is a document that allows you to talk about significant aspects of your life. A Profile Page is comprised of a high-quality, full-color photo of yourself (and your family, if appropriate) and a few paragraphs of text. Including a picture of yourself on the resume is optional; including a picture of yourself on the Profile Page is essential.

Your writing style should be narrative and conversational. Keep the details relevant to the nature of the ministry you want to do, if not the job to which you apply. I recommend two or three paragraphs but avoid the tendency to tell everything. While your writing is more conversational than professional, you are still constrained by the elements of C.A.R.: Concise, Actionable, and Relevant.

Pablo applied for a job in Michigan. He had never lived there, but his father was born in the area. Pablo's grandfather worked his whole life in the Detroit automobile industry. Pablo told me, "I love my granddad, and I 'get him:' practical, no-nonsense, and industrious. If you can't prove it in simple terms to a Journeyman, then it doesn't mean much for how he should live." Pablo shared these details on his Profile Page.

Carol was 26 and single when she graduated from seminary. In seminary, she worked—first as a volunteer and then in a paid internship—with young women in the youth group. She wanted a job that allowed her to continue working with women. On her Profile Page, she wrote about growing up in the Midwest, her testimony of faith, and her trajectory of vocational ministry.

I used her Profile Page as an example for years because of her picture. Stretched across the top of the page like a banner was a photo of Carol with her senior high school girls. They had their arms around her. They smiled. It was a candid picture with people milling about in the background. The picture conveyed one message: Carol cared for young women, and they cared for her in return. If you include a picture on both your Resume and Profile Page, use a professional photo on the resume and a more casual photo on your Profile Page.

You can share a brief testimony of faith on your Profile Page, but only if you have not done so in another document. For candidates seeking ordination, most denominational documents dedicate space for that information. If you do share your testimony, make it conversational more than theological.

Here are examples from other candidate Profile Pages:

- Bradford shared his love for the outdoors with a church in Denver.
- Christopher talked about growing up homeless when he applied to an inner-city church.
- Tom wrote about his dog in an application to a church on the edge of a well-used city park.

What you share should be true to who you are but not embellished, relevant to the nature of the work you seek, if not the specific job opportunity, and provide new information. That means it is information you have not already shared in another document of the resume packet.

References
There are several reasons to select who should serve as a candidate. Some candidates ask for references from influential people: a renowned pastor, an author, and the president or key faculty members from their seminary. This can leave the average candidate feeling at a disadvantage. While there may be upsides to having influential people serve as references, there are also potential downsides. And candidates without well-known references often do just as well, if not better, than their peers. (See Chapter 2)

Potential Downside to the Influential Reference

The best people to serve as a reference for you are people who have genuine experience observing your character and competencies. These are people to whom you reported or a peer with whom you have worked closely. In my experience, influential people are not the most informed about a candidate's skills, character, or abilities. In most cases, the influential Senior Pastor of a large church hasn't observed the youth intern closely or over a long enough period to know where she is strong and where she struggles. Even if you were the teaching assistant for a well-known professor, the extent to which he or she observed you is limited. Sadly, our weaknesses and shortcomings are the easiest to note in the short term. It takes greater exposure for people to see the extent of our strengths and abilities.

Also, listing a well-known person as a reference assumes that he or she is equally respected in the eyes of your resume readers. I have interacted with individuals, committees, and Elder Boards who, respectively, have found fault with every big name in the Western Christian world. Not everybody loves_____ (fill in the blank). One of the faculty I edited for while in seminary—he thanked me in the introduction to one of his books—is viewed as liberal by segments of the Christian world. Others have called him biblically unorthodox. Listing this widely known faculty member on my resume, far from helping me, would hurt my opportunities for employment in certain contexts.

The Best References

Select people with experience observing your ministry development over a lengthy period. Include three, four, or five references. Be sure that at least one of your references can speak to *each* of the critical areas of responsibility outlined by the job description. If the job you apply for involves supervising a team, find someone who has observed your team leadership. When the job involves teaching, select a reference who has observed you teach regularly over a period of time. These people can speak about your development and improvement, not just a snapshot of where you are in these capacities today. This may require you to have more than five references in the queue, using different references to fit the specifics of the job description.

In Chapter 8, I show that Behavioral Interviewing applies to how you answer questions from search committees. The experience you gain asking Behavioral Interviewing questions of your Network Partners (see Chapter 2) prepares you for this approach to identifying references. The STARR stories you tell during the interview will ideally involve people you've listed as references. When you ask these men and women to serve as references, take a minute to remind them about the events or situations you'll likely share during the interview process. This refreshes the situation in the mind of the reference. And if the person shares that story, it provides the search committee with a confirmation of perspective.

Be intentional. Think about why you wanted this person to be a reference. In what situations have they observed how you work and interact? How long have they known you? What negative situations might they have observed? You need to be able to tell a reference why you want them to serve in this role.

Lauretta applied for a position that required soft skills: care, counseling, relational development, and the ability to maintain a non-anxious presence in tense situations. She asked a former coworker, Robinson, to serve as a reference. After asking if Robinson would serve as a reference, she commented, "I know you've seen me manage several intense personal interactions. One that came to mind for me was when the Skogens went through their painful divorce. That was one of the hardest situations I've been involved with, but I was thankful for the opportunity to model a bold love to both parties. Thank you again for your support during that time." Lauretta and Robinson ended up reprocessing aspects of the situation right then.

Lauretta later used this situation as a STARR story in her first interview. And because she brought up the situation with Robinson, it was fresh in his mind when the committee asked him to share his observation of Lauretta managing a stressful situation.

Summary Questions:
- Who has observed you closely for an extended period?
- Why is each person equipped to serve as a reference for you?
- What shared ministry stories should you recall during your phone call asking someone to serve as a reference?
- Can at least one of your references speak to each significant aspect of the job description?

Denominational Forms

I like to joke that denominational data forms are like one pair of jeans designed to fit every person in the world. The jeans would fit two people perfectly. The rest of us need either suspenders or expanders.

The stage at which a church asks for a denominational form tells you something about the organization. Under-Resourced Churches ask for denominational forms at the beginning of the process. These churches view the form as the first litmus test to assess whether to move forward with the candidate. They tend to conduct data-dependent searches, reducing candidate evaluation to a narrow set of quantifiable skills (e.g., preaching, teaching, and leading) or commitments (e.g., theological, cultural, and organizational).

Resourced Churches tend to ask for denominational data forms later in the process. They know that the generic information of the form won't reveal the most relevant aspects of character and competency. Instead, they view the denominational form as a means of exposing potential red flags with respect to theological commitments or to explore views on pastoral practices.

Data forms—sometimes called informational forms—vary from one denomination to the next. These documents seek to capture demographic information, vocational and geographic preferences, and theological commitments. The goal of most data forms is to establish a baseline for committee-candidate engagement. Presumably, if certain data can be established at the front end of the hiring process, then the outcome is likely to improve. To the degree that candidates don't want to be associated with a particular view or practice, or work in a certain geography, or serve in a particular context—yes, the form works.

Thomas didn't want to live or work in the southwest or be a youth minister. His self-selection out of this region and these jobs increased the efficiency of committees looking for youth ministry candidates to serve in the southwest. The problem arises when Thomas doesn't have enough information to assess these positions. Thomas may remove himself from positions for which he would be a great candidate or, more often, apply for positions for which he is ill-equipped and unprepared, even though they are in a region where he wants to live.

Data forms rarely confirm which candidates are a good fit. Rather, these forms reveal which candidates *believe* they would *not be* a good fit. As such, differentiating yourself from other candidates through the data form is difficult—difficult, but not impossible.

Candidates experience the forms as generic, disjointed, and sometimes irrelevant. And yet you will be expected to complete one or more. Some are extensive and thorough. Others are just a few pages. Some require approval by a clerical supervisor or regional director. Without time or space to evaluate every denomination's data form, I will focus comments on two variations. This should give you the ability to extrapolate the necessary information relevant to other settings.

PCA Ministerial Data Form (MDF)

The Presbyterian Church in America (PCA) denomination produces 1,500 pages of data annually in its multi-volume Yearbook. The PCA pastoral form is called the *Ministerial Data Form* (MDF). It is eight pages long and divided into four parts. You can get a blank MDF from the PCA Administrative Committee.

Part One collects basic demographic information, past ordained experience, and a list of references. Part Two asks candidates to self-select from a list of preferred church types, sizes, positions, contexts, and geographic areas. Part Three asks candidates to select pastoral activities important to them. Part Four asks for narrative reflection on personal views and practices, though several of the questions are theological in nature.

Recent seminary graduates are inclined to check all the boxes in Part Two: the summary of preferences. I recommend leaving one or more items in each section blank. This shows you completed the form with a degree of thoughtfulness. Few candidates would be interested in, *and* qualified for, a senior position *and* a Youth Pastorate. Furthermore, I haven't worked with any candidate who could serve effectively in every region of the country.

In Part Three, Pastoral Activities, check the boxes that most align with the type of position you seek if not the actual job to which you apply. If you apply to be the Assistant Pastor of Outreach and Evangelism, be sure to check the "Evangelism" box. On the other hand, if you apply for a position that does not include regular preaching, do not check the "Proclamation of the Word" box. If a candidate puts a high value on the opportunity to preach when the position does not include that facet, a search committee or Senior Pastor may be inclined to dismiss the application. Senior Pastors do not want to get into situations where they must spend energy redirecting frustrated staff members away from duties outside their defined job responsibilities.

Part Four remains the most ambiguous section of the form. To begin with, the list is an agglomeration of unrelated items. There are theological questions that ask about a candidate's view of the Trinity and the Word of God. Other questions are about preference and practice. In my assessment, what binds these disparate questions together is concern. The origin story of the PCA—born painfully from a break with the PCUS—makes the denomination wary of theological liberalism and individual license. Only in this context does a question about "the Person and Work of Christ" fit naturally alongside a question about the "Use of Alcohol."

Fearing a key aspect might be overlooked, candidates regularly give unnecessarily long answers with support and quotations from Scripture, the Westminster Standards of Faith, or both. This does not differentiate you. Honestly, few if any committees read that kind of answer. The rare few that do are likely in Under-Resourced Churches.

In my survey of churches, committees say they are typically looking for two types of responses for each of the listed sections: alignment and accessibility. First, committees want to know if candidates hold views that are in accord with the church's standards: alignment. If there is a red flag, churches want to find it sooner rather than later. Second, committees want to know if candidates can explain the concept or principle in simple terms to someone in the church: accessibility. That is, can you have a hallway conversation on that topic that is understandable to the average congregant?

Limit answers to three or four sentences. One or two sentences should explain your view on the matter with a citation of scriptural support. The last sentence should answer, "How does this view impact your ministry?" For example, a candidate expressing her perspective on the "Views of Scripture" could answer: "I believe all Scripture is inspired by God and written by men (c.f., 2 Tim. 3:16; WCF catechism Q1 & Q2). This gives me confidence when speaking to a student about another religion like Islam. I can express with confidence the power of the Holy Spirit to persuade and convict through the Bible."

Presumably, when the questions pertaining to alcohol and tobacco were added to the form, there was wariness about indulgence. In the 1970's, smoking (tobacco) and, to a lesser extent drinking, were associated with antiauthoritarianism, a rebellious spirit, and a rejection of conservative values. Today, we find as many churches with tolerance of tobacco and alcohol as those with skeptical views.

Candidates tend to share their personal use of tobacco and alcohol alongside their theological views. I discourage this. To begin with, the title of the section is "Personal Views and Practices." The second sub-section is "Personal Practices," which implies that the first section, "Theological Conviction" does not explicitly pertain to practice and behavior. To that end, candidates don't usually answer the question about evangelism with how regularly they evangelize and with what methodology. Candidates don't answer the question about the Word of God with how much they read the Bible and when. Most of the topics in this sub-section are *held* more than *practiced*.

More importantly, if something can be misunderstood, it will be. Someone currently abusing these substances is not likely to reveal as much, for fear of being disqualified. Someone who believes drinking and smoking of any kind are sins is not likely to say as much, at the risk of being considered extreme by moderate congregations. This leaves only moderate users to answer the question honestly. But doing so in writing limits your ability to understand the context of the church and congregation. This is not the place for confession. Keep your responses to theological views. Save the conversation about your personal use for a phone call or in-person conversation.

Regarding the weekly schedule, present a 48- to 52-hour workweek. A pastor showing that level of commitment has credibility when asking a congregant to add 8-10 hours to his 40-hour workweek to serve as an Elder or Deacon. If you are in a current ministry position, you know what a ministry schedule looks like. If you are looking for your first ministry job, show your current schedule—study hours, classroom times, work, worship, and rest—along with an example of what you expect your schedule to be when in full-time ministry.

EPC Personal Information Form (PIF)
The Evangelical Presbyterian Church (EPC) *Personal Information Form* is a 22-page document. You can download a copy from the www.EPC.org website. Part One is a Statement of Consent. Part Two asks for personal data including vocational work history, ordination history, and education. This section allows candidates to write about special interests and hobbies, ecumenical activities, and types of supervision the candidate has found helpful. Part Three is narrative, asking for a brief history and testimony of faith. Unlike the PCA MDF, it also asks for reflection on leadership and worship styles, your call to ministry, and involvement in the larger church. Part Four asks about ministerial preferences and history. Part Five requires the candidate to self-assess gifts and abilities. This section also asks for a list of references. Part Six is a criminal-behavioral disclosure.

This data form is significantly longer than the PCA version. Once completed, the two are about the same length. Also, the EPC form has at least two pages of introductory text and four pages for references at the end.

Comparing the two forms, the PCA form places a much greater emphasis on quantifiable data while the EPC form emphasizes narrative storytelling. One strength of the PCA form is the clarity of expectation when it comes to areas of theology and personal practice. One strength of the EPC form is the number of questions that require reflection and invite transparency.

When completing the EPC form, or forms like it, your differentiation rests in what stories you tell and how you talk about your leadership style, gifts, and abilities. I recommend you review Chapter 2, where I talk about the power of stories. Here are a few added remarks.

Watch your use of first-person pronouns. Besides being repetitious, excessive use of first-person pronouns inevitably makes you sound like the focus of everything—that you are the hero or the victim, as opposed to being a participant in a wider story of leadership, organization, management, and faith. Also, watch what you say about and how you describe other people. Whenever possible, assume the best. And when you must share about a challenge or conflict, stick to factual information. Avoid assumption or speculation.

Do not exaggerate or embellish. But don't disparage yourself either. Ephesians 4:1-16 describes how Christ has given gifts to the leaders of his church. That includes you! Speak truthfully about how the Lord has gifted you for ministry and where the Body of Christ has affirmed and confirmed that in you. I find that the more honest we are about our areas of struggle, the more clearly and confidently we can speak about our areas of strength.

Web Presence
Churches research candidates online. This means you need to manage the narrative of your online presence. I am not talking about creating an artificial virtual identity. Rather, I am drawing from the adage, "If something can be misunderstood, it will be." This is never truer when looking for a ministry position. Because churches are doing research on you, tell them the story you want them to see, hear, and read. And make sure everything else is hidden or removed.

LinkedIn
You need a LinkedIn profile. LinkedIn is the leading platform for posting your educational and vocational history, achievements, and samples of projects, presentations, and sermons. Churches regularly search LinkedIn. But even search engine results regularly pull profiles from the site. LinkedIn has robust features that allow you to link to websites and upload resources. At a minimum, complete the vocational history and education sections. Consider asking connections to write recommendations for specific skills you have. And be sure to use a quality image. Once you have completed your profile, log out and view the page as a guest to see how it looks to others.

Social Media
Ten years ago, Facebook was still populated by the 20- and 30-something crowd. Pictures and personal videos dominated the site. News and political articles were infrequent. Today, Facebook is home mostly to the late adaptors—50-somethings and above. Political news items and commercial advertisements dominate the site. Older church leaders in your current and future congregations are active on Facebook.

If you have a Facebook, Instagram, or other social media profiles, check your privacy settings. Use the "privacy checkup" tab to see how your profile and posts appear to other users.

Be ruthless. If something can be misunderstood, it will be. One candidate was pressed extensively on a photo of him holding a girl in a bikini. One pastor was asked to seek another position after his wife repeatedly posted dogmatic views about political topics. Another candidate blogged extensively about governmental spending mismanagement in rural America, while applying for jobs in the rust belt of Michigan. His perspective was not popular among the churches in those areas. And one man, applying for positions in a Baptist church, was turned down when the church looked at his profile picture showing him with his wife eating pizza and *drinking alcohol*.

I recommend making all your past posts hidden from the public. You can always go back and select individual pictures or posts that you want everyone to be able to see. Or go back and repost those items that tell the story of your life and ministry. Just as questionable posts can raise objections, positive pictures and videos are powerful ways to convey the tenor of your life, marriage and family (if applicable), and ministry— opening opportunities for positive connection and communication.

These same principles apply to Instagram, Twitter, and other social media. But you need to think beyond these big-name traditional platforms. There are public, social elements embedded in almost all websites. A search engine once pulled up a review I'd written at Amazon on a controversial product. And Venmo transactions default to public unless you change your settings. A college student who was paid by a classmate through Venmo for lunch was interrogated about the transaction. The classmate had listed the reason for payment as "Gett'n high with the Weed'sters." Intended as a joke, the recipient was required to take a drug test.

A Website or Blog
Anybody can have a website or self-published blog. It's fine to have one or both, so long as the purposes for the sites are clear. When specific to the job search, avoid random reflections on life and culture. Few of us have enough followers to justify the self-promotion of our original ideas, and you cannot know how these are going to be received.

The best ministry website I ever saw was simple in design and presentation. It featured five pages and a top navigation bar. The first page had a photo of the candidate with his family and two paragraphs of text focused on getting to know them. It was like a digital Profile Page. The other four tabs linked to pages titled Music, Leadership, Preaching, and Resume. On these pages, a printed statement raised questions about that aspect of ministry, and below it, a two-minute video featured the candidate answering those questions talking about his skills, capacity, and experience. None of the pages required you to scroll down to see other elements. This meant that everything was visible above the page-break. The resume page featured text, audio, and video files of a resume, profile page, presentations, and two sermons, respectively. With the drop-and-drag builder of most website providers, this site probably took the candidate 30 minutes to build and deploy.

Promote your website or ministry blog on your social media feeds and profiles. Add a URL to your signature block of your email. These enable committees to begin engaging with your resume materials in a directed manner instead of through an unguided browser search.

Get an Editor and Feedback
Have all your materials, online and printed, edited for typographical and theological errors. Feedback from other ministry leaders in your tradition is essential. Simple mistakes create big headaches and have huge, unintended consequences.

One candidate, writing about his theological commitments, stated how his ministry was empowered through the certainty that God the Father *became* God the Son. The concept that there is only one Person in the Trinity, and that He merely appeared in different forms, is a theological error called Modalism. This heresy was rejected by the Church in the fourth century. When asked, the candidate sheepishly replied, "I meant to say that God the Father *sent* God the son." Other candidates have reversed two numerals in their phone number or left out letters in their email address.

Such simple mistakes are not beneath me. In my first ministry resume, I misspelled discipler, writing instead that I wanted to be a "Discipliner of young men." My editor commented in the margin, "Really? I find that disturbing." Yikes! I am so glad she caught the error.

Another time, while working as a Marketing Director, we launched a major ministry conference campaign. Anticipating the large call volume the campaign would generate, we purchased an additional 1-800 number. The campaign elements—a magazine, posters, fliers, and a mass mailing—went through dozens of editorial revisions and reviews. In the final editorial stage, the elements were green-lighted up to the last person. On a whim, he called the 800 number we printed on all the materials. Two of the numbers had been inverted. The number we printed was for a risqué service. We went back through the design file to see when the error first occurred. I had mistyped the phone number on the original word document summarizing the basic details of the campaign, at the first stage of production.

Action Steps

1. Draft a sample cover letter using the C.A.R and XOXO models. This draft will serve as the template for the actual cover letter you will send. Remember to make the middle paragraph specific to the job to which you apply.
2. Create your first draft of a Master Resume where you put all your experience, education, and interests. Cluster the information into related categories. Continue to expand this document throughout the process.
3. Using your Ideal Job Description as a guide, decide which of the resume formats best fits your experience. Create your first draft of your resume using the information from your Master Resume.
4. Review a Denominational Data Form. What are the areas that will take you the longest to answer? What are the questions about which you need to pray (e.g., position, location, responsibilities)? Schedule time to complete the form.
5. Review all your documents. What information do you want to share that you haven't already? Incorporate this information into the first draft of your Profile Page.
6. Make a note to review and revise these documents regularly.

Sample Functional Resume, Recent Seminary Graduate

John Doe
12345 Nowhere Road, St. Louis, MO 63141
John.doe@email.co
314.123.4567

Experience Highlights

Teaching

- Small Group Ministries – Planned, coordinated, and led weekly Bible Studies and Fellowship Groups with Reformed Campus Fellowship (RCF) as a student and intern
- Community Groups – Currently hosting and leading a Community Group at South City Church (PCA) Martin, Missouri

Discipleship

- Mentored freshman guys as an RCF Campus Intern
- Recruited and trained RCF students for leadership roles

Counseling

- Met individually with RCF male students every 1-3 weeks
- Worked with male students struggling with personal, substance, and sexual issues
- Fostered a Biblical world and life view in many RCF freshman and fringe students

Outreach and Hospitality

- Built relationships with international students and Visiting Scholars at North Carolina College of Medicine through English Conversation Clubs and hospitality ministry
- Shared the gospel with a Taiwanese student and incorporated him into RCF large group at North Carolina College of Medicine and have maintained this cross-continental relationship
- Hosted dinner for International Students and Supper Club for RCF students
- Coordinated Frisbee Golf trips with RCF students and nonbelievers, helping RCF students to establish and build redemptive relationships with nonbelievers

Education

Master of Divinity..May 2012
Covenant Seminary
Bachelor of Arts, English...June 2007
Furman University

Employment

Ministry Intern...2011-current
South City Church - Martin, MO
Reformed Campus Fellowship Campus Intern..2007-2009
North Carolina College of Medicine- Charlotte, NC
International Student Orientation Small Group Leader...Summer 2007
RiverBend Camps and Conferences- Hendersonville, NC
Youth Camp Counselor...Summer 2005

Sample Traditional Resume, Experienced Pastor

John Doe
12345 Nowhere Road, St. Louis, MO 63141
John.doe@email.co
314.123.4567

Employment History

Senior Pastor, South Park Church, Lincoln, TX (2016-2024)
- Weekly preaching, teaching, and discipleship.
- Provided spiritual leadership and pastoral care to the congregation.
- Developed and implemented a comprehensive vision for church's growth and ministry.

Associate Minister, Waynesville Presbyterian Church, Waynesville, MS (2010-2016)
- Provided pastoral care and support to individuals and families experiencing life transitions, illness, grief, and other challenges.
- Planned and led support groups for various needs, such as grief support, caregiver support, and newcomers' groups.
- Performed weddings, funerals, and other pastoral care services.
- Planned and implemented events that foster fellowship and connection among members, such as potlucks, game nights, and social gatherings.

Assistant Pastor of Young Adults, Auburn Presbyterian Church, Auburn, TX (2002-2010)
- Collaborate with other church staff and volunteers to create a vibrant and supportive environment for young adults.
- Build relationships with young adults outside the church through outreach initiatives and community engagement.
- Weekly teaching for large- and small-groups and preaching 6-8 times a year.
- Regular one-on-one discipleship of young adults in areas of vocation, relationship, personal growth and development, and spiritual identity.

Education

- Bachelor of Arts in English, Taylor University, Uptown, IN, conferred 1997.
- Master of Arts in Practiced Theology, The Fairmont Theology School, conferred 2001.

Awards and Acknowledgements

- Outstanding Community Service Award, South Park Chamber of Commerce, 2022
- Senior Homiletics Award, The Fairmont Theology School, 2001

References available upon request.

6

HOW TO UNDERSTAND SEARCH COMMITTEES

Chapter Summary
Church hiring processes are often inefficient. Candidates experience frustration as a result, and frustration is a limiting emotion. Understanding what is involved in a typical hiring process (and why) alleviates these adverse reactions, which increases your emotional capacity. You grow in resilience in the face of inefficiency and develop curiosity in moments of confusion. Deeper appreciation for those serving on a hiring committee positions you to do *for free* what you ultimately want to be *paid for*: to pastor and shepherd. This chapter clarifies the confusion associated with hiring committees and their processes, to help you develop beneficial responses.

The (A)Typical Process
Just for fun, I recently applied for a job at a large financial firm. I wanted to know how they managed their hiring process. In 15 minutes, I created a profile, answered the demographic and employment history questions, stated my desired salary, uploaded my resume, and submitted my application. Twenty seconds later, I received an email confirming receipt of my application with details about the next step, including how soon I would hear from a recruiter. This process was clear, unambiguous, specific, prompt, responsive, efficient, and professional.

By comparison, Charles applied for a Solo Pastor position in his final year of seminary. After sending the required documents and following up twice, he received no response. Four months later, having already accepted another position, Charles received an email that read, "Thank you for your application to be considered for our Solo Pastor position.

To move forward in the process, please email us links to two sermons you have preached in the last year." (Yikes!)

Stefan applied to be the Assistant Pastor of Discipleship. He received a follow up email asking him to answer five written questions. After completing these, he had a first interview with the search committee chair. Six months of silence followed. He finally picked up the phone and called the church. "Oh," the secretary said. "We hired a new Assistant Pastor two months ago."

In the late summer of 1997, I was wrapping up my first youth ministry job and applied for a similar position at another church in Alabama. (Remember this story. I'm going to come back to it.) After a phone interview with the Pastor, I was invited to visit the church. There, I met with the leadership council and youth ministry committee. At the end of my visit, the chair of the committee expressed enthusiasm about my candidacy. She suggested moving forward quickly and asked about my preferences for involvement in the upcoming summer youth trips: "As we plan for summer youth trips, which do *you* want to be involved with?" I returned home that Sunday evening convinced I had the job.

I never heard from the church again.

As opposed to the process for the financial firm, these experiences can be described as unclear, confusing, frustrating, unspecific, inefficient, unresponsive, one-sided, inconsiderate, and (sometimes) disrespectful. If you've spent any amount of time looking for a ministry position, you may relate to these experiences.

We can either resign ourselves to this flawed process or find ways to navigate it effectively. This description of a quality ministry evaluation process outlines best practices and prepares you for potential challenges.

An Ideal Interviewing Process
You learned about a position and want to apply. Committees typically ask for your resume packet electronically. They may also ask for links to sermons and a completed denominational form. Before sending any materials, see if the posting has a phone number. If it does, find a good reason to call the church. Pastoral ministry is primarily relational while most hiring processes are not. A phone call allows the person on the

other end to hear your voice and make a connection beyond the paperwork. Here are a few exploratory questions you can ask:

- *Seek Clarity*: The description wasn't specific. Should I also send references at this time?
- *Ask for Background*: I could not tell from the description. Is this a new position for the church?
- *Make a Connection*: I have friends who attended university there. Does the church have a college ministry?

Likely the receptionist either does not know the answers to your question or will not provide much of a response. Receptionists at larger churches are busy, and when also the Pastor's administrator they serve as a gatekeeper. Engage with kindness and curiosity. Don't be surprised or put off if you are treated like a salesperson. All you can do is try.

A positive phone call can make a significant impact. When seeking my first job, I called a church and initially received a lukewarm response. However, after mentioning a mutual connection, the receptionist became engaged. She and I spoke for 40 minutes. Ten minutes later, the Senior Pastor returned my call and invited me for a visit.

Another candidate called a church to ask if he could apply. The Senior Pastor, who rarely answered the phone, was the only person in the office that Friday afternoon. The two talked for almost an hour. The Pastor said, "We have two strong candidates already, and I wasn't looking at any more resume packets. But I've enjoyed our talk and want you to send me your paperwork today so I can present you to the committee this weekend." That candidate didn't get the job but reported learning so much about the interview process through the interaction.

In addition to emailing resume documents, also mail a physical copy. This gives you control over how your documents appear. Electronic documents may be printed in black and white or photocopied, degrading the visual quality. Physical copies don't have these problems, and mailing physical copies assures you the documents are received. Candidates who are not notified that their electronic documents were received can worry about whether they got through.

Physical mail reduces the chance of electronic email getting stuck in a spam folder. Finally, someone must handle physical mail: open the envelope, hold the contents, and examine the documents. Physical mail increases engagement.

A church often responds to applications with an initial questionnaire. Ministry jobs can receive up to 70 applications, many sent without reflection. One committee in the Pacific Northwest told me it received a resume from a candidate who wanted to serve only in the southeast. These questions help committees learn more about you and require candidates to be invested in the process.

The initial interview is often less structured and more casual. This is one of the few times candidates can direct the conversation. Chapter 8 provides tips for interview preparation. Churches use a "parallel model" for evaluation. Some candidates may still be completing the application (stage one), while others have answered written questions (stage two) or been interviewed (stage three). Committees are engaged with multiple candidates at different steps in the process.

When you become a finalist, the committee may assume a "series model" for the final stages of evaluation. Candidates are ranked and placed in order. Final interviews are conducted in numeric order. The committee only moves on to a later candidate if the first candidate is somehow disqualified or unwilling to accept the position.

Before 2005, committees often traveled to hear pastors preach. Today, most interaction occurs through phone or video. In the final stage, the committee invites the first candidate for a visit, either public or private. The congregation or the Session then votes. If the candidate receives a "no" vote, the committee repeats the process with the next candidate, and so on until a final candidate is nominated, approved, and called.

There are scores of variations. I've known churches to extend a job offer after an informal phone call and a short weekend visit. Other churches have taken almost two years and a dozen different candidate-evaluation stages before settling on their next pastor. It can be hard to wait for the timing of each committee, but expressing frustration to committees is generally unhelpful. Remember these three realities:

- Committees are made up of volunteers figuring out a process for which they have not been trained.
- You are modeling for the members of the committee what kind of minister you are—even in the face of an ineffective process.
- The Holy Spirit is at work in you and them through this messy process.

Who *Are* These People?

Candidates have greater patience with the apparent inefficiencies of the not-for-profit job process when they understand some of the reasons for these inefficiencies. This starts with understanding the nature of the search committee.

A ministry search committee is a collection of volunteers elected to a task for which they have not been trained—to determine the fitness of one candidate (among many) for a position about which they (the committee members) have minimal experience, limited understanding, and almost no organizational knowledge. A ministerial search committee is asked to find a spiritual leader with the training and experience requisite for the congregation and context to which he or she is hired. This task demands the committee have a patient humility that is direct and explorative, be self-reflective and, above all, dependent upon the Holy Spirit. The challenges of hiring, keeping, and sustaining ministry leaders in vocational settings are not primarily challenges of theological discourse or academic expression. They are primarily spiritual and relational. This is a serious undertaking.

What do you observe? First, these are believers in Christ willing to donate their time and energy to this work. Because they have little or no training, they are going to make mistakes. Most denominations don't have a standard (universal) process, leaving committee members to figure it out on their own. And even when there is a standard process, there are dynamics that change from church to church based on the uniqueness of the people and context.

We often apply familiar systems to unfamiliar situations. For example, a committee member might say, "I worked in HR, so I understand hiring." This is a false extrapolation. Edward Jones can assess investment knowledge, but it's harder for a ministry committee to determine spiritual maturity and emotional intelligence necessary to navigate the complex relationships of people on the worship team who are frustrated with and hurt by one another.

Ministry job descriptions are complex and ambiguous. The full scope of ministry work doesn't fit neatly into a job description or a 45-hour work week. Sermon preparation can vary, but pastors are expected to preach on Sunday; they must set aside time for sermon preparation in addition to responding to unexpected needs, like sharing the Gospel or comforting grieving families. These intrusions can't be resolved with overtime pay or an extra day off, and few people would knowingly take a marketplace position with such ambiguous expectations.

When faced with complexity, humans resort to simple systems of thinking to find precise categories of difference. Most often, this is a dichotomy: reformed or dispensational, expositional or topical, visionary leader or manager, faithful to the text or not, culturally relevant or outdated, extroverted or introverted. A church is growing or it's not. A pastor is either a good preacher or he's not. These are false models created to oversimplify complex realities.

It makes sense that the process of finding a ministry job (for you) and finding a pastor (for the church) is going to be unpredictable and inconsistent. And your frustration with search committees will lessen when you remember the scope of these complexities.

What is Going on Here?

There is always more going on in these processes than you will ever know. Let's go back to the church in Alabama that never called me back. In the weeks following my interview in 1997, I was racked with self-doubt. I felt certain the committee had discovered some sinful pattern or unhealthy tendency about me, probably from one of my references or current Senior Pastor. I got stuck ruminating on who might have told them what. There was that time I got angry with the owner of the local electronics store. He called my pastor and told him what I'd done. Another time I overslept and delayed the opening scene of a VBS play in which I had a lead role. Reflecting on my failures, I felt a combination of fear, frustration, and shame.

I moved on, eventually taking a position with Mission to the World (MTW). Two years later, making phone calls to recruit churches for short-term trips, the Alabama church showed up on my call list. My stomach dropped. Nervous, I picked up the phone and called the church. The secretary answered.

"Hi, this is Joel Hathaway. I work for MTW. Your church has taken a trip with us before. Can I tell you about our new mission trip opportunities?" The secretary listened and then told me about some of the factors that might affect the church's ability to take another trip.

As the conversation wound down, I took a risk and said, "I don't know how long you've been there, but a few years back I interviewed for your youth ministry job. I'm just wondering if you ever filled that position." The silence seemed to stretch on and on.

Finally, the secretary asked quietly, "When was that?"

I wanted to blurt out, "July 20, 1997, at 2:37 PM. at The Pizza Place, where Kathy, Chris, and Joy more or less promised me the job!" Instead, I answered calmly, "Sometime in the summer of 1997."

"Could it have been around July 20?" she asked. My heart skipped a beat. I swallowed hard.

"Yes."

She responded, "That was the Sunday our founding Senior Pastor announced he was leaving his family and the ministry to run off with the wife of another Elder. Their families were wrecked, and our congregation was devastated. Our church almost folded."

The Lord delivered me from a system that would have demanded more of me than my age and experience had prepared me for, only I couldn't know it. Other candidates have had similar experiences. Charles later found out that the committee had extended a call to someone only to have it fall through at the last minute. This led to a mini church split. Stefan found out that the search committee chairperson resigned a few weeks after his first phone conversation. The chairman exploded in one of the committee's meetings and later acknowledged what many people in his life suspected: that he suffered PTSD from his years in Vietnam.

153

There is exponentially more going on with these people than you can ever know. God knows and is at work. You only get glimpses into the lives of the volunteers on the committee. This is the point at which your professed faith and practiced belief matter. Are you praying for the churches and the committees representing them, even as you are considering applying? Are you praying for them as you wait for a reply? And will you be so bold as to pray with them when you have the opportunity, after an interview or in an email exchange?

A college friend had this quote on his door, rightly or wrongly attributed to George Bernard Shaw: "Find something you love to do and do it with such excellence that someone pays you to do it." Your role in the ministry search process is not primarily transactional. It is also relational and, above all, spiritual. Your application of the means of grace—prayer, reflection, and the Word of God—to yourself and on behalf of the churches with which you engage can be the difference in how you interpret the process.

Action Steps
1. What are you praying for yourself and your family (if you have one) as you prepare to engage with a search committee? Write down a list.
2. How can you honor the volunteer work of the committee members you are engaged with during the job search process? Write down three practical actions.
3. For what are you praying for the committee members and churches you are engaged with? Write it down.
4. Who are the trusted people you can talk to about the frustration and disappointment you experience? Make a list. Ask them to be available to give you time and space to process.

7

HOW TO RESEARCH MINISTRY OPPORTUNITIES

Chapter Summary
This chapter guides you through discovering and exposing the behaviors, patterns, and systems that make up organizations. Understanding an organization will enable you to assess the degree to which you are a good fit for it and vice versa. I will explain how to use the Narrative Approach when examining the job description, website, sermons, and the experiences of previous staff, in order to develop a road map for engagement. You will be introduced to the concept of Church Personality, specifically as it pertains to organizational, leadership, communication, and relational-emotional styles.

There is a great deal of information you need and want to know prior to accepting a new job. This can include:

- What is the history of the position: is it new or did someone have it before you?
- What is the history of the organization: its mission, vision, and values?
- To whom will you report and what are his or her leadership and management styles?
- How does the church deal with success and failure, disappointment and frustration?
- On what basis will you be evaluated for effectiveness, when, and by whom?
- Why did previous staff leave, and where are they working now?
- How does this organization invest in and develop its employees?

- How does the church celebrate and grieve?
- What situations make the leadership or people anxious?

The types of questions you should ask of an organization generally cluster into several areas:

- Organizational Structure
- Leadership and Management Style
- Communication Styles
- Relational-Emotional Systems

When an organization is deeply reflective and highly aware of these realities, when it has nothing to hide and everything to gain from full transparency, you don't have to dig for this information. But few organizations have the capacities for these behaviors—reflection, awareness, and transparency—to the degree you need them to be. None of us is fully reflective, aware, and transparent.

How to Understand Organization
All organizations, whether a large corporation or small church, have distinct personalities and cultures. While companies might call it their corporate ethos, churches often refer to it as their ministry values. These personalities influence how organizations react to situations.

When applying for a job, it's crucial to assess whether your personality aligns with the organization's culture. Deciding if a position is a good match requires understanding of the organization's values and culture— what does it say about itself and how does it treat its members. Online resources can be helpful for larger organizations—websites like *LinkedIn* and *Glassdoor*—which provide information about corporate finances, leadership, and employee experiences. However, less public information is available for smaller organizations.

When researching smaller organizations, look for consistency between their stated values and their observable actions including financial commitments, worship style, demographics, socioeconomic factors, and their overall philosophy of ministry. Inconsistent behavior may show internal divisions or a lack of self-awareness. By carefully examining an organization's consistency, you can decide if it's a good match for your skills and values.

Church Organization

You might be skimming this section thinking, "Church organization? Sounds dry!" Trust me! This will change how you see church life! Here's the surprising thing: the size of a church has a bigger impact on how it functions than its specific beliefs. Many experts have studied this, and I'll explain it using five different church models. Think of a church as a group of people, not just a building or a set of beliefs (though those are important too!). Just like any group, churches have predictable patterns of interacting, relating, and making decisions.

Architecture is a notable example. A giant stadium with fixed seating is designed for a large crowd focused on a central point. It wouldn't be ideal for small, intimate gatherings with conversation. The architecture doesn't force behavior; it reflects it.

Similarly, churches come in assorted flavors based on their size and how they function. We'll explore five main types: Flexible Church, Consensus Church, Organizing Church, Catalyst Church, and Relational Church. These categories aren't perfect. There can be a large Consensus Church or a small Catalyst Church. What truly sets them apart is their core values, especially in leadership, relationship, and communication styles. Think of it like personality Types similar to the Myers Briggs Type Indicator.

What Kind of Trampoline Do You Prefer?

The trampoline is the most basic example of a complex system. It has all the necessary elements of a functional organization: structure (the frame), support (the springs), and challenge (the net). Individuals express personality through structure, support, and challenge. Most groups have a primary and a secondary element. Organizations rarely express all three equally. An organization which has all three elements in equal measures is under the greatest possible tension, a state sustained only through deliberate and constant intervention. Tension has the potential to pull objects apart. While all three of these elements are under tension, the two elements of greatest opposition—and thus the greatest stress—are structure and challenge.

- Churches that prefer _structure_ live in an organized way. Roles are clearly defined, and job descriptions are specific. They prefer a communication style that is precise, detailed, and factually presented in logical and chronological ways. They prefer leadership that is stable, predictable, and decisive. The managerial style is objective, and outcomes based. Truth is presented in narrow black and white terms, with little room for exceptions. Churches that prefer _structure_ tend to express the MBTI preferences of *Judging, Thinking*, and *Sensing*, in that order.

- Churches that prefer _support_ prefer living in a harmonious way. Relationships are valued above results. Expectations of job performance change based on the relational needs of the community. They prefer a communication style that is detailed and chronological or creative and patterned, but communication must seek mutual understanding and honor the value of respect. These people are loyal and committed. They prefer leaders who speak kindly and aware of a wide range of emotional expressions. They prefer a consensus style of leadership. Churches that prefer _support_ tend to express the MBTI preference of *Feeling* and *Extroversion* (either *Sensing* or *Intuition*), in that order.

- Churches that prefer _challenge_ live in an adventurous way. Life includes a high degree of risk, whether in new experiences or innovative ideas. These churches rely on originality and energy to create innovative programs for relational engagement or unique concepts for intellectual stimulation. They prefer a communication style that is laced with metaphor and imagery. They follow visionary leaders who are verbally creative, dynamic, and often edgy. Leaders may be collaborative or heroic. Churches that prefer _challenge_ tend to express the MBTI preferences of *Intuition* and *Perceiving*, in that order.

Exit and Voice

In his book, *Exit, Voice, and Loyalty*, Albert Hirschman studied the decline of organizations. Specifically, he looked at a firm that produced a salable product and had customers. While churches are not businesses and congregants are not customers, there is immediate application of Hirschman's work to the non-profit sector.

Churches, like companies, experience periods of growth and decline. When a company is growing the top and bottom lines, leaders take credit and are publicly recognized through praise and promotion. When a church is growing, senior leadership acts similarly.

Neither response is particularly reflective. Almost nobody asks, "Why are we really growing right now?" As a result, when a company or church is in decline, few people have the ability to evaluate the cause and almost nobody has the data to substantiate their opinion.

In periods of decline, companies and churches alike often default to replacing senior leadership, saying—in essence—"She is no longer effective," or worse, "It is his fault." Without the data necessary to understand earlier periods of growth and the current period of decline, Hirschman found that the stakeholders who remain take a position of befuddled optimism:

> The performance of the firm or an organization is assumed to be subject to deterioration for unspecified, random causes which are neither so compelling nor so durable as to prevent a return to previous performance levels, provided managers direct their attention and energy to the task....[55]

Stated simply, the perspective is, "We don't know why we're declining, but so long as we find the right leader we will return to the glory days." And every organization and company have one or more "golden eras" to which it wants to return.

Keep in mind that the job for which you are applying is part of the technical solution to tension within the system—either as a way of supporting growth or reversing decline.

Hirschman saw that less committed members or customers have two primary ways of removing their support for the organization. "[S]ome members leave the organization: this is the *exit option*," while others "express their dissatisfaction directly to management or to some other authority...this is the *voice option*."[56]

In transient periods, congregants act and react like customers, exiting churches or using voice to effect change. These two forms of protest can be found in every church dealing with a challenge or crisis, by members and staff alike. Which option a congregation primarily employs depends on the central values of the organization. In your research, see if you can figure out which of these forms of protest is employed most often.

Organizational Models

Below is a description of the five models of organization style common in churches. Where possible, I have matched these models to the paradigms of other church and marketplace literature.

The Flexible Church

I define Flexible Churches as nascent organizations. While generally excelling at relational support, they tend to lack defined structure. They are bound by affinity more than theology or mission. Flexible Churches come in two types: stable and transitional. Examples of stable Flexible Churches include family churches with fewer than 50 people. These churches are stable in that they have no reason to grow or change. They are committed to harmony, adventure, and shared experiences, at the expense of efficiency and excellence.

I once consulted with a church like this. The service started eight minutes late as congregants visited with one another. An Elder started the service with announcements, including an update on a sick member. A congregant interrupted as he spoke, "I have a more recent update." The Elder invited her to stand and share what she knew. This woman talked for five minutes and ended by saying, "But Martha was at the hospital this morning, so she may have more recent news." Martha then stood and gave another five-minute report. It was 11:24 AM before worship began.

Church plants are an example of a transitional Flexible Church. These churches also lack the necessary structures of organization: routine, process, consistency, hierarchy, and governance. The difference is that, as these churches grow and mature, they develop processes. This moves them into one of the other four organizational styles. The purchase of a church building is one impetus for developing greater structure, but a new building is not enough to create all essential aspects of structure. In some situations, the purchase of a building codifies behaviors that compete with growth and organization. Culture determines structure.

I do not provide a chart for Flexible Churches because, in a cluster analysis, they are least like one another than churches in other groupings. Transitional Flexible Churches ultimately drift to one of the other scalable organizational styles, while stable Flexible Churches lack the essential elements to scale beyond the family or tribe.

The Consensus Church

Consensus Churches are formed around the value of agreement, and they are sustained through togetherness: harmony and homogeneity. Achieving these values requires an *in-reach* orientation. This means they regularly start "together" ministries: a school, a book club, youth sport programs, or VBS. They have midweek events like fellowship dinners and small groups. These programs and activities provide for the Love Languages of *Quality Time* and *Acts of Service*.[57] Expressions of Christian character usually take the form of practical service: a meal for a new mother, running an errand for a friend, or visiting a shut-in. A life verse for this type of church is Acts 6:1, "What about our widows?"

These churches value personal and practical information clearly presented. They aren't inspired by a theoretic exposé on a theological point. They exchange information in chronological and narrative ways. They "put more importance on people-oriented information."[58] Thus, a good sermon expounds the entirety of the passage covered, even if the sermon does not form a cohesive theme. Sermon illustrations reflect their value of people and harmony. Rather than movie references and hypothetical situations, they resonate with practical and pragmatic stories about people: the parable of the Sower (Matt. 13:1-9) or examples from their own community.

There is a natural outcome of valuing relational knowledge that is narrative, concrete, and specific. Namely, members of these churches express the desire to know *everyone* and, in turn, be known *by* everyone. This sense of knowing and being known is lost as groups exceed their channel capacity which, Malcolm Gladwell explains, "refers to the amount of space in our brain for certain kinds of information."[59] Gladwell is summarizing the anthropological work of Robin Dunbar. Put simply, the size of the group to which a species belongs is proportional to the size of the neocortex in that species. For humans, that number is 150. "The figure of 150 seems to represent the maximum number of individuals with whom we can have a genuinely social relationship, the kind of relationship that goes with knowing who they are and how they relate to us."[60] For most people, this is their relational *channel capacity*.

During town hall or congregational meetings, Consensus Churches want to give every member of their group the opportunity to share their perspective. Individually, they want people to listen patiently to the stories of their daily lives. In decision making, "consultative, group process solutions" are preferred over leader-imposed decisions.[61] They make sense of the world through recounting their experiences. Their mutual reality is shaped by a cohesive view of the concrete world and their daily experiences in it. How big can a church be before the value of knowing and being known is lost? Around 150 adults. Add in children and the church may grow to around 200, after which members commonly remark, "I just don't feel like I know everyone anymore."

In these churches, a collaborative leadership style is typically preferred. However, when dealing with groups that are resistant to change, a consensus approach is typically practiced. This organizational type faces several practical, pastoral, and communal issues. First, they have difficulty growing, especially as they approach a group size of 150 adults. As the congregation reaches channel capacity, it focuses on the people and needs *within* the church.

Following a traditional organizational life cycle, these churches are in substantial decline before they realize their need to replace demographic holes in the 25-35 age bracket. In terms of the trampoline, these churches tend to value *support* and *structure*, in that order. Growth beyond 150 members—or any other dramatic change—requires the church moving toward the center of the net (*challenge*). Growth involves community engagement, a skill neglected in the years of full channel capacity. Language shift from internal cares—"What about our widows?"—to confusion: "Why won't more people come to church?"

Members' desires to serve can sometimes lead to neglecting their own well-being or hiding their true needs. Ideally, serving others is driven by a desire to strengthen relationships. However, in less positive situations, some members may serve with the unspoken expectation that others will reciprocate. (This behavior is common among Enneagram Type 2.) When this doesn't happen—especially when a senior leader fails to acknowledge a member's needs—resentment and criticism arise. Members fear feeling unheard or overlooked during change or growth.

Because of their deep commitment, members are disinclined to leave. During periods of change, duress, or disappointment, members make greater use of voice over exit. They'll complain or criticize for a long time before deciding to leave; many never do. And they are likely to remain in an organization beyond institutional health and viability.

These churches populate their websites with practical and concrete information. A picture of the church building, the physical address, and the meeting times are listed prominently. These churches prefer pictures of their own people doing life together over stock photos. They typically avoid abstract images all together.

The "about us" page often has a lengthy narrative of the church's history, including significant people who played a role in the church's formation and growth. Theological details are often secondary, listed further down the page or on a separate page altogether.

These churches develop their websites for insiders, making much of the information inaccessible to outsiders. For example, events listed on the church calendar may neglect to list where the events occur or how to get involved as a newcomer. The assumption is that everyone should know. That is, everyone who is already part of the community.

Style	Description
MBTI	*SFJ (primary), *STJ (secondary).
Pursues	Harmony, relationships over results.
Websites	Directed to *Insiders*.
Pictures	Real (not stock) of people they value
Interview Style	Pragmatic, practical. Tells and connects with personal and historic narrative.
Trampoline Elements	*Support* (primary), *Structure* (secondary).
Tim Keller Label	Small Church (40-200).
Philip Douglass Style	Fellowship (pg. 37).
Love Languages	Quality Time (primary), Acts of Service (secondary).
Ministry Orientation	*Insider* orientation.
Leadership Agility	Pre-Heroic (primary), Heroic (secondary).

The Organizing Church

Organizing Churches are driven by commitments to order and excellence, focusing on programs that meet their high standards. They prioritize *in-reach* ministries, driven by the belief that they can better serve their community than others. Their Christian character is expressed through knowledge, truthful speech, and a commitment to holy living. They see excellence and accuracy as essential to fulfilling their mission.

To attract and teach others, Organizing Churches offer practical programs. They host mission conferences for learning, giving, and prayer. They run programs like summer VBS, ESL, financial literacy training, sports, book clubs, and age-based activities. Their approach is similar to that of ancient Israel: "As we faithfully live out our calling, outsiders will be drawn in."

These churches value *Acts of Service* (*Love Language*) that are concrete and measurable and *Words of Affirmation* that are honest and specific. Praise must be backed by evidence, as they are cautious of unsubstantiated statements.

Organizing Churches favor concrete, specific, and factual communication. Sermons are often verse-by-verse, detailed, and draw from history, current events, and their own community. Christian education takes place in large rooms and employ the didactic style. Classes focus on what is true and what to do.[62] covering topics like church history, confessions, and practical models (e.g., marriage, parenting, outreach).

Information flows through established organizational channels, from leadership to the congregation. To start new initiatives, members typically seek approval. Congregational meetings are efficient, with questions welcomed but lengthy discussions discouraged.

These churches often adhere to the 5-Ps: position, person, platform, pulpit, and proclamation. The *position* defines the scope of expectation. The right *person* embodies specific character traits and embraces organizational values. These values form the foundation for the ministry *platform* of the congregation which is *proclaimed* from the *pulpit*. It follows that job descriptions emphasize the aspects of preaching and leadership. Leadership tends to be heroic, potentially limiting individual responsibility and teamwork. The authors of *Leadership Agility* explain,

> [H]eroic leadership overcontrols and underutilizes subordinates. It discourages people from feeling responsible for anything beyond their assigned area, inhibits optimal teamwork, and implicitly encourages subordinates to use the heroic approach with their own units.[63]

Members are highly loyal and use their voices to influence decisions. This might involve seeking formal leadership positions or using established communication channels. If these efforts fail, they often express public dissent (voice) and may eventually leave (exit).

This can sound terribly negative. It isn't always. In the 1970s, a group of churches seeking theological renewal within the Presbyterian Church in the United States (PCUS) left (exit) to form a new denomination: the Presbyterian Church in America. As the PCUS took more progressive stances on theological issues, those committed to an historic, orthodox interpretation of the Bible spoke up (voice). When their vocal opposition failed to achieve reform, they left (exit), giving up positions, church buildings, homes, large pensions, and lifelong relationships. I've interviewed 20 of the men who voted to leave. They told their stories through tears. These pastors believed they made the right decision despite it being painful. When voice failed, they chose exit.

On the other hand, the statement I heard most when interviewing congregants who remained in the PCUS (now PCUSA) is that "blood is thicker than water, and those who left violated our primary commitment to each other." Ignoring the theological issue for the moment, this perspective reflects more the Consensus Church value of putting loyalty to people over commitments to ideology.

Organizing Churches are built around a strong preacher with management skills. When preaching and programs no longer resonate with the community, decline occurs. Decline or disunity provoke a change in leadership, assuming the problem lies in ministry implementation (the leader) rather than the ministry approach (the church).

In positive times, these churches and leaders are often "calm, stable, and steady."[64] When relational challenges arise, they rely on technical processes and transactional communication. Members use analysis to diagnose problems and implement technical solutions. If unsuccessful, they may resort to criticism and eventually consider leaving.

Websites for Organizing Churches are professional, emphasizing the physical church building. They might show a picture of the sanctuary without the people. These churches tend to avoid images that lack concrete specificity. Their preference for *in-reach* orientation tends to carry into their web presence. They emphasize details: where to come, when, how to get there, and what to look for.

Smaller congregations can fall into the habit of using the website to speak to insiders. One declining Organizing Church changed their homepage to read simply, "Meet at the Johnsons' house to pray for our unbelieving neighbors this Sunday."

Style	Description
MBTI	*STJ (primary), *SFJ (secondary).
Pursues	Excellence, results over relationship.
Websites	Directed to the Insider.
Pictures	Real (not stock) of buildings, spaces, icons, and people they value.
Interview Style	Pragmatic, practical, detailed, structured. Seeks information; less interested in narrative.
Trampoline Elements	*Structure* (primary), *Support* (secondary).
Tim Keller Label	Medium Sized (200-450), Large Church (400-800), or Very Large Church (over 800).
Philip Douglass Style	Organizer (pg. 232).
Love Languages	Acts of Service, Words of Affirmation.
Ministry Orientation	Insider orientation.
Leadership Agility	Heroic Styles.

<u>The Catalyst Church</u>

Catalyst Churches are characterized by their emphasis on vision and innovation. Leaders in these churches are driven by a clear vision to achieve specific organizational goals. They "have original minds and great drive for implementing their ideas."[65] Their Love Languages include creative *Words of Affirmation*—specifically in recognition of their unique solutions or verbal creativity (Enneagram Type 4)—and personal and original *Gift Giving / Receiving*.

Catalyst Churches prefer a communication that is colorful and metaphorical.[66] They value articulate communicators who can effectively convey their worldview and organizational values. Their leaders use vivid imagery and storytelling to convey their vision and inspire others.

Leaders "exhibit insight, devotion, originality, and interpretive skill in their preaching, teaching, and counseling ministries."[67] They are comfortable preaching a long text, skipping over the exegesis and application of entire verses to draw out the pattern within the data. Members, in turn, may "enjoy debating, challenging, and questioning ideas and theories with a cool, logical, and detached approach."[68] Worship elements are led and conducted with accuracy and artistic excellence. Errors and flaws are felt acutely by the leaders and the congregation alike.

Their leaders pursue excellence to bring effective, original solutions to problems. They focus on a few ministries and look to do them well. Once a problem is solved, a system fixed, or a program launched, these leaders hand it off to managers. This frees leaders to solve the next problem or achieve the next stage of the larger vision. Leaders approach issues logically and analytically. Their cool-headed reasoning is appreciated when facing organizational and theological issues, but they can be perceived as aloof when addressing relational conflict or tension.

The same logical analysis comes to play during organizational transition and conflict. Members use voice to seek change—presenting their case with the same carefully constructed argumentations. Those who cannot see or do not agree with the reasoning of their argument are perceived as narrow, lacking in vision, or too shaped by tradition. If the case is not resolved to their liking, they can pivot quickly and exit the organization.

In fact, people with this organizational preference are the least likely to weather a challenging season. They are quickest to exit when they no longer agree with the vision and direction of senior leadership.

Because they value excellence *and* creativity, their websites tend to be professional. If they include a picture of the building, it is a unique photo with emphasis on a particular architectural element, unusual lighting, or an unexpected camera angle. They like to include people in their pictures when the images convey an organizational value. Pictures may be cropped to focus on the hands or highlight a particular pose. These churches rarely include the history of their congregation because tradition isn't as important as other values. Instead, a concise, clear mission statement and list of core values are featured more prominently.

Style	Description
MBTI	*NTJ (primary), *NFJ or *STJ (secondary).
Pursues	Innovation and achievement; results over relationships.
Websites	Directed to outsiders; intended to inspire.
Pictures	Artistic and creative of people and projects they value.
Interview Style	Forward looking, visionary, structured. Interested in concise, image-driven narrative.
Trampoline Elements	*Challenge* (primary), *Structure* (secondary).
Tim Keller Label	Large Church (400-800), or Very Large Church.
Philip Douglass Style	Strategizer (pg. 192).
Love Languages	Words of Affirmation, Gift Giving / Receiving.
Ministry Orientation	*Outsider* orientation.
Leadership Agility	Catalyst, Co-Creator, or Synergist.

<u>The Relational Church</u>
The Relational Church values creating space for relationships and beauty to thrive. These congregations are driven by the aspiration to see people changed—emotionally, intellectually, and spiritually—*through* relationships with one another and with God. Leaders are followed because of their warmth, originality, and imagination. Their Love Languages include creative *Gift Giving / Receiving,* and *Words of Affirmation* that specifically recognize their uniqueness.

Like the Catalyst Church, communication is creative, laced with metaphors and analogies. Because they see a future that isn't fully formed or in focus, they tell stories of a better world: stories full of pictures that convey the future. Illustrations draw from novels, movies, painting, and thematic events throughout history. The goal is to provoke strong emotions that motivate the pursuit of harmony. Members value creative communicators who can convey a view of the world where their relational values shape reality.

Sermons "ponder the meaning and implication of passages of Scripture, sounding the depths of each verse and exploring the richness to develop insights of human behavior."[69] Pastors often preach from long texts, skipping over the exegesis and application of entire verses, to draw out specific images within the data. Or they can preach from a single verse, poetically conveying the verbal richness within the passage. "[M]embers are particularly interested in discovering how relational dynamics are supposed to work from a biblical perspective. Demonstrations and practical examples are of use to them."[70] Worship elements are conducted with beauty and excellence, but mistakes can be overlooked as members pursue harmony by extending grace.

Their leaders pursue their own personal growth first. Then they seek the development of others within the bounds of kindness, respect, and inspiration. Their creativity gives birth to many different ministries, diluting the impact of any individual ministry. Members get bored with programs that don't allow space to develop deep, relational connections and tire of programs that don't provide inspiration for personal and community growth.

Leaders tend to approach issues relationally and personally. Their warm approach is appreciated when facing relational challenges and theological issues, but they can be perceived as inconsistent or inadequate when addressing matters and issues that require a more analytical response.

The same relational harmony comes to play during organizational transition and conflict. Members use voice to seek change—appealing to respect and harmony when presenting their case. Those who dismiss the relational and personal aspects of an argument are perceived as rigid and cold, lacking in relational intelligence. If their case is not resolved to their liking, they may try to use voice with peers (not just leaders) to seek justice. They tend to exit organizations more slowly than members of either the Catalyst or Organizing Churches, but more quickly than members of a Consensus Church.

Because they value imagination and creativity, their websites tend to be professional. They include unique photographs of buildings, common spaces, the communion table, and an ornate pulpit: images that help create the ideal world they can visualize. They like to include pictures of people interacting in a shared experience. These churches rarely include the history of their congregation because tradition isn't as important as other values. Instead, a descriptive, creative mission statement and list of primary values are featured more prominently.

The desire to honor the unique ministry expressions of others means that the Inspirational Church can be unfocused and overextended in its ministry pursuits. Even when there is a degree of consensus, there is likely a wide variety of *in-reach* and *out-reach* oriented ministries. The role of leaders is to ensure that organizational vision is prioritized, ministry mission is never undermined, and ministry implementation is pushed out to the congregation.

Style	Description
MBTI	*NFJ (primary), *SFJ (secondary).
Pursues	Results through relationships.
Websites	Directed to everyone who embraces their values.
Pictures	Real (not stock) of people together.
Interview Style	Relationally focused, caring, interested in narrative and story.
Trampoline Elements	*Challenge* (primary), *Structure* (secondary).
Tim Keller Label	Small-sized (40-200), Medium Sized (200-450).
Philip Douglass Style	Inspirational (pg. 75).
Love Languages	Words of Affirmation, Physical Touch, Gift Giving.
Ministry Orientation	*Outsider* orientation.
Leadership Agility	Catalyst, Co-Creator, or Synergist.

What is *This* Church's Personality?

Dr. Philip Douglass' book, *What is your Church's Personality*, is the brilliant application of the personality inventory to organizational dynamics. Not only is this an acceptable extension of typology, but a necessary one. Murry Bowen, pioneer in the field of family system theory, wrote, "The more one observes families, the easier it is to detach from the narrow conceptual boundaries of individual theory; and the more one detaches from individual theory, the easier it is to see family patterns."[71] The family, he explained, is a number of different kinds of systems.[72] Collective organizations are amplifications of the family system to the level of the organization or corporate—in our case, what we call a *church*.

Douglass categorizes churches into one of eight organizational styles, with each style featuring the dominant expressions, values, commitments, and preferences of the corresponding MBTI Types. He summarizes his data visually in this chart (used with permission):

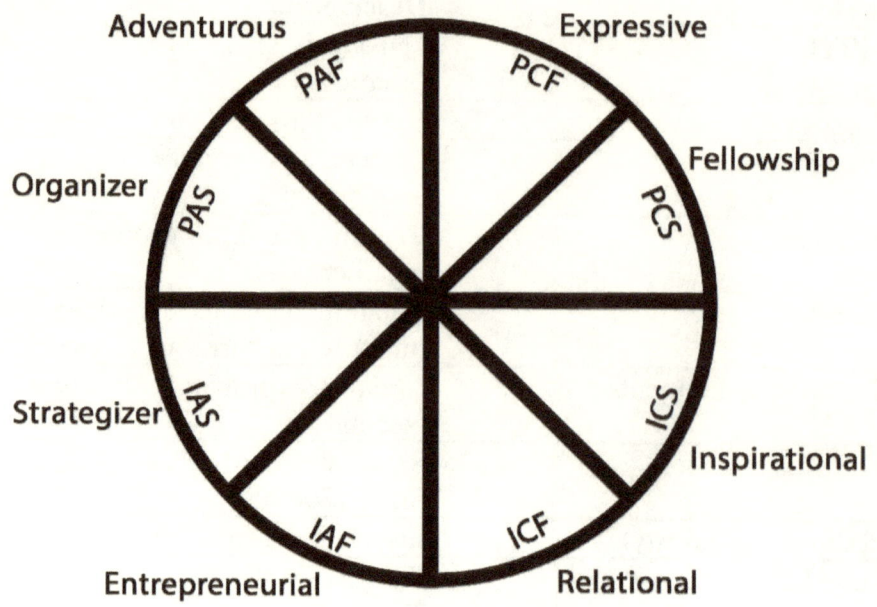

The classification of each organizational style reflects a combination of three dichotomies:

- Practical (P) v. Innovative (I)
- Analytical (A) v. Connectional (C)
- Structured (S) v. Flexible (F)

Whether or not you have the categories to classify your observations, all your research on a church *is* personality evaluation at an organizational scale. This is the equivalent of doing research on the "culture" of a public company.

Likely you've had the experience of "picking up on something that doesn't sit right." You don't have terms or categories for what you are feeling, but your sense is accurate. This feeling—call it your gut or intuition—may be non-concrete but that doesn't make it untrue. Often our inability to label experiences comes from a lack of clinical knowledge and practical experience. Learning to classify feelings with specific language provides clarity.

Dr. Douglass' approach is a good model for this type of classification. I believe his work gives words to name what you observe through your interactions and in your observation from the website, sermons, and previous staff. Let me encourage you to read the first 33 pages of *What is your Church's Personality?* This outlines the framework of Douglass' approach. As you begin to build an active file on a specific church, try to identify which of the eight organizational types it falls into. Even if you aren't exactly right—and it's worth mentioning that most organizations have both a dominant style and a secondary style—this process increases your capacity to differentiate organizational preferences and patterns from one church to another. It also helps you create and ask better questions during the research and interview stages of the process.

The Goal of Your Research
When you research a position, your goal should be to develop a realistic and coherent view of the organization. Every piece of data should be viewed as a puzzle piece. Your job is to put them together into a cohesive image, as you search for elements of continuity and discontinuity. At the end of the process, you should feel confident about your assessment of a church and position, including the dynamics, culture, and values of the organization. I call this the Narrative Approach to data gathering.

This may sound obvious, but there are alternative approaches to data gathering. One alternative approach is to view each piece of data— aspects of the job description, language on the church website, email interactions, and phone calls—as confirmation of preconceived expectations. This is a Quantitative Approach to data gathering, repeatedly asking, "Does this new data substantiate my expectation and perspective or not?" This approach is less effective because it ultimately puts every interaction into binary categories: yes or no, affirmation or denial, substantiate or undermine, integrity or incongruity. Then, when you have an interaction with one person that seems in tension with or, worse, contradiction to another interaction, the conclusion is that one of them must be untrue.

A Quantitative Approach to human assessment asks, "Is Joel emotionally healthy?" The person asking this question must then assess all data points to determine a conclusion. This exercise leaves the researcher at a decisive terminus: yes or no. The structure of the question does not allow space or time for growth, change, or development. Reality is too complex for that. Human behaviors and interactions are not so easily bifurcated. Asking instead, "Is Joel growing in emotional health?" allows room for change and sanctification, but it is still a binary question requiring a quantitative analysis.

By comparison, a Narrative Approach (Qualitative) asks, "How is Joel growing in emotional health?" (Notice the similarity in structure to Behavioral Interviewing questions.) This changes the process of data gathering completely. Now there is variance, nuance, and the need for narrative analysis.

Along those lines, a candidate who asks, "Does this church present a realistic view of itself?" must eventually conclude affirmation or denial (binary). Denial means he should not go there. Affirmation means he should at least consider it. What this approach doesn't allow for is your own interpretive bias and the limitations of your assessment. More than building a cohesive view of reality, the Quantitative Approach affirms preconceived expectations.

But what if collections of people—what we call organizations—are moving toward greater awareness of reality through interaction? This changes the question: "How is this church moving toward greater awareness of their organizational dynamics?" Now the static Polaroid becomes a static panorama, and in time the static panorama becomes a dynamic film—moving and changing through time. You are no longer trying to answer, "Is this a good and safe place for me to work?" Instead, you explore, "In what ways am I equipped with the necessary skills and capacity to navigate the particular struggles of these people, in this organization, in this place, in this cultural moment?"

Using the Narrative Approach to research, candidates should view each piece of data as a snapshot—a small, 2 x 2 Polaroid. The Polaroid image isn't untrue. It just isn't big enough to capture the entirety of a situation. A Polaroid of small stones and a Polaroid of giant boulders appear indistinguishable. This mathematical feature is called a fractal. In either event, reality is irrelevant unless the picture comes with the instructions on how to drive over the rocks. Suddenly, it matters whether the stones are 6 centimeters or 16 meters.

Consider a pastor who starts meetings late and is unwilling to end them at a reasonable hour. How significant is it that the Senior Pastor refuses to put a time limit on the Session meetings that start at 6:00 PM and run well past 1:00 AM? Is this a pebble or a boulder? This single observation has meaning and value but has greater or less meaning and value in the context of more information. Each new bit of data is another Polaroid, offering a panoramic view of reality. There will always be unknowns— gaps between the images—but the emotional-relational map created through repeated interactions provides sufficient information to determine the consistency (as opposed to inconsistency) of the church in question.

Start by reading the job description and exploring the website. Exchange emails and phone calls. Answer written questionnaires and write thank you notes. Listen to the concerns behind the questions and note the stories of hope, disappointment, joy and sorrow. Use these snapshot moments to build a dynamic panoramic of the church.

"Active File" Data Management
Before you jump in with both feet, develop a system for information management. After reading just one job description, you will have highlighted words, noted observations, and made a list of questions. Candidates are tempted to rely on memory to keep track of all this information. But as the number of interactions increases, along with the number of positions you explore and apply for, memory is insufficient. You need an information tracking system.

The two most common systems for keeping track of information are an Excel spreadsheet or a physical folder. If you choose to use an Excel spreadsheet, have one worksheet for each job you apply for. Personally, I prefer physical folders over digital files. This allows me to manage the physical documents related to each job. On the outside cover, draw boxes where you can put "at a glance" information, such as:

- Contact Date/Time
- Key descriptors of church (from job description, website, interaction)
- List of Questions
- Names/roles of people involved in the process.
- Timeline for hiring.
- Other Important Information

The Job Description

Your first exposure to most positions is the job description. I've already mentioned how most job descriptions are created in a vacuum and should be viewed as the beginning of the conversation. When it comes to researching the commitments, values, and culture of a church, a job description gives you an initial snapshot of the organization—what traits they value (character), what skills they are seeking (competencies), and what duties they want you to fill (responsibilities).

I recommend printing a physical copy of the job description. Highlight the nouns (who and what) with one color and the verbs (actions) with another color. This "coding" allows you to find the themes of the job description. You will be able to see if those themes find support in how the church describes itself on the website, what language is used by the Pastor in his sermons, and how the search committee interacts with you.

Try to engage with the job description with curiosity. Reserve judgment until you have more information. After reading about a youth ministry position, instead of concluding, "I don't want to do youth ministry!" (judgment), try asking questions about the role: Why are they currently looking for a youth minister? Where did the last youth minister thrive and flourish? What are the hopes of the church in hiring the next youth minister? (curiosity)?

Note any areas of discrepancy or inconsistency. Look for an opportunity to ask the committee about your observations. For example, one youth job description required the candidate "be active in the community supporting the activities of students, and building relationships with youth not currently involved in a church." A few lines down, the job description stated, "The Youth Pastor will hold regular office hours between 9:00 AM and 4:30 PM." These two responsibilities are in tension with one another. How would you inquire about this apparent discrepancy? The "I'm curious about" or "Tell me more" approaches might serve well: "I noticed you want the Youth Pastor both to hold regular office hours *and* be regularly engaged in the community. Can you tell me more about how those two responsibilities work together?"

Pay attention to words that allow for a variety of meanings, such as: engaging, leadership, energetic, and passion. Each of these words begs the question, "With respect to who or what?" People consider me friendly, warm, and initiating in relationships, but I am an introvert who is quiet, reflective, and prefers to spend downtime alone. Compared to many other introverts, I seem energetic and extroverted. Compared to my extroverted wife, I am introspective and quiet.

Forms of the word *leadership* are used in most ministry job descriptions. A survey of 1,124 job descriptions found that *lead, leadership,* and *leader* appeared in 953 (85%) of the job descriptions. But what do those words mean? Within the field of leadership studies, there are six major leadership *theories*.[73] Bill Joiner and Stephen Josephs, in *Leadership Agility*, present five levels of leadership *development*. And various books and websites have dozens of other keywords and descriptions qualifying different leadership styles. The word *leadership* is used so often and in so many different situations that it has come to have no definition that is transferable from one context to another. You must determine what is meant when the term is used.

Non-Profit Job Description Language
Here is a list of the top words by frequency, taken from 254 job descriptions from 2018-2021. I only looked at words that have 50 or more occurrences:

Pronouns (top 5)	Frequency
our	1441
we	1217
their	445
his	412
you	380

Notice the absence of third person pronouns: him, her, them, theirs. In contrast, the word "others"—as in *other* people—shows up 143 times. Also notice the directionality of the pronouns. Pronouns focused on people inside the church—*our* and *we*—had a higher recurrence rate than those words referring to people outside the church.

Noun (top 5)	Frequency
team/teams	537
leadership	439
vision/visionary	287
disciple/discipleship	270
outreach/evangelism	262

Administration is at the bottom of the list, with only 51 occurrences. This is a disappointing but not surprising fact, considering the disparity between ministry expectations and ministry reality. In Chapter 1, I quote from *Pastors In transition*, in which the researchers found the gap between the *ideal* ministry position as described by pastors and the *real* positions these pastors filled. Pastors desired to spend time preaching, teaching, and engaged in other pastoral duties, but instead spent most of their time on administration. My takeaway is that people who write most job descriptions do not have the knowledge necessary to know what to emphasize. This is attractive for those who desire to *pastor* but inconsistent with the reality of having to *administrate*. This puts the burden of exploration upon you, as the candidate, to discern.

Verb (top 5)	Frequency
serve/serving/service	820
work/working	613
lead/leading	569
develop/developing/development	543
able/ability	432

Most traditional *pastoral* duties show up lower in the list, including:

- #6: Teach/teaching (379)
- #11: Preach/preaching (242)
- #14: Equip/Equipping (161)
- #17: Counseling (131)
- #26: Study (100)
- #27: Encourage (99)
- #28: Minister (99)
- #33: Shepherd/Shepherding (76)
- #39: Visit (57)

The mere use of any of these words is not enough to determine the importance of the duty or responsibility, but the over- or under-use of a term should at least elicit questions for you to explore during the interviewing process.

Website
The website provides you with another opportunity to learn about the church. Your goal when evaluating a church website is to look for points of agreement or continuity and points of disagreement or discontinuity compared to what you observed in the job description.

Photographs
Pay attention to what photographs are used. As mentioned in Chapter 2, how a church uses pictures tells you something about its organizational style and values. Are the pictures comprised of people or buildings? Are the pictures professional or candid? Do they include real church members or stock photos? Are the pictures intended to convey a specific event—worship—or are they artistic—like an out-of-focus shot of the communion table?

Smaller, less connected churches with a local focus (rural) use stock images of people or none at all. Churches that value the Myers Briggs function *Sensing* use an image of the church building on their home page, and throughout the website they use candid images of people involved in actual tasks: greeting one another, worshiping, or sitting around a table eating.

Larger churches that are more connected geographically focused (urban and suburban) use professional imagery. The people are actual church members, not stock photos. They include a picture of their building, but it is only one of several beautifully captured aspects of the church architecture and people. Churches with a preference for *Intuition* are most comfortable using abstract pictures to capture or convey aspects of their organization.

About Us, Mission & Vision
Pay attention to the "About Us" section of the website. Churches with a preference for *Sensing* use this section to give the entire history of the church, from the early days as a small group and the first leaders, the most effective pastors, and meaningful moments in the life of the

organization. The emphasis is on "us"—the story of that church and their history together. Churches with a preference for *Intuition* tend to write less about the history of the church and more about its current mission. The emphasis is on "you"—the visitor to the website, and how you and the community fit into the developing story of the church.

Sometimes there is a separate section on the mission and values of the church. Churches with a preference for *Sensing* and *Thinking* often emphasize theological distinctives, while churches with a preference for *Intuition* tend to emphasize the implications of these theological distinctives as they shape engagement with the world.

- *Historic Approach*: Welcome to the website of First Presbyterian Church of Jackson, Mississippi. We are thankful for your interest in First Presbyterian Church. The First Presbyterian Church of Jackson has been a steadfast witness to historic, Reformed, Christianity for over 175 years. (fpcjackson.org/about/ and graceandpeacefellowship.org/about-us/who-we-are/)
- *Practical Approach:* Sunday mornings at Riverwood begin with Sunday School at 9:15 AM. As you drive into the parking lot, the building to your immediate right (with the tall steeple) houses our nursery, Sunday school classes for children of all ages, and an adult class in the fellowship hall. On your left as you enter the parking lot is the Administrative Building. This building is home to our church offices and a conference room where another adult Sunday school class meets. The Sunday school youth class meets in the second building on your left (which we refer to as the *Youth Barn*). (riverwoodchurch.org/about/what-to-expect/)
- *Mission-Vision Approach*: Our vision is to see individuals, families, greater Atlanta and the world come into a life-transforming encounter with the kingdom of God. (www.perimeter.org/about)
- *Conversational Engagement Approach:* Redeemer Presbyterian Church, New York, NY does not even have an about us section. Where you would expect to find it, there is the statement, "Skeptics Welcome." (https://downtown.redeemer.com/skeptics_welcome).

None of these approaches is uniquely right or intrinsically wrong. I point them out to illustrate diverse ways a church seeks to orient a community to its (the church's) identity: *in-reach* or *out-reach*. You are likely drawn to one of these approaches over the other, and you will fit better in a church that has a similar orientation.

Staff Page
Look at the staff page. How are staff members dressed: professionally or casually? What biographic information is prioritized? A church that shows staff members dressed in business-professional attire and emphasizes the academic degrees each has received usually prioritizes "excellent preaching" and "visionary leadership." A church that shows staff members dressed in casual or business-casual attire and emphasizes family or hobbies in the biographical information often prioritizes "visitation" and "relational development."

Church Calendar
Peruse the church calendar if it's available. What types of groups does the church sponsor and where do they meet? Organizations that view the physical church building as the nexus of spiritual life—*in-reach* oriented—conduct their activities in the church building. Organizations that view the gathering of God's people anywhere the essence of spiritual life—*out-reach* oriented—conduct their activities out in the community. Also, note on the calendar what types of activities the church sponsors for Easter and Halloween.

As you explore the website ask yourself if the website is primarily talking to members of the church (insiders) or to visitors to the website (outsiders). How churches use their websites says something about how they view evangelism, outreach, assimilation, membership identity, and participation. In most cases, the construction of the church website is not made up of neutral features. Images, words, and layout convey the same values and commitments practiced in the church's culture, leadership, management, and mission-implementation. In this sense, the website is a mirror of the emotional and organizing processes at work in the church. Make notes of your observations in your active file.

Sermons

One of the clearest ways to identify the priorities of a congregation is by listening to sermons, specifically those of the lead pastor.

- What books of the Bible has the Pastoral staff preached through?
- What theological elements are emphasized: the evil of the world or the goodness of the God who made it?
- What characteristics of God are most often cited: justice and holiness or goodness and mercy?
- What are the main points of application: repent and believe, or have confidence, or live rightly?
- Who is at risk of God's judgement: the people *out there* or people *in here,* or both?
- Who is the focus of the application: the congregation or the world?
- Who needs this message: believers or unbelievers?

I recognize this list includes several false dichotomies. God is just and holy even as He is good and merciful, "for all have sinned and fallen short of the glory of God and are justified by His grace as a gift" (Rom. 3:23). Still, we are prone to fall to one side of the spectrum or the other in our theology.

The emphases of pastoral staff in sermon delivery usually reflect the theological commitments of the church. Here are some examples of what I mean. I consulted with one church that wanted to know when to interrogate their candidates on the topic of Critical Race Theory; the church was in a rural, racially homogeneous region. The Pastor of a different church preached passionately against the sexual wickedness of the world "out there" with no application of the Scriptures to the people listening to his sermon. In another situation, at a recent presbytery examination, pastors peppered a candidate about his views on a conference. Despite his humble acknowledgment that he wasn't familiar with the content of the conference, some of the Pastors continued to query him by stating what they understood the conference to be about and then asking the candidate to express his views on their summary. And in yet another example, a woman on one search committee asked a candidate, "What is your view of divorce?"

182

These statements and questions come from places of deep commitment and, I propose, fear. The world doesn't fit into dichotomies, but that doesn't stop us from trying.

When listening to sermons, remember that you are not just listening for theological accuracy. Can you see yourself and your family regularly sitting under, listening to, and growing from this communication style and homiletic focus?

Former Staff

Where the job description, church website, and sermons provide static information about a particular organization, interviewing former staff can provide a dynamic perspective. This isn't always possible, of course. Smaller churches don't have a history of multiple staff, and the retiring Solo Pastor has been there for 20 years or more. And maybe you just can't find the names of the previous staff or can't find a good way to connect with them. I find it harder to gain information about former staff from jobs listed on job boards.

Here are ways to connect with former staff members:
- Ask the committee who was in the position previously and if they would be willing to connect you to them.
- Ask pastors serving in other churches in the region, presbytery, or synod if they know and can connect you to former church staff.
- Look at the church website to see who regularly preached at the church in the past.
- Check to see if your denomination has pastoral and church yearbooks, or if regional directors have knowledge of people who were previously employed at the church.

Search the Internet to see what you can find out about the former staff. Where are they employed now? How do they describe their vocational history on LinkedIn? What can you discern about them from their public profile on Facebook or Instagram? Be sure to document all your observations and questions in your active file management system.

Before interviewing former staff, be as transparent as the situation allows. I usually encourage candidates to ask the committee how they would feel if you spoke with a former staff person. And whenever possible, have a mutual friend or acquaintance connect you. This can alleviate your uncertainty or suspicion (on the part of the former staff).

When interviewing former staff, be clear that you are motivated by curiosity and that you appreciate anything you can learn. Ask open ended questions, like those that start with, "What can you tell me about...," e.g. the past candidate's experience, the church, the leadership, the congregation, the community, the worship service, the music style, the youth group, key families, and so forth. You need to avoid the appearance of looking to dig up past problems or expose current issues. Your goal is to observe and learn, not trick or trap.

As you engage with a particular church, try to make a timeline of the vocational (employment) history of the church. Pay attention to how long former staff members stayed at the church and what types of positions they moved into in their next jobs. The vocational trajectory of the former staff provides insight into the health of the organization and leadership.

Robert interviewed for a youth position in the southeast. A mutual friend connected him with Alan, the former youth minister. Alan was no longer in ministry but had moved into a position at a technology firm. Alan was guarded in his interaction with Robert, giving vague answers. Robert decided to ask one more question before giving up:

> "Who was in the position before you?"
> "His name was Taylor. He held the position for only 18 months," Alan said.
> "Do you know where he's working now?"
> "I think he also left ministry a few years after leaving the job."
> "Was he the first person to have the job," Rob asked?
> "No, that would be Jonathan. He stayed 3 years and is working as a Youth Pastor at a similar sized church in another state."

The health of this church is reflected in its timeline of staff members. Healthy churches regularly send staff members off for positions of greater leadership, influence, and longevity such as when the Youth Pastor left after five years to become the college pastor of another congregation, or an Associate Minister left to become a Solo Pastor at another church. These are progressive transitions.

184

But churches with substantial leadership issues or organizational dysfunction are often marked by a series of short-term staff members or pastors who leave for similar positions in other churches, stay in subsequent positions for shorter amounts of time, and eventually leave the ministry completely.

The Necessity of Nuance

Up to now, I've made a number of assumptions about personality and preference. I recognize there are people who are skeptical of personality assessments. Part of their suspicion arises from the multiplicity and diversity of models. There is the RightPath, FIRO-B SkillCheck, StrengthsFinder, Career Beliefs Inventory, and The Big Five. Other inventories, like the MBTI, are viewed with suspicion for making regular revisions to the instrument. I find that people either love these rubrics or hate them. Christians also have taken staunch positions for and against these inventories, labeling them either (positively) portals to relationship-saving insights or (negatively) unbiblically humanistic.

How we view these metrics affects how we use and apply them. Some proponents have used such metrics to the detriment of themselves and others—wrongly using these models to reduce, classify, categorize, or limit others: "You can't do _____ because you are a _____ Type on the Myers Briggs." A common response to this misuse is, "I feel put in a box." On the other hand, others use their Type to justify character flaws and competency deficiencies. Still others outright reject these models as unsubstantiated "psychobabble." This latter group, universalizing their own experiences, does equal harm to other people who think, process, and communicate differently. These models are intended to encourage exploration and curiosity, not excuse our excesses or give us power over others.

None of these metrics are unique. An overlay of four such metrics—the MBTI, Love Languages, Enneagram, and DiSC—reveals considerable consistency. For example:

- INF* Types on the Myers Briggs are often Enneagram Type 4, S/i on the DiSC, and have the Love Languages of *Physical Touch* and *Words of Affirmation*.

185

- *STJ Types on the Myers Briggs are usually a Type 1 or 8 on the Enneagram, D/i or D/c on the DiSC, and have the Love Languages of *Quality Time* and *Gift Receiving*.

Each of these inventories tries to explain something about our individuality as people that a post-enlightened, scientific-data dependent education and post-reformation theology tend to deny or at least ignore. Yes, we are all humans made in the image of God; and, no, we are not all the same.

Models are important for us to navigate the world. Our God-given limits as image bearers make our assessments of the world imperfect and incomplete. We are not omniscient. Imagine the information necessary to walk across a seminary campus if you did not have working models of spatial geometry, physics, ecology, biology, and meteorology. None of us knows all there is to know about any one of these subjects—many of us know very little—but all of us can surmise that fixed, inanimate objects do not independently move, the special theory of gravity remains consistent, trees do not suddenly behave like the Whomping Willow from Harry Potter, and tornadoes do not inexplicably appear and disappear like the microscopic black holes of quantum mechanics.

Without models, complex decisions become elongated, tenuous, and delayed such that, under the weight of everyday decisions, we would collapse within a couple of hours. And without exposure to variation and the ability to differentiate between types, we become stunted. As philosopher Thomas Kuhn put it, "To reject one paradigm without simultaneously substituting another is to reject science itself. That act reflects not on the paradigm but on the man."[74] We only develop a refined (nuanced) perspective where there is variety or difference *and* the ability to classify such.

In his book *Make it Stick*, Peter Brown quotes a physician, Douglas Larsen, reflecting on the role of variation in developing a refined perspective. Larsen said, "The reason variety is important is it helps us see more nuances in the things that we can compare against... That comes up a lot in medicine, in the sense that every patient visit is a test. There are many layers of explicit and implicit memory involved in the ability to discriminate between symptoms and their interrelationships."[75]

The Bible is full of evidence of these models. By all accounts, the Apostle Paul had a preference for *Introversion*, choosing to communicate predominantly through writing. The Corinthians accuse, "His letters are weighty and strong, but his bodily presence is weak, and his speech of no account" (2 Cor. 10:10).

The Apostle Peter, the energizer bunny of the apostolate, had a propensity for *Extroversion*. Referring to Peter, Scripture uses the verbs *said, replied, answered, spoke, declared,* and *denied* no less than 39 times in the Gospels and Acts.

Luke had a preference for *Sensing*—oriented to present realities, factual and concrete information, seeing and recounting specifics. John had a preference for *Intuition* as shown by his imaginative and verbally creative writing which focuses on patterns and meanings in data and his trust of inspiration: "In the beginning was the Word...." Even Jesus points out the proximate meteorological and astronomical models employed by the ancients when He said to the crowds, "You know how to interpret the earth and sky..." (Luke 12:56).

The beauty of these assessments is their ability to help us understand ourselves against the backdrop of a Genesis 1-2 creation and a Genesis 3 fall. Redemptively, my intuition allows me to see relational needs in others. Sinfully, my intuition causes me to jump to false conclusions, fueled by my insecurity. Practically, knowing that I am intuitive helps me understand why I talk about my day in terms of highs and lows with no consideration for chronology. Knowing I am intuitive helps my wife understand why I *don't* remember specifically what my supervisor said to me in the hallway and can only tell her how it made me feel.

More importantly—and this is where I think we often fall short—when used in Gospel ways, these metrics enable us to love, serve, and communicate in ways that honor other's uniqueness. Too many of us stop with the application of these metrics to ourselves: "I am a
_____(preference of choice). That's why I
_____(justification of behavior)."

Most of these inventories state that you should *never* "apply" them to other people. Riso and Hudson in *The Wisdom of the Enneagram* write, "We feel strongly that is it always more problematic to use the

Enneagram to type others than it is to use it on ourselves."[76] And Myers, McCaulley, *et al*, in the *MBTI Manual* write, "Verification of the accuracy of the indicated type *by the respondent* is essential. MBTI results do not 'tell' a person who she or he is. Rather, individual respondents are viewed as experts who are best qualified to judge the accuracy of the type descriptions...."[77]

Starting from a Reformed, orthodox, Christian worldview, I believe these inventories, where true and valid, should lead to the place all truth leads: to love of God and love of neighbor. Knowing my wife has a preference for *Sensing* means I work to remember specifics about my conversation with my supervisor and communicate my day chronologically. Wherever we experience disconnect in our communication, relational, and organizational styles, we need to ask: besides sin, what else might be the cause? What differences in my neighbor require me to engage outside my preferences?

People who refuse to allow any inventory, assessment, or model to broaden their perspective invariably universalize their own experience. The Myers Briggs didn't come up with the binary choice option. It's in all of us. The disciples asked, "Who sinned, this man or his parents?" The Samaritan woman asked, "Where should we worship: on this mountain or that mountain?" Joshua asked, "Are you for us or for our enemies?" I really love this last one because the angel to whom Joshua was speaking gives a third alternative: "Neither" (Joshua 5:13-15).

The default for Christians is to think in terms of sin and righteousness. The Elders at one Fellowship Style Church (SFJ) fired their pastor who had a preference for *Extroversion* and *Intuition* because, "That man doesn't know his Bible." What they meant and further explained was that the Pastor didn't go line by line and phrase by phrase but took large sections of Scripture and tied them together with a driving image.

Another pastor quit his church because, in his judgment, the Elders were not fit to serve. They lacked compassion and were aloof, never gave positive feedback, and challenged every idea he presented during their hours-long Elder meetings where he talked through all his big-picture ideas. The Pastor's personality was ENFJ while the dominant group personality of the Session was ISTJ.

One elder (ESTJ) at another church opposed a plan to let young families have a community group at 5:00 PM on Sunday evenings because it conflicted with Sunday evening worship: "The Elders have decided Sunday evening worship is good for our people, and so these people should come." These young families *didn't* come to evening worship because it was too hard on their infant children. Moreover, they weren't going to start coming just because an Elder declared it. The Pastor (ESFJ) supported the Elder over the Assistant Pastor (ENFJ) who first presented the idea of a Sunday evening community group.

What only a few people knew is that this Elder had made similar inflexible demands on his own children as they were growing up. His adult children still lived in the community but had stopped going to church. Now we've drifted from the Myers Briggs to Bowen's Family System Theory. To this Elder, not going to evening worship was a sin, but when these young families chose not to go to evening worship, they were a painful reminder that he could not force his grown children to do what, when younger, he should have been wooing them to love.

Did this Elder respond the way he did because he was an ESTJ or because he was a Type 1 with a 2 wing, or because he was a D/c (on the Disc profile), or because he was experiencing cutoff from his children and conflated his role as an Elder with that of a father? Yes, and no. Each model provides a degree of insight into the vast complexity of the human condition and reality. This is why Katherine Myers and Isabella Briggs wrote, "I am like every INFP. I am like some INFPs. I am like no INFPs."

In the absence of alterative models, we must conclude that either the Elder is right and the young families neglecting evening worship are wrong, or the other way around. We then look for scriptural support to justify this conclusion. In the absence of an alternative models, we default to false dichotomies.

No single rubric is helpful in every situation. Knowing when and how to apply them requires wisdom. And there will always be tension. On the one hand, these assessments say never to tell another person how he or she would come out on the inventory. At the same time, we have not tried to fulfill the greatest commandments if we stop at self-knowledge. Loving our neighbors demands we seek to understand them: their core beliefs and fears, deepest desires, and hopes. Loving our neighbor also means we don't put them in a box, dismiss, or control. Instead, we give others the necessary space to grow uniquely as the Lord desires.

Your first challenge is to discover your personality, whichever assessment you choose. Your second challenge is to understand the results sufficiently so that you can explain them simply, illustrating how you demonstrate that facet. Few committees are versed in the Myers Briggs, so saying you are an ESFP means nothing. Instead, say that you are energized by being with people, exploring new aspects of God's created world, having new experiences, and gaining new insights into topics of shared interest, while growing in relationship with God and others. Rather than saying you are an Enneagram Type 1, say that you are thoughtful and methodical, seeking out the right way to carry out plans and achieve a goal, inviting others into that proven approach in pursuit of the best results.

The Example of Trips
In 1990, I took a five-hour trip with my father. We rode in silence the whole way. As an INFJ, I interpreted his silence as a judgment: *I was not worthy of his pursuit.* I said in my heart, "I will never neglect my children in silence."

In 2010, I drove my oldest son to baseball practice. I peppered him with questions about his day, his interests, and his heart. He gave one-word responses. Almost frustrated, I finally asked, "Would you like me to stop asking you questions?" He sighed with relief, "Yes. I haven't had any time to myself today, and I want time to think." To his immense joy, we drove the rest of the trip in silence.

In 2012, I drove a well-known pastor back from a week-long speaking engagement. We got in the car at 9:00 PM. He immediately put in his earbuds and disappeared behind his computer for two hours. When we arrived in Indianapolis, he asked if I felt up to the task of driving us home that night instead of the next morning. I agreed. He thanked me as he put his earbuds back in. We rode in silence until we pulled into his driveway at 3:00 AM. "Thank you," he said again and left.

Knowing how God made me helps me understand what I wanted from my father and why. Being willing to explore how my very-different son wants to be engaged frees me from universalizing my own experience, honoring his uniqueness, and thereby avoiding the repeated pattern of resentment: him declaring in his heart, "I will never talk my son's ear off." Finally, knowing myself and others enables me to interpret similar situations—my father, my son, and the well-known pastor—through radically different lenses. These situations while similar on the level of concrete details, are radically different when I willingly set aside my default mode of viewing the world—I am right, they are wrong—and embrace the wide and wild complexity of God's creation.

What about you: what differences do you notice in your interaction with others? Where do you "just click" and where is there "constant friction"? What models help you make sense of the world, growing your comprehension and appreciation of other people?

Action Steps

1. Create your Active File data management system, whether digital or physical. Chart the types of information you want to capture on each of the jobs for which you apply.
2. Go back through the job descriptions you are considering. Code nouns, verbs, and other significant phrases using different colored highlighters.
3. Practice your skills of observations by exploring several websites. Make notes on what you observe—where there was continuity or discontinuity.
4. Peruse the first part of *What is Your Church's Personality*. Read the chapter featuring the ministry approach that you resonate with most. How does this information help clarify what you should look for in your next organization?

8

HOW TO PREPARE FOR THE INTERVIEW

Chapter Summary
If you are like most candidates, you are bursting to prove yourself by the time you get an interview lined up. You've learned the skill of Behavioral Interviewing and practiced it with Network Partners. You've worked your network with a concise, active, relevant email blast. You've researched positions extensively and have lengthy files on many of them. A church has taken an interest and scheduled an interview. You are ready to share what you know, speak about what you have learned, and talk about what you have done. Instead of seeing the interview as an opportunity to talk, this chapter provides a structure for engaging with anticipated and actual questions. Using the Behavioral Interviewing skills developed in Chapter 2, candidates can impress committees as much by the questions they ask as by the answers they give. This chapter coaches you in exploring the questions (and assumptions) behind the questions, helping you craft your responses to address spoken and implied concerns. Additionally, you will learn how non-profit organizations typically approach conversations about the salary package. The chapter ends with recommendations on following up with churches after the interview.

Elements of the Interview
When conducting qualitative research, a researcher must read extensively and conduct long interviews using the constant comparative method to identify the scope of relevant research. This arduous work, the Literature Review, takes up the largest section of the dissertation. The chapter does not give the researcher any space to share his or her thoughts. The researcher must keep opinions out of the dissertation until Chapter 5.

By the time you get an interview, you just want to prove what you know. You've conducted thorough research and networked. This feels like your "Chapter 5" moment: you are ready to share what you know, speak to what you have learned, and talk about what you have done.

Stop. Take three deep breaths. Now remind yourself to practice patience. The process ahead is as least as taxing on your time, energy, and nerves as everything you have done up to this point. Adjusting your expectations to meet the reality of this stage of the process helps mete out your energy, enthusiasm, and words.

Most candidates report the following steps after applying for a position:

- Initial conversation to set up interview: This is usually with one committee member or pastor (for support roles).
- Initial interview: Broad scope. The first interview tends to be less structured and more casual.
- Committee talks to references.
- Second interview: Focuses on specific strengths and struggles of the candidate as they pertain to the needs of the church. More conversational: candidates get time to ask questions.
- Personal visit: Often under the radar and not as public candidate, unless the church is smaller, in which case usually only one visit.
- Second visit: Public visit.
- Job offered.
- When do you share what with whom?

Initial Conversation

Often your first interaction is little more than courtesies and logistics. You and the committee member introduce yourselves. It is possible the committee member has a surface-level question or two for you, but a significant portion of the time is spent working out details for your interview. This is not the time to ask pointed questions about the job, the organization, or the process. Given the time and the flow of the conversation, you might be able to squeeze in one information-gathering question. Here are three examples:

- I could not tell from the job description: is this a new position for the church? (This is a closed question.)
- I noticed on the website that you have a partnership with the

Boys and Girls Club of America. Can you tell me more about the history of that relationship? (This is a context specific and open-ended question.)

- I read the profile of the Senior Pastor. Tell me about his time at the church.

Initial Interview

Churches chronically ask bad questions of candidates, at least in the initial stages of the interview process. You can expect questions to be generic, technical, theological, and hypothetical—rarely behavioral. Here are actual questions committee have asked of candidates.

Generic Questions:
- Tell us about your time in seminary.
- Tell us about your current job.
- Tell us how you came to know the Lord.

Technical Questions:
- Tell us about your weekly schedule.
- What is your process for sermon preparation?
- What are your views on Critical Race Theory?

Hypothetical:
- We recognize we need to grow in discipleship. What would you do to increase the number of men in discipleship groups?
- We want to reach out to a new neighborhood. How would you go about developing relationships with new people?
- If we are going to grow, we need to do a better job with evangelism. What is your approach to outreach and evangelism?

Exercise: Pick one of questions above and write a paragraph response. Keep your answer where you can reference it as you read the chapter.

When asked these types of questions, most people believe providing a technical or hypothetical answer is better than nothing. This tendency increases in situations of power imbalance, like an interrogation or interview. Power imbalance is a normal part of human relationships. Parents have power over children. Employers have power over employees. In job interviews, those conducting the interview have power over those being interviewed.

Here is the rationalization behind offering hypothetical answers to hypothetical questions.

- <u>Premise One.</u> Because these people are responsible for finding a candidate, they must have specific skills or abilities in mind when asking these questions.
- <u>Premise Two.</u> Because they have unique skills or abilities in mind, they must know what they are doing by asking hypothetical questions.
- <u>Conclusion.</u> Because they know what they are doing, they have a specific purpose for asking the questions they ask in the way they ask them.

In fact, reality looks more like this: Members of the search committee have been tasked to find a candidate for their job. And while each brings their own educational background and experience, few of them have any experience navigating the peculiar elements of a pastor search process. Therefore, they often ask questions that can be improved upon.

Most people answer technical questions with technical answers, and that is fine. But we can get into real trouble when we answer hypothetical questions with hypothetical answers. Stated more strongly, candidates have gotten into real trouble answering hypothetical questions with hypothetical answers.

Dryden was seeking a youth ministry position. During one interview, the committee chairman described a high school down the street from the church. None of the kids from the school was involved at the church. The chairman asked Dryden how he *would* "break in" and make relationships with people at the school.

Dryden answered, "I *would* approach it like I did in my current town. I started by introducing myself to the administration and praying with the principal. I got permission to leave flyers with the teachers. I *would* have breakfast with interested students on Day of Prayer, and eventually got permission to have lunch once a week at the high school. Once I've established relationships with the administration, I *would* look for opportunities to substitute teach in the school so I could get more time with the students."

Notice that Dryden used "would" to describe both his past (completed) and future (hypothetical) actions. Two years later, the committee chairman led the charge to have Dryden fired. This man had a series of complaints—including the youth group's not growing and how Dryden preached (which he rarely did).

But the chairman's biggest allegation was that Dryden was "a liar." "You lied," the chairman accused. "You said you were going to reach out to the local high school, meet teachers and administration, and eat over there. You never did any of those things."

In fact, Dryden tried all those endeavors and was rebuffed. The principal wouldn't let him in the school. The teachers didn't respond favorably to the flyers Dryden left for them. There was a Day of Prayer, but the students who attended were already involved in other churches. Dryden thought he was communicating what he would *try*. The chairman heard Dryden communicating what he would *accomplish*.

Answering hypothetical questions is dangerous. You simply don't have enough information to speak with clarity, authority, or certainty about what course of action to take or what solutions to propose. And you never know exactly how your answer is being received. Likely, how your answer is being perceived has as much to do with your personality type—*Judging* verses *Perceiving*, and *Thinking* verses *Feeling*—as it does with your actual words. People with a preference for *Perceiving* interpret most conversations through the lens of possibility, while those with a preference for *Judging* interpret most conversations through the lens of certainty: settled and decided. Considering these normal communication differences, the potential for being misunderstood goes up when you are speaking to a group of people you don't know about and situations about which you don't have enough information.

When answering a hypothetical question, start with what you don't know and then lead into what you have done before: "I don't know all the particulars of your context. I would like to spend the first six months getting to know the church and current ministries. But let me tell you about a time when I was asked to solve a similar problem." This kind of answer doesn't commit you to a course of action, while at the same time it clearly conveys your ministry and leadership capacity.

The Softball Question

Many churches want the initial interview to be a conversation. Some even report that the time will be split between asking and answering. In fact, you can expect to have only a little time to ask questions during the initial interview. However, there is one time in almost every interview when the candidate can dictate the direction of the conversation: the opening question. What question do you think is most often asked first in an interview? It is the opening question: "Tell us about yourself."

Exercise. Think about that question for one full minute. Write down the possible answers to that question before reading further.

The question is so open-ended that you could answer it in a hundred ways. Sometimes candidates give a summary of their faith journey or a snapshot of vocational history. Some share about their family, and others talk about why they are excited about the interview.

While none of these is wrong, this information has already been conveyed in another place: the resume, the profile page, or the denominational data form. I recommend using this softball question to set the stage of the conversation. Be prepared to answer with a STARR story of your own.

Lance had eight years' experience as an Assistant Pastor in two churches, with limited preaching opportunities. He was applying for a Senior Pastor position at a mid-sized church. He knew most committees would have questions about his ability to preach weekly. When asked to talk about himself, he answered:

> You have my resume, which outlines my family, faith, and work experience. I want to share a meaningful story from the last time I preached. My Senior Pastor fell ill on Thursday and asked me to fill the pulpit on short notice. With just two days for preparation, I focused on 2 Corinthians 1:3-7, which speaks about God's comfort. After the sermon, a private, older woman approached me. She shared that she had recently been diagnosed with stage three cancer. Her eyes filled with tears as she explained how my message reminded her of God's comfort, easing her fear during such a challenging time. In that moment, I realized that's the kind of ministry I want to be part of.

Another example: Natalia had served as a volunteer women's ministry director for five years. She was interviewing for a paid women's ministry position at another church. The job description for the new position emphasized the need to lead a team of strong women in paid and volunteer positions. When asked to talk about herself, she answered:

> You've seen my resume, so let me share my passion for ministry collaboration. Ministry thrives on teamwork. In my current role, I lead the women's ministry committee. As an extrovert, I love engaging with others, but I noticed some women became disengaged. When longtime-volunteer Sandy resigned, I invited her for coffee to discuss her decision. She appreciated my leadership but pointed out that, in my enthusiasm, I sometimes talked too much, limiting other's input. She was right. I apologized and asked her to stay on and help. We implemented a system where I would speak for 10 minutes during the vision planning stage. The rest of my input would focus on asking clarifying questions. It was Sandy's job to give a summary of decisions at the end of the meeting. This increased collaboration resulted in one of our best Bible studies the following year. That success was a team effort, which is what I love about ministry.

These stories take about three minutes to tell. (Natalia's is a bit longer, but she also talks faster!) Lance and Natalia aren't the heroes: Lance didn't comfort that woman. He was used by God to convey God's comfort for this woman. Natalia didn't come up with the best ideas but demonstrated that she could learn from her mistakes and get a team of people engaged for effective ministry. These narratives don't answer every question—about Lance's ability to preach weekly or Natalia's leadership style—but they draw attention to both candidates' abilities to learn, grow, and stretch under challenging situations.

I recommend writing out a succinct STARR story for each of the main points of the job description. Read these stories. Practice them aloud. If a story takes longer than three minutes to tell, shorten it. Each story should illustrate *one* skill or capacity used in *one* situation. You should be able to summarize your STARR story into a single narrative pitch: Lance had to preach on short notice, and the Lord used that to bless a congregant. Natalia learned that asking powerful questions increased team collaboration.

What to Share, When, with Whom?

One common pitfall among ministry candidates involves what to share, when, and to what extent during the interview process. Most candidates are invited to speak with openness about their weaknesses, flaws, and failings. Committees that do not explore this area of your character and competence are living in an idealistic and artificial world.

Personality shapes how you answer questions about your current weaknesses and past mistakes. On the Myers Briggs Type Indicator, people with a preference for *Thinking* tend to define weakness in terms of performance and results. *Thinking* Types struggle receiving praise when they do not think it merited. In turn, when they think they deserve it, they expect to be ushered into places of greater leadership and influence. People with a preference for *Feeling* tend to define weakness and failure in terms of relationships. They tend to focus on situations in which they or someone else violated their core values of harmony.

Self-awareness also plays heavily in how you answer questions about weakness and failure. All personality Types can be emotionally aware. However, because of how western culture developed, we have historically undervalued emotional intelligence. This makes it difficult to understand much less appreciate internal motivation and emotional processes. This is especially difficult for *Thinking* Types, who find their reliance on reason and objectivity reinforced in the values of our corporate-minded culture.

I recommend the following books for growing in self-awareness and mindfulness. Read with discernment. Find the gold within the dross. Look for God's common grace expressed through the words of those who may not know Him.

- *The Anger Workbook: An Interactive Guide to Anger Management*, by Les Carter and Frank Minirth. (Harper Christian Resources, 2012).
- *Generation to Generation: Family Process in Church and Synagogue,* by Edwin H. Friedman. (The Guilford Press; Illustrated Edition, 2011).

Back to the matter of vulnerability, part of the problem rests in the conflation of vulnerability, transparency, and humility. Humility is freedom from pride: a realistic assessment of yourself in areas of strength and struggle. Humility has to do with character. Vulnerability is the ability to be wounded whether physically, emotionally, or mentally. Transparency is the quality of openness, usually with respect to personal and relational matters. These are three distinct things.

Thirty years ago, few were transparent about their sexual struggles. Today, the topic regularly comes up in my coaching conversations with candidates. The assumption is that speaking transparently about one's sexual struggles is evidence of vulnerability and a sign of humility. Often it is neither. The indiscriminate sharing of information is not evidence of humility; it can be evidence of imprudence or immaturity. Revealing information that can be used against you requires a high degree of trust between the speaker and listeners.

Transparency without vulnerability is informational reporting. Transparency without humility is arrogance. Vulnerability without humility is sympathy-seeking. Vulnerability without transparency is shallow self-protection.

Avoid confusing honesty with transparency. In cases of employment law and medical ethics, it is illegal to be transparent fully with the wrong people. In matters of church discipline, it is unwise to be fully transparent with those beyond the scope of the situation. Often, it is unloving and unkind to be fully transparent with everybody, all the time.

For example, after the firing of an Assistant Pastor, a group of congregants wanted more details. The Pastor and Elders said, "We have shared what we can. Everything else is covered by employment law. We cannot divulge further details."

While serving on a school board, we had a legal case involving three parties. There was pressure by a small group to make "all the details" known to exonerate the accused. But full disclosure would have brought unnecessary criticism on others, potentially splitting the school and church. You will face situations like these in which honesty—speaking truth—requires you to speak with limited transparency.

You are going to be asked about your weaknesses and struggles during the interview process. The context and timing of the question should influence your response. The degree to which committee members have been vulnerable and transparent gives you some indication of the level to which you should do the same.

Soren was in the second round of interviews for a solo pastorate for a suburban congregation of about 80 members. Should he receive the job offer, this would be a revitalization effort. The last pastor of the congregation had championed ministry to women in the sex trade, a growing issue in a nearby city. This created several challenges for the church, located 20 miles away. Congregants didn't have the time or capacity to be in the city, so the Pastor was doing the work alone. And the church was already stretched thin trying to minister to and support two women who were trying to come out of that context. The Pastor interpreted the congregation's reluctance as a lack of support for his vision. As his resentment grew, so did his focus on ministering to these women. In time, the Pastor fell into sin and eventually left the ministry.

As a result, the search committee at this church was sensitive to sexual issues. They asked candidates, "Do you struggle sexually and, if so, in what ways?" This is a technical question. For most candidates, an honest answer requires transparency and vulnerability. As a married man, Soren shared his occasional temptation with pornography, who his mentors were in this area, safeguards he put in place for his own protection, the work of the Holy Spirit and progressive sanctification, the encouragement of his wife, and the guidance of a counselor. He was honest without being gratuitous or crude.

Because of Soren's answer, the committee decided not to engage Soren further and dismissed him from their process. Soren had assumed the directness of the question was an invitation to be honest and that transparency would be well received. It wasn't.

Given its past, the committee wanted to find specific challenges their next pastor might face. But they were put off by Soren's transparency. Initially, the search committee couldn't describe why Soren's answer made them uncomfortable. During a lengthy meeting in which I asked questions, one member finally remarked as other members nodded in agreement, "Honestly, we just want someone who doesn't struggle sexually." The next day, the search committee removed all questions about sexual struggle from the interviewing process.

This committee wasn't ready for an honest answer to a difficult question. They were reacting, first to the moral failing of their last pastor and then to Soren's honest and transparent response.

A better question would have set the stage and invited reflection on the topic, something like, "We live in a highly sexualized culture. When you experience sexual temptation, what safeguards do you put in place to be affirmed in the Gospel and encouraged by mentors?"

In the following chart, I've listed several questions that committees have asked. The second column is a technical response to these questions. The third column lists alternative responses which are more thoughtful and relational.

Committee Question	Natural (Technical) Response	Thoughtful (Relational) Response
How have you experienced sexual brokenness?	Give an overview of the nature of your sexual story including areas of struggle.	"I am glad to talk about ways I have sought healing in this area. Help me understand more of the church's experience?"
Tell us about a time you experienced failure.	Might talk about sexuality, or relational conflict, or vocational failure.	"I have experienced failure in many areas of life at some point. Can you give me a little direction as to what you are asking?"
What is your view of divorce?	"I think the Scriptures are clear that divorce, except in cases of unfaithfulness, is unbiblical."	"I can give you the biblical position, but I'm not sure that's what you're asking. What is your experience with divorce as a church?"

What is your view of hell?	"The Bible says that those who die apart from Jesus will spend eternity in hell…"	"I can give you a theological answer, but it would be helpful for me to understand more about your exploration of this theological topic."

Most loaded questions come from places of pain, heartache, and difficulty. The woman who asked about divorce wanted to know if her physically abused daughter would be welcome at the communion table. The man who asked about hell had been criticized by the last pastor, who believed and taught that hell wasn't real and that unbelievers ceased to exist at death (Annihilationism).

Before speaking transparently, I recommend using feedback from mentors and trusted friends to identify your areas of strength and struggle. Write a short response for each. Seek further feedback on those responses before using them in the interview. You can be honest in your vulnerability without being completely transparent.

References
After the first interview and before the final interview, committees check your references. Selecting good references is itself challenging. How to select and prepare your references to serve well in the process is covered in Chapter 5. To complicate matters, few committees are equipped to assess references effectively.

Despite selecting the most qualified individuals to represent you in this process, many references are cautious in their assessments. They are guarded, sharing only positive aspects of their experiences with you. Current and former colleagues, including direct reports, express hesitation to speak candidly. Some fear legal consequences. Others, including current employers, are reluctant to share negative perspectives of candidates with whom they have experienced significant, unresolved conflict or workplace issues. A few may do this out of humility, believing that a difficult employee might perform better under different circumstances. However, at least a dozen supervisors have admitted to providing positive references for troublesome employees in hope the candidate would "move along" without further conflict.

Committees generally ask many of the same generic questions of references that they ask candidates. The best step you can take is to prepare your references to share their experiences of you that pertain directly to aspects of the job for which you apply. Does the job require leadership, administration, vision, and management? Make sure that at least one of your references can speak to each of these skills. When possible, let references know the STARR stories you intend to share during the interview process, especially when those people took part in or observed those events. At the very least, encourage your references to tell their own STARR stories—historical narratives—to substantiate their testimony. Refer to Chapter 2 and 5.

Follow Up Interviews
There is no pattern for follow up interviews. Ideally, the first interview adheres to a highly structured interview protocol. This means that the committee asks all the candidates the same questions, preferably in the same order. This information, together with any written materials, should make the follow-up interview more semi-structured. This means the questions asked, and order of them, in follow-up interviews are specific to you, and different from those asked of other candidates.

Unfortunately, committees are not often this organized. Candidates report that follow-up interviews don't adhere to any predictable order. Ideally, follow-up interviews allow you more time to ask your questions. If they do not, at the end of the conversation ask, "I also have questions. When would it be proper to ask those?"

One way to prepare for a follow up interview, regardless of the structure, is to have a new set of STARR stories. Ask your references if they have been contacted by the committee. If so, inquire as to what questions were asked. Prepare stories that show your character, capacity, and skill in areas where you are strong, but also prepare thoughtful responses demonstrating your ability to learn and grow in areas of weakness or struggle. Draw from language you developed to express aspects of your personality (Chapter 4) but explain them in simple terms using concrete situations. Remember to be honest, even if you cannot be fully transparent in what you share.

Compensation Package

In a marketplace job, compensation is usually one of the first topics discussed. In ministry, compensation is usually one of the last topics discussed. Churches want to know that candidates are interested in their position for the nature of the work and the people, not the money. And when the topic of money finally comes up, there is not generally room for a wide range of negotiation. Non-profit work is compensated at non-profit rates.

In a 2016 report, the Bureau for Labor and Statistics reported that non-profit pay is on par when compared to for-profit counterparts. The report goes on to state that in the aggregate non-profit employees are compensated at a higher rate, earning "$5.13 per hour more than workers at for-profit establishments."[78]

However, in my experience, evaluating over a thousand church-based positions, compensation is either on par with or below comparable positions in the marketplace. Churches are dependent on the tithe of their congregants. In most churches, tithing and benevolent giving is low and declining. Even in churches where members donate at a high rate, pastoral compensation is moderate at best.

Understanding Compensation

Your compensation package is more than your paycheck. Non-profit compensation packages include benefits such as:

- Salary
- 401k or 403b retirement savings plan
- Holiday, Vacation, and Sick-time paid leave
- Medical, dental and vision insurance
- Defined work hours
- Subsidized training or education
- Reimbursement spending account

Ministry positions might also offer non-monetary benefits. Some churches own a house (e.g., parsonage or manse) for use by their minister. And I have known many rural churches that include benefits such as free eggs, milk, chickens, and beef. Be sure to clarify what compensation and benefits are included in your salary package.

The Presbyterian Church in America created an introductory resource explaining the differences between a marketplace compensation package and a ministry compensation package. You can find this and other helpful information at: https://genevabenefits.org/. The US Government's Bureau of Labor and Statistics also has expansive information on salary and benefits, which can be accessed here: https://www.bls.gov/ncs/.

How these benefits are structured depends on your ordination status. Ordination comes with specific tax benefits. The "dual tax status" of ordained ministers means you bear responsibility for all your FICA taxes. At the same time, you qualify for a tax-deductible housing allowance. If you are ordained or seeking ordination, I strongly recommend you hire an accountant who specializes in clergy taxes. Well-meaning accountants in your church might offer to help you with your taxes. Unless they are skilled at navigating the complex dual-tax status, you are as likely to be harmed as helped. If you insist on doing your own taxes, I recommend the book "The Church and Clergy Tax Guide." There is an updated edition for each tax year.

Call Package Language
Pay close attention to the specific language of your ministry call package. Read these two example paragraphs below.

- "That you may be free from worldly cares and avocations, we hereby promise and oblige ourselves to pay you the sum of $60,000 per year in regular monthly payments, inclusive of benefits, such as a housing allowance, medical insurance, annuity, automobile allowance, books, conferences, and vacation of four weeks, during the time of your being and continuing as the Pastor of this church."
- That you may be free from worldly cares and avocations, we hereby promise and oblige ourselves to pay you the sum of $60,000 a year in regular monthly (or quarterly) payments, and other benefits, such as, manse, retirement, insurance, vacations, moving expenses etc., during the time of your being and continuing the regular pastor of this church.

Did you catch the significant difference? It is the phrase in the first example "inclusive of." This means the offer of $60,000 includes *all* your financial benefits. You are responsible to pay for your own insurance, mileage allowance, and any resources you need or conferences you choose to attend.

Notice in the second example the phrase "and other benefits..." This means you will be paid $60,000 a year *plus* all the added benefits listed. These two- and three-word differences are the difference between a $60,000 paycheck and a $35,000 paycheck.

Prior to accepting an offer, have several trusted ministry leaders read the offer with you. Better yet, contact the PCA Geneva Group and ask for a free consultation to discuss the particulars of your offer. You do not have to be ordained or minister in the PCA to access these resources.

Negotiating Pay

In most cases, candidates are unable to negotiate a significant pay increase. A co-instructor, Rev. Chris Florence, reminded students that churches aren't trying to take advantage of candidates. Usually, they offer to pay what they can afford. You might be able to negotiate a 4-6% increase in pay, but you will need to make a case for the request.

Rolland was at the airport. His interviewing trip was ending. The Senior Pastor told him, "I've enjoyed my time with you. The Session agrees. I'm wondering, if we offer you a position, are you likely to accept it?"

Rolland and his wife looked at each other, "Yes, if you were to offer the position, I think we would be inclined to accept it. As you know, our biggest hesitation is the finances." Rolland was given his first look at the compensation package the night before the trip began. He and his wife ran the compensation package against their budget. There was an almost $10,000 gap, due largely to the increased cost of living where the church was located. Trusting the goodwill of the Senior Pastor, they shared details of their finances with him.

"Let's keep talking," the Pastor said. He prayed with them and said goodbye. When the plane landed, Rolland's phone buzzed with a voicemail from the Senior Pastor: "Rolland, I called the Session and told them you were the person I wanted to hire. I also told them we needed to come up with another $10,000. They agreed."

In this case, Rolland trusted the Senior Pastor with financial details, and the Senior Pastor stewarded that information well, resulting in a significant increase in the compensation package.

In another example, Collin accepted the job offer as the Solo Pastor of a rural church. He presented the details of the job offer to his presbytery. His presbytery was tasked with examining the terms of the job offer, to ensure Collin was not putting himself and his family in a precarious situation. One committee member stood up and said, "Collin, clearly you are excited about the opportunity to be a parish pastor. Please explain how you plan to provide for your family on $20,000 a year."

Collin explained how he and his wife were empty nesters with limited expenses. The rural area had a lower cost of living. The church was offering a parsonage. The couple would go down to one vehicle, and they wouldn't be driving it much.

Collin added, "And while it's only $20,000 in cash, the church has committed to providing me the beef from one cow twice a year, all the milk my wife and I want from a local dairy farmer, and all the fresh vegetables we can eat."

The committee member stood up again and said, "So with all those added benefits, what are you going to do with the $20,000?" (The entire committee laughed.) Collin's small church couldn't increase their compensation package the way Rolland's Senior Pastor did. It found alternative ways to provide for the needs of their pastor.

Get a handle on the cost of living in the area you are moving into. Know what you need to live on. And start with an assumption the church is not trying to take advantage of you.

Insurance
Clarify the church's policy on health and life insurance. Some churches provide it as part of a group policy. Others give you cash equivalent, asking you to find your own provider and plan. Others are part of co-ops, and some push candidates toward government subsidized offerings (e.g., The Affordable Care Act). I recommend you explore all your options including the added benefits of gap insurance offered by companies like Aflac.

Clarify *when* insurance coverage begins. Standard practice is to ask for a date that allows a one-month overlap with an existing policy to ensure there are no issues. And there can be serious issues.

Corinne accepted a new position requiring her to move from South Carolina to Idaho. Her existing insurance policy was set to expire on August 15. The church in Idaho agreed to start her new policy the next day. During the three-day drive west, Corrine started experiencing internal discomfort. By the time she arrived in Idaho, she was experiencing waves of debilitating pain. She went to the emergency room, where she was diagnosed with a severe case of Crohn's disease. She was hospitalized for almost a week.

The hospital bills started arriving; she thought there was a mistake. She discovered that the person responsible for processing her insurance at her new job put the wrong start date on the policy: August 18. Her old insurance had expired, and the new provider considered her hospitalization a preexisting condition. In the end, the hospital, the church, and Corrine shared in Corinne's $125,000 medical expenses.

As another example, my wife and I moved to St. Louis for seminary. I declined to pay for the extended COBRA insurance. We were in good health, and I figured we were safe to wait until we arrived in Missouri to secure new insurance. But in the busyness of the move and starting graduate school, insurance became an afterthought. A month after school started, I applied for a new policy. Days after mailing our forms, and before we were notified of coverage, my wife informed me that she was pregnant. When I notified the insurance company, they let me know that the pregnancy would not be covered.

A one-month policy overlap would have provided my wife and me—and Corinne in her situation, with peace of mind at minimal cost.

Ministry Reimbursement Account
When structuring your compensation package, ask the church to keep ministry expenses in a reimbursement account instead of giving it to you as part of your salary. If you receive these funds as part of your salary, you will pay Social Security, Federal taxes, and State taxes. When the funds are kept in a reimbursement account, you can submit receipts from meals, events, and trips. The reimbursement is not taxable.

Start Date

Clarify the start date. You are going to want enough time to leave your current position well, to move yourself and your family (if you have one), and to get situated into your new housing. Ideally, the start date provides a period for rest in situations where you are coming off an extended season without rest.

Severance

The topic of severance can seem strange when talking about your compensation package. And in most cases, it would be out of order. Still, there are unique situations in which having a conversation about severance is not just appropriate—it is essential.

Shawn was pursued by a large urban congregation. The church had a tumultuous history. Several pastors had been disciplined for moral issues. One had been arrested. The church had split twice. Support staff left, often citing dysfunctional leadership and personal burnout.

The church had reached a place of apparent stability. They had a vibrant elementary school. Attendance and giving were on the rise. And the search committee was convinced Shawn should be their next pastor.

Shawn asked, "What happens to my family and me if we get here, and things go sideways quickly?" The search committee didn't know how to answer. They discussed possible ways to give support to Shawn and his family in the event of conflict.

"I don't want to wait until things get bad to try and figure out how to take care of my family. Before I accept your position, I want to negotiate my severance package." Shawn is still at the church ten years later.

Pastors who take risky calls, moving his family to a difficult area to revitalize a dying church, may also want to negotiate severance. There comes a point in congregational life when the rate of decline cannot be halted by endowed funds or meager growth. What is the Pastor's exit strategy, so that he is not left without income?

These are hard conversations that should not be entered into lightly. And they are hard conversations that you sometimes *must* have. Seek advice from confidants as you navigate and negotiate these interests.

Follow Up to the Interview

Relationships depend on effective communication. That includes your communication with a prospective employer. The fact that you are dealing with a group of people, a committee, can complicate communication. Many aspects of the post-interview process—next steps, timing, and committee action—are out of your hands. But there are ways you can keep the ball in your court.

As with your Network Partners (see Chapter 2) send a handwritten note to the committee immediately after your interview. And you can send more than one. If you interacted with the Pastor and the search committee, send each a note. If you have a second interview, send another note. After the site visit, send a note to the people who were meaningful in planning your visit.

When you *hand write* a note of gratitude and appreciation to a search committee for the opportunity to talk with them, when you *hand write* that you will pray for discernment in their deliberations, when you *hand write* that you hope to talk with them again—you are breaking down the business processes that dominate the modern job search with elements that are personal, relational, and emotional—in a word, ministry.

After sending a note, wait. Wait for the search committee to conduct other interviews. If they take a *series* approach to candidate evaluation, they may be reviewing the initial written responses of some candidates even as they are scheduling follow up interviews with earlier candidates. You can't rush a committee, but that doesn't mean you shouldn't follow up after a reasonable time.

Near the end of your first interview, try to clarify expectations. Ask when you should expect to hear from the committee next. Ask when the church hopes to have someone in the position. In my experience, the reply will be vague. Honestly, most committees don't know how long it will take for them to work through the next step of the process, and most of their estimates are widely inaccurate.

If the church doesn't plan to hire someone for six months or more, follow up with the committee once a month. Keep your tone casual and curious. Every interaction you have with a committee is the opportunity to show your personal, relational, and ministerial abilities. Ask questions. Avoid making statements.

- Do this: "As I seek direction and discernment in my vocational pursuits, I continue to reflect on our earlier interactions. The Lord continues to bring your church to mind. I am praying for your work as a committee. At your convenience, can you provide me an update on the progress of your search?"
- Not this: "I'm still seeking a ministry position and was really drawn to your church. When can I expect to hear from you about next steps?"
-

As the church gets closer to the stated hiring deadline, you may follow up more often—every two or three weeks—especially if you have continued in the process through multiple interview stages.

Whenever possible, follow up by phone. In one of your follow-up emails, ask if you can set up a time to talk. If you get the opportunity, use the call to ask questions, seek clarity, and pray with and for the committee and its process. The committee may not want to talk by phone, so don't push the issue. But it is better to ask and be turned down than not to ask and miss the opportunity to connect personally.

Action Steps
1. Make a list of the questions you most want to prepare for during an interview.
2. Think about the questions you may be asked, which bring you the most concern. How will you answer these questions?
3. Make a list of people willing to help with a mock interview.
4. How will you advocate for time to ask your questions?
5. Write out a STARR story for each main responsibility listed on a job description for a position to which you apply. Keep it short and simple. Memorize and practice telling the stories.
6. Do you tend to share too much or share too little? Talk with a confidant about what would be right to share and with whom, especially in areas where you struggle.
7. Review your personality type—Myers Briggs, Enneagram, or others. How do your preferences inform the way you answer questions about weakness and failing?
8. Look at several sample call offers. Highlight sections of the job that stand out to you.

HOW TO PREPARE FOR THE CHURCH VISIT

Chapter Summary

A site visit allows you to confirm your observations and pursue unanswered questions. Getting the correct information depends on who you meet with and in what context. And you will want to know how free you are to discuss aspects of the job, the organization, and the salary package. The schedule of your visit will dictate your focus and attention. You must prepare to ask for input into the schedule and make your desires known. This chapter outlines elements of a good visit. We'll look at ways to look for confirmation of your previous observations of the system and practice "thinking systems, watching process."

Visiting the Church

The number of visits to a church, and what happens on each visit, depends on the position to which you apply. Often senior leader candidates—including Senior and Senior-Associate Ministers—may have two visits to the church. Churches with more resources are more intentional with site visits. Besides that, there seems to be little correlation between the number of visits the committee plans and the seriousness of their consideration of the candidate.

In a two-visit situation, the first visit is covert: *under the radar*. That is, the candidate meets with key constituencies of the church—including the search committee, senior leadership, and other significant influencers. The candidate worships with the congregation as a guest of one of the committee members. But most people in the congregation are not aware that he or she is a candidate. The second visit is a public visit.

In a one-visit situation, the visit can be either an under-the-radar visit or a public visit. Support-role candidates typically don't have a public visit during the evaluation process. This reduces the potential for attachment confusion—the possibility of congregants latching onto the appearance, age, family dynamics, personality, or gifts of a candidate who is not ultimately offered the position. Under-the-radar visits also protect candidates who have not announced to their current congregation that they are interviewing for other positions.

Unless you are a senior leader making a public visit, you may have little say in how public or private your visit is. There are, however, places where you should give input into the visit.

The Schedule
Committees tend to schedule too many activities for candidates. Because they are paying for travel expenses, often including a flight and hotel stay, committees want to make the most of their interactions with a candidate.

Santos and his wife were interviewing for an Assistant Pastor of Youth. When the committee invited them to visit, Santos asked for a schedule. The chairman replied, "We haven't written anything down, but we want you to meet with the committee, the Session, the youth-ministry planning committee, and our staff. These will be separate meetings of course. And then you'd worship with us on Sunday as my guest. I'll get something to you in writing later this week. Also, my wife and I would love to host you two in our guest room."

As the schedule got firmed up, it became clear to Santos and his wife that the church had not allowed for any time to see the city, explore neighborhoods where they might live, or rest between scheduled activities. Santos wrote back to express his appreciation for the organization, and asked if they could provide a little more down time. His wife was going to be worn out by the travel and back-to-back meetings, while trying to manage their two-year-old.

Santos also asked for time to drive around with a realtor. Santos suggested times in the schedule that seemed to make the most sense, but said he was open to redirection. In the end, they settled on a schedule that accommodated both the committee's goals and the desires of the candidate. Make a list of important aspects of your site visit.

What if you are invited to stay at the house of someone in the church? Consider the potential costs. Thatch got up at 4:00 AM for an early flight to his site visit. By 9:00 PM, he was ready for bed. When the last meeting ended, his host—the chairman of the committee—took him home, but then continued to talk with him standing in the kitchen until 11:00 PM. The next day, Thatch was completely wiped out.

I once traveled ten hours to preach at a small, rural church. I arrived at the Pastor's home at 10:00 PM to find the Pastor irate and his wife in tears. The three Elders at the church had called a congregational meeting without the knowledge of the Pastor, voting to dissolve the pastoral relationship. Despite knowing the Pastor was about to receive a house guest (me), the Elders had come by three hours earlier to tell the Pastor he had been fired. I spent the next four hours listening to and praying with the grieving couple and their teenage children.

Staying in the home of a church member can be wonderful as long as you know what you are getting into. Find out how private the space is. If you know you'll need to get to bed, state this ahead of time: "I'm glad to stay with Mandy and her family. I will be tired from the long day and need to go to bed by 10:30 PM." If other accommodations are offered, inquire as to which would be most conducive to a good site visit. In a smaller church, turning down the hospitality of a member to stay in a hotel may appear standoffish and financial frivolous. Whatever you decide about staying in the home of a church member, pray that the Lord would make that a meaningful interaction for you and your host.

Similar relational dynamics must be considered should you ask to meet with a realtor. The committee may try to connect you with a realtor in the congregation. You must decide your comfort level with this conflation of roles. What happens if you don't get along with the church member? Do you risk weakening relational equity early on by deciding to work with someone else?

In a similar experience, I served in youth ministry in a small town. I asked for recommendations for a hair stylist and was quickly referred to an older woman in the church who owned a salon. When I switched stylists a year later, I was told it hurt her feelings. Feelings can get hurt quickly, and it can be challenging to repair strained relationships. On the other hand, I was recommended to a primary care physician who was a church member. Thirty years later, he remains the doctor I hold in the highest regard for his service, professionalism, and courtesy.

One way around this situation is to find a realtor on your own, prior to firming up the visit schedule. Then, should the committee refer a realtor, you can graciously decline saying you had already scheduled another realtor and wanted to honor that commitment. You saw it as an opportunity to meet someone in the community not involved with the church. You can more easily switch away from the services of a non-member to those of a member than the other way around.

Here are some questions to ask yourself prior to firming up the visit:

- What are your options for housing?
- How much down time or processing space do you need and want? What is the minimum amount you require?
- What types of services are you looking for, such as a realtor, primary or pediatric doctor, banker, or schooling options? What options can you find and secure on your own and which do you need the committee to help with?
- Will you have access to your own vehicle? What are the benefits or constraints of having and managing your own transportation?
- If your family is traveling with you, are the necessary accommodations being made for their needs?

Along with the schedule, ask that the committee provide the names and roles of the people at the scheduled meetings. This allows you the time to familiarize yourself with whom you'll be interacting.

Clarify Who Pays
Usually, without question, the inviting church pays for expenses related to the visit. There have been a couple of situations in which candidates were surprised, after the fact, to be asked to reimburse the church for visit-related expenses. One committee offered a candidate the choice of staying in a host home or a hotel. She selected the hotel. After getting home, the committee sent her a bill for the two-night stay saying they had not budgeted for it. (This proved to be just one of many red flags.)

A committee that expected having members drive you around may be surprised to be asked to cover the cost of a rental car. The easiest way to avoid any confusion is to simply ask: "Will I be expected to cover any of the costs related to the visit?"

After the Visit
Send a handwritten note to each of the people who played a significant role in your visit, including the search committee, dinner or lodging hosts and—if applicable and appropriate—the Senior Pastor.

Think Systems. Watch Process.
Caden noticed a couple strange comments during his interview with a New England church for an assistant pastorate. He wasn't exactly sure why the last Assistant Pastor left or the one before that. Answers from church leadership had been vague. During his site visit, he remarked on aspects of the church's architecture. The Elder with whom he was talking replied, "Yea, some of us don't like that. In fact, there are things we hope to change once you get here."

When Caden asked the Pastor what he wanted to see change or develop, the Pastor talked about his grand vision for numeric growth. Where the Session's perspective was specific and detailed—major changes to the Christian Education and discipleship programs—the Senior Pastor's responses were vague. Caden chalked it up to differences in leadership or personality style and accepted the position.

Six months into the job, he began seeing the dysfunction between the Senior Pastor and the Elders. During one meeting, the conversation got so intense that the Senior Pastor left. One Session member turned to Caden and said, "This is why we hired you. We need your help forcing him out!" Caden resigned the next morning.

Caden noticed the inconsistencies during the interview process but, he later admitted, didn't know how to connect those inconsistencies to the larger system. This requires that we think systems and watch process:

> The first step toward mature leadership is learning to think in a different way about how people in a living system affect each other and react to each other. This way of thinking requires learning to recognize how anxiety holds chronic systems in

place and how each person in the system has a role to play in keeping things in balance. This is thinking systems....[79]

Harrington, Creech, and Taylor name four behaviors of a chronically anxious system. These are:

1. Conflict
2. Distancing
3. Overfunctioning-underfunctioning reciprocity
4. Projection onto a third person

The conflict (1) between the Senior Pastor and the Session at Faith Church had come to a breaking point. They had settled into a fake peace (2) that avoided any issue that could generate anxiety. Caden noticed the overfunctioning-underfunctioning reciprocity; specifically, the Session had shifted their focus to addressing issues in their own way to the exclusion of the Senior Pastor. The Senior Pastor, for his part, willfully ignored this breakdown in relationship, choosing instead to play Pollyanna: *everything is good.* And both parties conspired to triangulate with a third person, namely the newly created position of Assistant Pastor: Caden.

Additional Examples of Complex Relational Systems

Aiden
Aiden served for ten years as the Solo Pastor of a small, rural church. The congregation met under one roof but was comprised of two distinct groups of people. There were the original residents of the region: blue collar, middle to low income, and with little higher education. And there were the "Renovators:" high net worth and highly educated young couples who moved to the area to escape the sprawl of west coast cities. Aiden was aware of the different needs, concerns, interests, and capacities of these disparate groups. Neither group was growing nor engaged in outreach to their respective communities. Their differences and geographic distance from one another meant there were no natural places of shared life or ministry collaboration.

Aiden and the Session entered a period of prayer, reflection, and study on the topic of Church Revitalization. They settled on the decision to multiply the congregation through an intentional separation. In phase

220

one, the two congregations would meet separately for worship. Aiden would preach a series on the mission, vision, and values for each group.

Phase two involved replanting the Renovators into a community center located in the higher income community. As that congregation grew, the Session would hire a second pastor to shepherd the congregation that remained in the old church building with the people who lived in that area. The resources of the Renovators would serve as the financial basis for this under-resourced congregation.

The Session laid out the plan for the congregation during a special meeting. Over the course of two hours, they unpacked the details of the plan. Then they opened the floor for comments and questions. The first person who stood up was an influential leader among a majority of the congregation. He had no formal role or title but vast informal power.

"This is the dumbest idea I've ever heard," he said, and sat down. Nobody else spoke, either to ask questions or clarification, or to offer a perspective. The opinion leader had spoken for the people. In their minds, the matter was settled.

Aiden reflected later that he and the Session made several mistakes. First, by trying to guide the people through an inductive process, they caused the congregation to feel manipulated into a decision that was predetermined. Also, Aiden observed, it was foolish to think the average congregant, over the course of two hours, would arrive at a conclusion that the called leaders had come to through six months of prayer and discussion. He and the leadership should have led outright, instead of seeking consensus.

Most importantly, they didn't account for the emotional component. Change is scary at any age and harder at some points than others, but the emotional reality of considering new relationships, a new building, new place, and new leaders was too much. This is the emotional component existing in every system. Heifetz and Linsky note that "fear of loss" is one of the "five major constraints" that hinder people from embracing change.[80]

Blake

Blake was called as an Assistant Pastor to a city church. Cost of living near the church meant the congregation was spread out over a large geographic area. When his new Senior Pastor urged Blake to find living on the cheaper, East Side, Blake thought nothing of it.

Blake was hired to develop and implement a program of outreach and assimilation. His work took place on Sunday at the church building, and in the neighboring communities during the week. Blake was told he could attend Session meetings *if he wanted to,* but the Senior Pastor urged him to use that time in more beneficial ways.

"Send me a ministry update report the Friday before the Session meeting," the Senior Pastor said. "I'll include your report in my update to the Session."

Blake found out that the last Assistant Pastor also missed most Session meetings without any issues. While Blake felt removed from the Leadership Team, skipping Session meetings meant he could spend time with his young family. (Midweek, it was a two-hour, round-trip drive to the church.) But it also meant he had limited access to the Session.

Ten months into his position, Blake and the Senior Pastor began to experience recurring conflict. Blake's initiating style pushed him to seek resolution. Increasingly, the Senior Pastor distanced himself. Blake responded by overfunctioning, putting in far more hours than he should to the neglect of his own health and his family. Unfortunately, because he was distanced, physically and relationally, from church leadership, nobody saw his efforts.

Eventually, Blake emailed the Senior Pastor and asked if he could come to the next Session meeting to discuss their issues. The Pastor emailed back saying Blake could come, not to the next meeting but the one after that. Blake had no interaction with the Senior Pastor during those seven weeks except for brief exchanges of information on Sunday morning.

Blake arrived at the Session meeting early. It was only his second Session meeting in 12 months. He expected to have the opportunity to share an update on his ministry progress, talk about his commitment and work ethic, and bring up the issue of conflict. Instead, the leader of the meeting presented Blake with a list of failures and shortcomings as reported by the Senior Pastor over the previous year. Blake said he addressed many of their concerns in his monthly reports.

"We haven't been receiving your ministry updates," the Session. (The Senior Pastor had not been passing them on.) In the end, the Session determined too much relational damage had taken place. Blake's employment ended with three months' severance, citing the unity of the church and leadership dynamics.

Distance may be individual, or it may be corporate. Blake is not the only pastor to find himself distanced from other influencers to diminish any threat to those in the system with power. By "inviting" Blake not to attend Session meetings, the Senior Pastor effectively created a firewall between Blake and the Session. Everything the Session was hearing—and it wasn't much—came second hand, from the Senior Pastor's perspective. The Senior Pastor and the Session had colluded—willingly or unwillingly—to triangulate against Blake, thus creating closer ties between themselves and cutoff with Blake.

Blake reflected later that it felt strange for the Senior Pastor to discourage him from attending Session meetings. He noticed something odd in the process but did not think about the larger system.

Peyton
As part of the Leadership Team, Peyton was expected to be at a monthly Monday evening meeting. Her Senior Pastor liked to host the event at his house. The extended team included five Elders, four Deacons, three part-time staff in addition to Peyton, the Senior Pastor, and a full-time Worship Director. Dinner usually ran from 6:45 to 8:00 PM., followed by prayer. With breaks and interruptions, the business part of the meeting didn't usually start until after 9:00 PM. Business was unstructured. No decision would be made without unanimity.

Most weeks the meeting ran past midnight, and most weeks Peyton excused herself at 11:30 PM. Tuesday started for Peyton at 6:00 AM, as she got her children ready for school, followed by a 7:30 AM Bible study. The day ended with a congregational-care team meeting that ran until 10:00 PM. Peyton led both the Bible study and the meeting as part of her job requirements.

223

Peyton finally approached her Senior Pastor about the lateness of the Leadership Team meeting, and the toll it took on her and the strain it put on her family. The Pastor looked at her from across the desk.

"Either you are committed to this church and my leadership, or you aren't."

She responded, "I am committed to supporting your leadership and the church. I'm asking if there is a way to shorten the meeting."

"I won't do that," he said. "I want every person in that room to say whatever is on their mind."

"I respect that, but often we end up having the same discussions month after month without any resolution. Could we implement a docket or itinerary to keep us on track?"

He replied, "That feels constraining to me. I think everybody likes the free-flow structure of our time.

"What would be the downside of ending the meeting by 11:00 PM?" Peyton asked.

The Pastor looked away and said, "Nobody else has a problem with the time. If this job is too much for you, we can revisit that." Peyton wanted to say that none of the other people had a young family to care for or ministry commitments early the next morning. The meeting was over.

With the details I've provided, this is a harder situation to diagnose. I think we would all want to see more sympathy from the Senior Pastor for Peyton and her situation. At the same time, we don't know the background as to why the meeting starts and ends so late, or what challenges the Senior Pastor has had to negotiate. What questions would you ask to diagnose this situation? What relational patterns would you look for? What would it mean to watch process and think systems?

Six months later, the Senior Pastor's ministry came unraveled. One of his children publicly renounced his faith and the church. During the stress, it came out that the pastor's marriage had been on the rocks for years. His inability to make tough decisions of leadership—with the losses, disagreement, and disappointment—led to ministry ineffectiveness. Before stepping down, he told Peyton how he had lived in fear of disappointing *anybody* and was terrified of conflict. The Pastor's insecurity undermined his ability to lead at church, and conflict at home taxed his capacity to take a strong position anywhere else. In the end, all he could do was minimize conflict.

Peyton reflected that she should have sought to understand the perspectives of others on the Leadership Team. She hadn't paid attention to the relational dynamics between the Pastor and his wife, and only later was able to make sense of several strange interactions.

Learning to Watch Process, Think Systems

Read *The Leader's Journey*, at least Chapters 3-5. Anything I could add to the thoroughness of the text would be extraneous. Next, look for and examine other case studies. These can be written narratives or narratives you get from other ministry leaders. Observing situations from an external position often gives objectivity without personal interest. Freed from obligation and emotion, you can see the patterns of anxiety within the system. When you find yourself in analogous situations, you can identify the symptoms more easily. Finally, reflect on your experience.

- When do you get emotionally hijacked?
- When are you likely to lose your cool?
- What triggers you?
- In what systems are you prone to get most anxious?
- In what situations do you tend to lose the ability to be a calm presence?

In my wallet is a card bearing the two questions Herrington *et al* ask:

1. What is my role in keeping this problem in place?
2. How can I change my role?

Healthy differentiation is a lifelong process. Nobody arrives at perfection in this lifetime. In my observations of people, I have seen extended periods with minor change interrupted by sudden periods of exponential growth, whether we call it the *Tipping Point,* the cumulative effects of an *Atomic Habit,*[81] or progressive sanctification.

I was unaware of my lack of differentiation until I was almost 30. Five years later, my wife urged me to seek counseling for my emotionally reactive patterns. At the age of 40, I began to see and understand the role I played in my family of origin and my marriage. As I write, I am a few weeks away from being 52, and I am struck anew by my role in some of the chronic patterns of conflict and anxiety in my life.

In seasons of apparent stagnation or plateau, remember who you are: a child of the King. In the seasons of sudden growth and development, remember who to credit. You are not the Christ but—collaborating with the indwelling Holy Spirit (Rom. 8:26-30)—you *can* and *do* change.

As you engage with the process of finding a job, pay attention. What stands out to you? What catches your attention? What observations do not fit within an understanding of the system? Equally important: what is going on inside of you as you interact with the situation? From the moment you first engage with a church, you become part of the emotional system of the organization.

Action Steps
1. Make a list of aspects you want to prioritize during a site visit. What desires do you have for that time?
2. How can you be curious about the structure of the visit without being judgmental? Practice writing out your questions.
3. How can you advocate for yourself during the visit—whether asking for margin between meetings, or time to drive around alone? Practice these requests with a confidant to get feedback.
4. How can you capture the names of the people to whom you want to send a follow-up note? Plan for securing names and addresses either during your visit or immediately after.
5. Reflect on a time you had a weird feeling about a situation. Write down the factual data you had along with the emotions you experienced. In retrospect, how is this an example of "thinking systems and watching process?"
6. Think about a time when you were in a chronically anxious situation. How did it affect you? How did you respond? In what ways could you have responded differently? How can you prepare for similar, anxious situations?

Bibliographic Endnotes

[1] Hanna, David P. *Designing Organization for High Performance*. New Jersey: Financial Times Press, 1988; pg. 36. Quote widely attributed to Arthur W. Jones, British organizational designer for Proctor and Gamble.

[2] Hoge, Dean R. and Jacqueline Wenger. *Pastors in Transition: Why Clergy Leave Local Church Ministry*. Grand Rapids, MI: William B. Eerdmans Publishing; pg. 117.

[3] Hoge, Dean R. and Jacqueline Wenger. *Pastors in Transition: Why Clergy Leave Local Church Ministry*. Grand Rapids, MI: William B. Eerdmans Publishing; pg. 118.

[4] Funyak, James Daele. *The Role of the Pastor in the Process of Developing Ordained Leadership*. St. Louis: Covenant Theological Seminary, 2014; pg. 46.

[5] Spurgeon, Charles Haddon "Christ's Pastoral Prayer for his People: John 17:9-10." *The Metropolitan Tabernacle Pulpit, Vol. 39*. In public domain.

[6] Knee, Jonathan A. "Must I Bank," *The Wall Street Journal*, April 23, 2008.

[7] Rumsfeld, Donald. Press briefing as United States Secretary of Defense, February 12, 2002.

[8] Creech, R. Robert. *Family Systems and Congregational Life: A Map for Ministry*. Ada, MI: Baker Academic, 2019; pg. 5.

[9] Hoge, Dean R. and Jacqueline Wenger. *Pastors in Transition: Why Clergy Leave Local Church Ministry*. Grand Rapids, MI: William B. Eerdmans Publishing; pg. 80-81.

[10] Wasserman, Nina. "A Closer Look at Behavior-Based Interviewing," *Inc Magazine,* March 1, 2000. https://www.inc.com/articles/2000/03/17957.html.

[11] Livermore, David. *Cultural Intelligence: Improving Your CQ to Engage Our Multicultural World.* Ada, MI: Baker Academic, 2009; pg. 138.

[12] Brown, Peter C., Henry L. Roediger III, and Mark A. McDaniel. *Make it Stick: The Science of Successful Learning.* Cambridge, MA: Belknap Press: An Imprint of Harvard University Press, 2014; pg. 136.

[13] Stoltzfus, Tony. *Coaching Questions*, Redding, CA: Coach22 Bookstore LLC, 2008; pg. 12.

[14] Bolsinger, Tod E. *Canoeing the Mountains: Christian Leadership in Uncharted Territory.* Downers Grove, IL: IVP Books, 2019; pg. 19.

[15] Casson, Michael H., Gonzalo Chavez, Ralph Jagodka, and Brigitte Madrian. "What Career-Focused Curriculum Looks Like." *Harvard Business Publishing,* June 20, 2021. https://hbsp.harvard.edu/inspiring-minds/what-career-focused-curriculum-looks-like/.

[16] Hoge, Dean R. and Jacqueline Wenger. *Pastors in Transition: Why Clergy Leave Local Church Ministry.* Grand Rapids, MI: William B. Eerdmans Publishing; pg. 5.

[17] Gladwell, Malcolm. *The Tipping Point: How Little Things Can Make a Big Difference.* (Kindle Edition) Boston: MA, Little, Brown, and Company 2006; pg. 38.

[18] Gladwell, Malcolm. *The Tipping Point: How Little Things Can Make a Big Difference.* (Kindle Edition) Boston: MA, Little, Brown, and Company 2006; pg. 38.

[19] Gladwell, Malcolm. *The Tipping Point: How Little Things Can Make a Big Difference.* (Kindle Edition) Boston: MA, Little, Brown, and Company 2006; pg. 45.

[20] Gladwell, Malcolm. *The Tipping Point: How Little Things Can Make a Big Difference.* (Kindle Edition) Boston: MA, Little, Brown, and Company 2006; pg. 46.

[21] Gladwell, Malcolm. *The Tipping Point: How Little Things Can Make a Big Difference.* (Kindle Edition) Boston: MA, Little, Brown, and Company 2006; pg. 48.

[22] Gladwell, Malcolm. *The Tipping Point: How Little Things Can Make a Big Difference.* (Kindle Edition) Boston: MA, Little, Brown, and Company 2006; pg. 54.

[23] Gladwell, Malcolm. *The Tipping Point: How Little Things Can Make a Big Difference.* (Kindle Edition) Boston: MA, Little, Brown, and Company 2006; pg. 53-54.

[24] Schell, Edwin Haskell. *Technique of Executive Control.* New York, NY: McGraw-Hill, 1926; pg. 31.

[25] Whitehead, T.N. *Leadership in a Free Society.* Cambridge: Harvard University Press, 1948; pg. 79.

[26] Henkel, Shi. *365 Foolish Mistakes Smart Managers Make Every Day: How and Why to Avoid Them.* Ocala, FL: Atlantic Publishing Group Inc, 2006; pg. 172.

[27] Green, Alison. "The Boss Who Takes Spa Vacations With Her Employee." *Slate Magazine,* August 6, 2018.

[28] Gladwell, Malcolm. *The Tipping Point: How Little Things Can Make a Big Difference.* (Kindle Edition) Boston: MA, Little, Brown, and Company 2006; pg. 48.

[29] Myers, Isabel Briggs, Mary H. McCaulley, Naomi L. Quenk, and Allen L. Hammer. *MBTI Manual: A Guide to the Development and Use of the Myers-Briggs Type Indicator, 3rd Edition.* Washington, DC: Consulting Psychologists Press, 1998; pg.64.

[30] Gladwell, Malcolm. *The Tipping Point: How Little Things Can Make a Big Difference.* (Kindle Edition) Boston: MA, Little, Brown, and Company 2006; pg. 33.

[31] Maher, Michael. *The Seven Levels of Communication.* Dallas, TX: BenBella Books, 2016.

[32] Abbott, H. Porter. *The Cambridge Introduction to Narrative.* Cambridge, England: Cambridge University Press; pg. 1.

[33] Doriani, Daniel M. *Getting the Message.* Phillipsburg, NJ: P&R Publishing, 1996; pg. 61.

[34] Grenny, Joseph, Kerry Patterson, Ron McMillan, Al Switzler, and Emily Gregory. *Crucial Conversations: Tools for Talking When Stakes are High, 3rd Edition.* New York, NY: McGraw Hill, 2021; pg. 98.

[35] Merriam, Sharon B. *Qualitative Research: A Guide to Design and Implementation.* Hoboken, NJ: John Wiley & Sons, 2015; pg. 1

[36] Kim, Daniel H. *Introduction to Systems Thinking.* Waltham, MA: Pegasus Communications, Inc., 1999; pg. 2.

[37] Heifetz, Ronald A., and Marty Linsky. *Leadership on the Line: Staying Alive Through the Dangers of Change.* Brighton, MA: Harvard Business Review Press, 2017; pg. 51.

[38] Brown, Peter C., Henry L. Roediger III, and Mark A. McDaniel. *Make it Stick: The Science of Successful Learning.* Cambridge, MA: Belknap Press: An Imprint of Harvard University Press, 2014; pg. 112.

[39] Brown, Peter C., Henry L. Roediger III, and Mark A. McDaniel. *Make it Stick: The Science of Successful Learning.* Cambridge, MA: Belknap Press: An Imprint of Harvard University Press, 2014; pg. 104.

[40] Brown, Peter C., Henry L. Roediger III, and Mark A. McDaniel. *Make it Stick: The Science of Successful Learning.* Cambridge, MA: Belknap Press: An Imprint of Harvard University Press, 2014; pg. 60.

[41] Gladwell, Malcolm. *The Tipping Point: How Little Things Can Make a Big Difference.* (Kindle Edition) Boston: MA, Little, Brown, and Company 2006; pg. 37.

[42] Heifetz, Ronald A., and Marty Linsky. *Leadership on the Line: Staying Alive Through the Dangers of Change.* Brighton, MA: Harvard Business Review Press, 2017; pgs. 51-74.

[43] Heifetz, Ronald A., and Marty Linsky. *Leadership on the Line: Staying Alive Through the Dangers of Change.* Brighton, MA: Harvard Business Review Press, 2017; pg. 13.

[44] Peterson, Eugene H. *Under the Unpredictable Plant.* Grand Rapids, MI: William B. Eerdmans Publishing, 1994; pgs. 38-39. Peterson recounts confronting his Elders in frustration. Nearing burnout, he accuses them of not knowing how to run the church. An Elder loving responded, "It sounds to me like you don't know how to be a pastor either. How about you let us learn how to run the church and we let you learn how to be a pastor."

[45] Colino, Stacey. "The Let-Down Effect: Why You Might Feel Bad After the Pressure Is Off." *U.S. News,* January 6. 2016. https://health.usnews.com/health-news/health-wellness/articles/2016-01-06/the-let-down-effect-why-you-might-feel-bad-after-the-pressure-is-off

[46] McPherson, Miller, Lynn Smith-Lovin, and Matthew E. Brashears. "Social Isolation in America: Changes in Core Discussion Networks over Two Decades." *American Sociological Review* (2006), 353-375. https://journals.sagepub.com/doi/abs/10.1177/000312240607100301.

[47] Juhnke, Gerald, and W. Bryce Hagedorn. *Counseling Addicted Families: An Integrated Assessment and Treatment Model, 1st edition.* Oxfordshire, England: Routledge; 2006; pg. 267.

[48] Herrington, Jim, Trisha Taylor, and R. Robert Creech. *The Leader's Journey: Accepting the Call to Personal and Congregational Transformation.* Ada, MI: Baker Academic, 2020; pg. 53.

[49] Bowen, Murray. *Family Therapy in Clinical Practice*. New York, NY: Jason Aronson, 1978; pg. 119.

[50] Burns, Bob, Tasha D. Chapman, and Donald C. Guthrie. *Resilient Ministry: What Pastors Told Us About Surviving and Thriving*. Lisle, IL: Intervarsity Press, 2013; pg. 15.

[51] Sawhney, Vasundhara. "Why We Continue to Rely on (and Love) To-Do Lists," *Harvard Business Review,* January 3, 2022. https://hbr.org/2022/01/why-we-continue-to-rely-on-and-love-to-do-lists.

[52] Tuff, Chris. *Save Your Asks: Evolve Your Networking Currencies. Grow Your Influence. Triple Your Business.* New York, NY: Panta Press, 2022; pg. xvii.

[53] Burnison, Gary. *Lose the Resume, Land the Job.* Hoboken, NJ: Wiley Publishing, 2018; pg. 22.

[54] Burnison, Gary. *Lose the Resume, Land the Job.* Hoboken, NJ: Wiley Publishing, 2018; pg. 22.

[55] Hirschman, Albert O. *Exit, Voice, and Loyalty: Responses to Decline in Firms, Organizations, and States*. Cambridge, MA: Harvard University Press, 1970; pgs. 3-4.

[56] Hirschman, Albert O. *Exit, Voice, and Loyalty: Responses to Decline in Firms, Organizations, and States*. Cambridge, MA: Harvard University Press, 1970; pg. 4.

[57] Chapman, Gary. *The 5 Love Languages: The Secrets to Love that Lasts*. Woodmere: NY: Northfield Publishing, 2024.

[58] Myers, Isabel Briggs, Mary H. McCaulley, Naomi L. Quenk, and Allen L. Hammer. *MBTI Manual: A Guide to the Development and Use of the Myers-Briggs Type Indicator, 3rd Edition*. Washington, DC: Consulting Psychologists Press, 1998; pg. 42.

[59] Gladwell, Malcolm. *The Tipping Point: How Little Things Can Make a Big Difference.* (Kindle Edition) Boston: MA, Little, Brown, and Company 2006; pg. 179.

[60] Gladwell, Malcolm. *The Tipping Point: How Little Things Can Make a Big Difference.* (Kindle Edition) Boston: MA, Little, Brown, and Company 2006; pg. 179.

[61] Myers, Isabel Briggs, Mary H. McCaulley, Naomi L. Quenk, and Allen L. Hammer. *MBTI Manual: A Guide to the Development and Use of the Myers-Briggs Type Indicator, 3rd Edition.* Washington, DC: Consulting Psychologists Press, 1998; pg. 42.

[62] Chapell, Bryan. *Christ-Centered Preaching.* Grand Rapids, MI: Baker Academics, 2005; pg. 54.

[63] Joiner, William B., and Stephen A. Josephs. *Leadership Agility: Five Levels of Mastery for Anticipating and Initiating Change Leadership.* San Francisco: Jossey-Bass Publishers, 2006; pg. 10.

[64] Myers, Isabel Briggs, Mary H. McCaulley, Naomi L. Quenk, and Allen L. Hammer. *MBTI Manual: A Guide to the Development and Use of the Myers-Briggs Type Indicator, 3rd Edition.* Washington, DC: Consulting Psychologists Press, 1998; pg. 66.

[65] Myers, Isabel Briggs, Mary H. McCaulley, Naomi L. Quenk, and Allen L. Hammer. *MBTI Manual: A Guide to the Development and Use of the Myers-Briggs Type Indicator, 3rd Edition.* Washington, DC: Consulting Psychologists Press, 1998; pg. 64.

[66] Douglass, Philip D. *What is Your Church's Personality?: Discovering and Developing the Ministry Style of Your Church.* Phillipsburg, NJ: P&R Publishing, 2008; pg. 207.

[67] Douglass, Philip D. *What is Your Church's Personality?: Discovering and Developing the Ministry Style of Your Church.* Phillipsburg, NJ: P&R Publishing, 2008; pg. 210.

[68] Douglass, Philip D. *What is Your Church's Personality?:
Discovering and Developing the Ministry Style of Your Church.*
Phillipsburg, NJ: P&R Publishing, 2008; pg. 224.

[69] Douglass, Philip D. *What is Your Church's Personality?:
Discovering and Developing the Ministry Style of Your Church.*
Phillipsburg, NJ: P&R Publishing, 2008; pg. 81.

[70] Douglass, Philip D. *What is Your Church's Personality?:
Discovering and Developing the Ministry Style of Your Church.*
Phillipsburg, NJ: P&R Publishing, 2008; pg. 87.

[71] Bowen, Murray. *Family Therapy in Clinical Practice.* New York: J.
Aronson, 1978; pg. 156.

[72] Bowen, Murray. *Family Therapy in Clinical Practice.* New York: J.
Aronson, 1978; pg. 158.

[73] The six historic theories of leadership are the Great Man Theory,
Trait Theory, Behavioral Theory, Management Theory, Relationship
Theory, and Situational Theory.

[74] Kuhn, Thomas S. *The Structure of Scientific Revolutions.* Chicago,
IL: University of Chicago Press, 2012; pg. 79.

[75] Brown, Peter C., Henry L. Roediger III, and Mark A. McDaniel.
Make it Stick: The Science of Successful Learning. Cambridge, MA:
Belknap Press: An Imprint of Harvard University Press, 2014; pg. 56.

[76] Riso, Don Richard, and Russ Hudson. *The Wisdom of the
Enneagram: The Complete Guide to Psychological and Spiritual
Growth for the Nine Personality Types, 11th Edition.* New York, NY:
Bantam Publishing, 1999; pg. 17.

[77] Myers, Isabel Briggs, Mary H. McCaulley, Naomi L. Quenk, and
Allen L. Hammer. *MBTI Manual: A Guide to the Development and
Use of the Myers-Briggs Type Indicator, 3rd Edition.* Washington,
DC: Consulting Psychologists Press, 1998; pg. 5.

[78] "Nonprofit pay and benefits: estimates from the National Compensation Survey." *Monthly Labor Review*: U.S. Bureau of Labor Statistics, January 2016. https://www.bls.gov/opub/mlr/2016/article/nonprofit-pay-and-benefits.htm.

[79] Herrington, Jim, Trisha Taylor, and R. Robert Creech. *The Leader's Journey: Accepting the Call to Personal and Congregational Transformation.* Ada, MI: Baker Academic, 2020; pgs. 49-50.

[80] Heifetz, Ronald A., and Marty Linsky. *The Practice of Adaptive Leadership: Tools and Tactics for Changing Your Organization and the World.* Boston, MA: Cambridge Leadership Associates, 2009; pg. 247.

[81] Clear, James. *Atomic Habits: An Easy & Proven Way to Build Good Habits & Break Bad Ones.* Garden City, NY: Avery Publishing, 2018.

About the Author

Joel Hathaway was born to ministry-minded parents in Memphis, TN. At the time, his father was an ordained minister in the Bible Presbyterian Church (BPC), Collingsworth Synod. Joel pursued his academic interests at the University of Alabama, earning a Bachelor of Arts in English Literature with a minor in Studio Art, in 1995.

Joel's ministry career started in Cleveland, MS, where he served as Youth Director at Covenant Presbyterian Church from 1995 to 1997. The Lord then gave him a wider view of the global Church through Mission to the World (MTW), the mission-sending agency of the Presbyterian Church in America, where he managed short-term mission trips from 1997 to 2000.

In 2000, Joel moved to St. Louis, MO, to study at Covenant Theological Seminary, where he earned his Master of Divinity in 2004 and his Doctor of Ministry in 2016. Over the years, he has worn many hats at Covenant Seminary, including Admissions Recruitment Coordinator, Director of Communications and, currently, Director of Alumni and Career Services, as well as Director of the Doctor of Ministry Program.

Joel's research into pastoral retention and longevity grows out of a desire to see pastors and their families thrive. He regularly consults with churches seeking pastoral leadership, and he coaches candidates pursuing ministry positions. He is the author of *Finding a Pastor*, a resource that helps churches navigate the Pastoral search process.

Churches and candidates interested in exploring best practices for pastoral placement can reach out to Joel at: joelhathaway@joelhathaway.com.

www.ingramcontent.com/pod-product-compliance
Lightning Source LLC
Chambersburg PA
CBHW021230130626
46554CB00004B/1428